PLACES
of
PILGRIMAGE

Bernard Jackson

PLACES
of
PILGRIMAGE
Bernard Jackson

GEOFFREY
CHAPMAN

Cover photograph (Iona Abbey) by Tim Cann, reprinted by
permission from *Legendary Britain: an illustrated guide*,
published by Blandford Press, an imprint of Cassell.

All photographs within the book are by Bernard Jackson,
except that on page 11, which is by Robert Kelly.

Geoffrey Chapman
An imprint of Cassell
Artillery House, Artillery Row, London SW1P 1RT

First published 1989

British Library Cataloguing in Publication Data
Jackson, Bernard
    Places of pilgrimage
    1. Europe. Places of pilgrimage.
    Visitors' guides
    I. Title
    914'.04558

ISBN 0 225 66534 4

Typesetting by Area Graphics Ltd, Letchworth, Herts

Printed and bound in Great Britain by
Biddles Ltd., Guildford and Kings Lynn

CONTENTS

To my mother, Agnes,
for her intelligence and inspiration

INTRODUCTION

There was a period in mediaeval European history known as the Golden Age of Pilgrimage. During the four centuries leading up to the Reformation thousands of shrines and churches throughout Christendom became focal points where pilgrims of every social rank gathered to ask a favour, to seek a cure, or simply to pray. According to the French chronicler Radulph Glaber, Europe went into a frenzy of religious fervour. 'Some three years after the year 1000 there was a sudden rush to rebuild churches all over the world, and above all in Italy and France.' Although most of these churches were in perfectly sound condition, Christians everywhere vied with each other to improve them. 'It was as if the world itself had thrown aside its old rags and put on a shining white robe of churches.' And yet despite the fact that we in the twentieth century are supposed to be entering into a secular age and that religious belief and practice is on the decline, places of pilgrimage have never been so popular. One fact that goes some way to explain this apparent paradox is that cheap travel has certainly made it much easier for the modern pilgrim to jet in and out of a pilgrim centre within a matter of a few days. Mediaeval man, on the other hand, would have taken many months to accomplish the same, once-in-a-lifetime spiritual journey. But that is not the whole story: the so called secular age does not attract everyone, and those who continue to maintain more traditional religious attitudes are often anxious to make a public gesture in defiance of the rising tide of secularism.

To retrace our steps along this age-old pilgrim route to the time of the first pilgrim, we have to go back to the time soon after the death of Christ. About thirty years after the crucifixion, St

Peter, the chief apostle, made his way from Jerusalem to Rome. His mission was to establish the Christian Church in the capital of the Roman Empire, which was then the centre of the civilised world. By moving from Jerusalem to Rome, Peter was switching the focal point of Christianity from a Middle Eastern to a European setting. Because of constant and cruel persecution (Peter himself was, according to legend, crucified upside down in what is now the site of St Peter's Square) the growth of the young Church was slow. It was only when the Roman Emperor Constantine became Christian in the fourth century that the followers of Christ became acceptable and respectable. Instead of having to worship in secret, the Christians could now practise their faith in the open. In fact Constantine built the original St Peter's Basilica over the tomb of Peter, on the Vatican Hill, which was to last a thousand years. It is at the time of Constantine that the idea of making a journey, or a pilgrimage, to a holy place first shows itself in Christian terms. Constantine's mother was Helen or Helena. She came from Asia Minor and married Constantius Chlorus by whom she had a son, who later became the Emperor Constantine. In her later years Helen became a Christian as did Constantine. The elderly Helen set out for Jerusalem in search of the True Cross, only to discover that the Emperor Hadrian had built a temple to Venus over the crucifixion site. Constantine ordered the temple to be destroyed, and it is popularly believed that Helen then found three wooden crosses in a rock cistern near to the hill of Calvary. One of those crosses was declared to be the one that Jesus Christ had died upon about two hundred years before. So, Constantine's mother Helen became the first Christian pilgrim; she had travelled to a holy place in order to associate herself with what she believed happened there. Helen then spent her remaining years in Palestine.

For the next several centuries serious pilgrimages were focused on a handful of important Christian centres, all with strong early Christian connections. There was, of course, the Holy Land itself, where St Jerome, an early pilgrim, went to live in Bethlehem for the last 35 years of his life. There, in a stone cell underneath what is now the Church of the Nativity, he translated the Bible from Greek to Latin. Rome naturally was another site where Christians gathered, and to which they made long and dangerous journeys to be where Peter had been martyred. Anglo-Saxon kings retired in Rome and in the eighth century a Lombard king walked to Rome with his wife and children to accept a monastic habit. By the ninth century even Irish monks began to regard Rome as a place worthy of some spiritual importance, in spite of their Celtic traditions. Another popular shrine of the same century was Santiago de Compostela on the northwest coast of Spain. Legend there had it that St James the apostle (the Greater) went to Spain to spread the Gospel and when he returned to Rome he was beheaded in AD 44. His disciples then bore his body, and his head, back to Spain, where he was buried. For several centuries his remains were forgotten but by the eighth century a French book of martyrs reveals that 'an extraordinary devotion paid by the inhabitants' to the bones of the apostle was evident in Santiago.

Canterbury was another shrine of European importance, particularly during the years immediately after the death of St Thomas Becket in 1170. After a somewhat halting start, for at this time many shrines were cropping up in many places, Canterbury was to become a very distinguished place of pilgrimage. Geoffrey Chaucer firmly established Canterbury in the minds of English speaking people at least, by writing his famous *Canterbury Tales* in 1387, in which he describes a mixed bag of pilgrims who set off for Thomas's shrine from the Tabard Inn in the Southwark area of London. Curiously, another shrine which became a great favourite with both commoners and kings was the shrine of Walsingham in the flat lands of Norfolk in the east of England. For those who could not get to either Jerusalem, Rome or Santiago a trip to Walsingham was an acceptable substitute. Incidentally, although I have been to Jerusalem, Rome and Santiago I have not included them as chapters in this book. Whole libraries have been written on the Holy Land, so a chapter here would hardly do justice to a country crammed with Christian significance. Similarly the Eternal City has been much written about in the past, and a brief treatment here would not be appropriate. As for Santiago, although very rich in its history, today it is mainly a tourist attraction. The famous Hostal de los Reyes, once a sanctuary for pilgrims from all Europe, is now a five-star hotel in the Cathedral Square. However, to this day they still swing the massive *bota fumeros* or thurible across the nave of the cathedral in a shower of sparks and white-scented smoke. As well as being a devotional piece of apparatus, it is also said to have been very appropriate when the cathedral was filled with good-hearted but unwashed pilgrims who'd just completed their long journeys when hygiene was of little or no priority! But of the five important and ancient places of pilgrimage, I have included Walsingham in this book: a fascinating village surrounded by ploughed fields and often wide, clear blue skies overhead. The story of Walsingham is fascinating too, with its Holy House, its ancient ruins and its ecumenical aspect, so appropriate in the twentieth century.

In fact, Walsingham was the first place of pilgrimage I visited at the behest of the BBC. I covered the pilgrimage there one year for a religious current affairs programme. I then suggested a series of six which I thought would make 'a good listen', as they say in broadcasting circles. Well, they were 'a good listen', so another half dozen were commissioned. The fact that Croagh Patrick and Lough Derg shared the same programme accounts for twelve programmes and thirteen chapters in this book. I think it is only fair to make it plain at this stage that, strictly speaking, I did not visit the shrines, the churches and the grottoes as a pilgrim. I had a job to do, I was always somewhat outside what was actually happening in front of me. That is not to say that I didn't enjoy my travels. Quite the contrary. Like any other modern pilgrim, I travelled by car, boat, train and aeroplane, often along with others. In fact, at times I met up with 'regulars' in different places. There wasn't one trip which didn't live up to my expectations. Someone once asked me why I liked going on pilgrimages and I found myself answering that it was not unlike a game of golf in that it combined so many things at the same time. Any golfer will tell you that apart from getting that tiny ball down a tiny hole, there's the fresh air, the exercise and of course the pleasure of gathering at the nineteenth hole after a good game for a little light refreshment. And in the same way, a pilgrimage also has many facets to it, all of which could be said to be beneficial. Indeed, many a mediaeval pilgrim returned from his or her journey fitter and healthier than on departure. The fresh food, the fresh air and the exercise all contributed to the well-being of the traveller, probably more so than was realised. And in a sense it is not unlike that today; the modern pilgrim can have that same sense of adventure a journey often brings; everything is different – most of all the company – and the complete change of scene adds stimulus to a frame of mind and body which is perhaps dulled by routine. But all that apart, at every shrine I found a purpose, a genuine piety and a single-mindedness which all contributed to a very powerful atmosphere. The spiritual climax after a long and perhaps difficult journey is really something to witness. I remember the waves of hymn singing which washed over me at Lourdes, at Czestochowa and at Fatima. Only the most cynical could remain unmoved.

Of course, each pilgrim centre I have visited has been very different, not only in location and history but also in appeal. People go on pilgrimage for much the same reason as they have always done, almost regardless of the location of the shrine. I have seen fanatical fervour at Poland's principal shrine of Czestochowa, where I watched enormous groups of young and old people, who had walked hundreds of miles over many days, sweeping up to the majestic monastery of Jasna Gora to pay homage to Jesus Christ and the Virgin Mary. In Fatima in Portugal I saw pilgrims walking a kilometre or more on their knees on rough ground, and with bloody knees they approached a tiny chapel where the Virgin Mary is said to have appeared to three young children. I found in Lisieux in northern France a gentleness and a mysterious quality which probably has something to do with St Thérèse whose memory is kept alive there. Canterbury, on the other hand, was full of a grand history stretching back to the time of St Augustine, whereas Iona in Scotland had a remote and harder edge to it. Lough Derg in Eire I found tough, weatherbeaten and penitential. And at Lourdes, a thousand miles away, I discovered a place full of gentleness and kind understanding for those who are sick and handicapped.

Over the two-year period I toured Europe to visit the various shrines, my main yardstick was that they should be popular in the strict sense that many people go there regularly. Invariably each location provided me with ample atmosphere and touching human stories which all add up to worthwhile and very popular radio listening. In this book I have set down the story of each shrine, which I hope the reader will find of interest. And who knows, perhaps for those who have never ventured on a pilgrimage, this book may encourage them to do so. Apart from the physical and spiritual benefits such a journey, I believe, can bestow, the modern pilgrim should know that he or she is joining into a continuous and ever-swelling river of souls which has been running down through the centuries, and will probably continue to run for many centuries to come.

BERNARD JACKSON
Harrow 1988

IONA

Over fourteen hundred years ago an Irish Celtic monk called Columba came to the Scottish island of Iona, built a monastery and began to spread the Christian Gospel in the west of Scotland. Six centuries later, when that Celtic tradition had died away, Benedictines came and re-established Columba's monastery. This second settlement lasted until the Reformation in the sixteenth century, when it was destroyed. Gradually the deserted site crumbled into disrepair, and nothing was done about it until the turn of the nineteenth century, when the then-owner, the Duke of Argyll, handed over the ruins to the Church of Scotland, which formed a group called the Abbey Trustees. The abbey was then restored over a ten-year period, and in 1905 it was rededicated to the worship of God. The real link with the present came in 1938, when a far-seeing Scottish Minister of the Church of Scotland, George Macleod, came to Iona with some fellow ministers and craftsmen, and together they started upon the complete restoration of the abbey outbuildings. That was the beginning of the now world-famous Iona Community, whose influence is still spreading. To understand these historical and modern strands in their true context, we must first take a step back into the sixth century, when Columba from Ireland first set foot on this wild and wonderful island.

Columba was born at Gartan, County Donegal, on 7 December 521. He was born into a Christian community which was Celtic in origin, and which had existed in the British Isles long before Augustine of Rome came to Canterbury in 597. The Celtic Church reached the British Isles in either the second or the third century, and there were Celtic Christian communities in Cornwall, Wales, Scotland and Ireland. Essentially, Celtic Christianity was the same as Roman Christianity except for minor differences such as the observance of the Easter festival, the manner of administering Baptism and the form of tonsure for clerics. In matters of basic theology and religious practice they were indistinguishable. Columba was connected to the Royal line in Ireland, but he chose instead to dedicate his life to God, and became a monk. He studied under two eminent Irish scholars of the time – Finnian of Moville and Finnian of Clonard. He was ordained priest at the age of thirty in 551. During the next twelve years Columba made his mark in Ireland as a strong leader and innovator, and he founded several churches and two monasteries: Daire Calgaich (Derry) and Dairmagh (Durrow). In May of 562, when he was forty-one years old, Columba left Ireland and sailed to the northwest with twelve followers. Celtic monks of the sixth century were essentially missionaries, and the charismatic figure of Columba had in his heart the fiery zeal to spread the Gospel in a land where little of Christ was known.

It is not altogether clear exactly why Columba left Ireland, where it seems he was well established and there was much mission work still to be done. However, there is a theory which could possibly account for Columba's departure, and it concerns an argument he is reputed to have had with one of his old tutors – Finnian of Moville. In those days, before printing was invented, books were a rare and highly valued commodity; they all had to be copied laboriously by hand, and naturally their owners guarded them jealously. Finnian had in his possession a copy of St Jerome's Latin translation of the four Gospels – the Vulgate. Somehow Finnian had obtained his copy directly or indirectly from Rome. As soon as Columba saw the book he greatly desired to make a copy of it for his own use. To him it would have been of enormous value as a monk and teacher. Columba was also an expert scribe and illuminator, which further attracted him to Finnian's copy. (I have heard it said that the Book of Kells, now in the library of Trinity College in Dublin, had its origins on Iona before being taken to Ireland, and therefore could have been at least partly illuminated by Columba himself. However, this priceless and beautiful ornamented manuscript of the gospels in Latin was more than likely written some time during the eighth century, much after Columba.) Realising that Finnian would probably forbid him to make a copy Columba set about the task in secret. This is how an

Irish 'Life' describes Colum Cille (another name for Columba) at his clandestine copying:

> At night time, while engaged in that transcription, the fingers of his right hand were as candles which shone like five bright lamps whose light filled the entire church. On the last night when Colum Cille was completing the transcription of that book, Finnian sent for it. When the messenger arrived at the door of the church, he was astonished at the great light he saw within and fear seized him. Timorously he glanced through a hole which was in the valve of the door of the church and when he beheld Colum Cille . . . he dared not address him or demand the book of him. It was revealed to Colum Cille that the youth was watching him and he became very angry and addressing a pet crane of his he said, 'If God permits, you have permission to pluck out the youth's eye who came to observe me without my knowledge!' With that the crane drove its beak through the hole of the valve towards the youth's eye, plucked it out and left it resting on the youth's cheek. Thereupon Finnian was displeased and sained [blessed] the youth's eye so that it was as well as ever.

Obviously Columba had a bad temper!

In spite of Finnian's wrath, Columba felt that he had done nothing wrong, and the case was referred to Diarmit, King of Ireland. After due consideration judgement went against Columba, who was both enraged and deeply disappointed. The incident between the two men grew into a dangerous issue, and Columba gathered forces against the king for what he considered to be an unjust decision. The Battle of Culdreihmne ensued, the king's troops were routed and 3,000 of his men lay slain on the battlefield. In sorrow and guilt at being the cause of so many deaths, Columba sought exile in reparation for his deed, and that exile was Iona. However, Columba's biographer, Adamnan (a later abbot of Iona), prefers to tell us that Columba left Ireland for Iona simply because of his strong missionary zeal.

There is a pointer which, in a way, favours the first theory rather than the second; on the south side of Iona there is a bay called Columba's Bay, where the saint first made land in his coracle (small boat) with his followers. Nearby is a hill called 'The Hill of the Turning Back to Ireland' (Carn Cul ri Eirinn). Columba is said to have climbed that hill as soon as he landed, and because he could still see his native Ireland from there, he decided that this was no suitable place to settle. For him, true exile meant a place where there existed no sight of the place he had sought to leave. Instead, Columba chose the other, eastern side of the island to found his monastery, near to where the present abbey stands and roughly on the same site.

Opposite the west door of the abbey is a hill called Tor Abb. It is believed that Columba's own cell was sited here. It would have been a crude, beehive-shaped hut made of wood and turf peat; fine stone churches and cathedrals were not to come for many centuries. Remains of a timbered building have been found near to the road which passes the abbey near St Oran's Chapel (the oldest building on the island). Each monk would have had his own cell on the site, with the larger building serving as the church, perhaps a chapter house and a refectory. The complete site would have been enclosed by a boundary wall which has been traced, and which would have included most of the present-day buildings, although Columba's settlement would have been far larger and wider.

For the next 34 years Columba and his followers set about their task of spreading the Christian Gospel to other islands, the mainland and the whole of the west of Scotland. Celtic Christianity later spread down into northern Britain. After the death of Columba St Aidan continued the work, and in his lifetime he preached the gospel well down into the middle part of England. In later centuries Celtic monks were to be found in places as far afield as Italy and Germany, but it is uncertain as to how Christianity was carried there and by whom.

In 597, the year of St Columba's death, Augustine of Rome landed on the Kent coast in the south of England and established Roman Christianity at Canterbury. During the next half century Celtic Christianity was coming down the British mainland from the north, and Roman Christianity was spreading in the south. Eventually differences had to be settled, and this was done – after a fashion – at the Synod of Whitby in 664. The two sides met, and it was decided that the Roman view should prevail. This decision marks the beginning of the end of Celtic Christianity, although for

Iona. St John's Cross (replica)

about another century monasteries such as the one on Iona would have been little affected by the new authority. But eventually Roman or Augustinian Christianity gained an ever-stronger hold on Britain.

A further setback came to Celtic Christianity and to Iona with the Viking raids in the eighth century. In 806 the monastery was devastated and 68 monks were slaughtered by pirates at Martyrs' Bay. The Community was forced to abandon the island settlement and return to Ireland. The monks took with them the remains of their founder Columba, but returned to Iona in 818 to make a fresh start. Seven years later, however, the monks fell victim to another massacre. Gradually other monasteries on the mainland became more important and influential than Iona, although during the next 200 years (850–1050) most of the kings of Scotland chose to be buried on the island, including, it is said, Macbeth and Duncan. Irish, French and Norwegian kings also recognised Iona as a holy place, and their bones came to rest on the Scottish isle. As Celtic monasticism waned, the Benedictine way of life grew in importance and in the early thirteenth century the last of the Celtic monks left Iona forever. They had been on the island for 600 years. At about the same time, a Benedictine monastery was founded on the island and the settlement named after St Columba. The Benedictines remained until the Reformation in the sixteenth century.

The buildings and the monastery were destroyed and all the manuscripts disappeared. In the late seventeenth century Iona became part of the Duke of Argyll's estates, and in 1899 the eighth Duke gave the monastery ruins to the Church of Scotland. Immediately plans were set in motion to restore at least the abbey itself, and in 1905, on 9 June – St Columba's Day – the restored abbey was rededicated to the worship of God. Columba himself is said to have foretold this second coming of Christianity to Iona in a Gaelic poem:

> Iona of my heart
> Iona of my love
> Instead of monks' voices
> Shall be the lowing of cattle
> But ere the world come to an end,
> Iona shall be as it was.

Along a winding lane, and near the old nunnery – still in ruins and too expensive to renovate – there is a plaque fastened to the wall. On it is a quote from the famous Dr Samuel Johnson, who came to Iona in 1773 with Boswell (he made a tour of the Hebrides and Scotland, and spent one night on Iona before returning to Mull):

> That man is little to be envied
> Whose patriotism would not
> Gain force upon the plain of Marathon
> Or whose piety would not grow warmer
> Among the ruins of Iona.

Just a little way along is Maclean's Cross, and on the right, towards the abbey, is the whitewashed building of the St Columba Hotel. Almost opposite is a house set back from the road a few yards, where the Community Warden lives with his wife and family. And there, to the right, is the abbey itself, with its wonderful backdrop of the Island of Mull in the distance across the Sound. Just before you reach the abbey, there is St Oran's Chapel (Reilig Oran) which stands amidst the ancient burial ground of many kings. The chapel dates from the eleventh century, the oldest building on the Island, and it is used for quiet prayer and meditation. The cemetery is still used by the islanders. A cobbled roadway leading towards the abbey was uncovered in 1962 and originally laid by the Benedictine monks. Centuries ago this road led up from the village to the abbey grounds. The abbey itself is quite small, although the original was even smaller, and it is the focal point of a neat set of buildings. All have been renovated in beautiful matching stone, and on a sunny evening when the light reflects off those warm reds and browns, you could be back in the Middle Ages and the time of the Benedictine monks. Little of the twelfth-century abbey remains, apart from some sections of the tower and some parts of the walls. The old, original west door was moved during the renovations and now stands far up the church on the left and serves as a splendid sacristy door. The west door is now the main entrance to the abbey, and just outside are two large stone crosses and the remains of another. Farthest away from the door is St Martin's cross which has stood there for 800 years. In front of a small chapel to the left of the west door is St John's cross. That chapel is said to contain the remains of St Columba which the monks brought back with them from Ireland when they made their second settlement. The original cross of St John would probably have dated from about AD 800, but the present one is a replica. Only the shaft of a slightly later cross of St Matthew stands beside the well facing the west door.

The man responsible for reviving interest in Iona back in 1938, and founding the Iona Community, is Lord Macleod; he was made a Life Peer in 1967 and regularly sits in the House of Lords. Lord Macleod is a tall man with a white moustache and he wears a deaf-aid; with the aid of a stylish cane, he walks quickly in spite of his 86 years. We sat in a tiny room, just off the abbey cloisters, and Lord Macleod told me how he, as the then Reverend George Macleod, came to Iona in the years of the Great Depression. 'I came to Iona because I felt that in my parish in Govan, which I had for eight years, there was a need for understanding what it was to be unemployed. I was amazed when I first went to Govan, because the people who were not coming to church, were, none the less, behaving very much like Christians. They were feeding the hungry, clothing the naked and generally helping anyone in trouble. There were 10,000 people in that parish at the time, all living in tenement flats. Some of them, who had no money, had to go to the workhouse, and whole families would be split up – perhaps never to meet again. That was the sort of thing that was going on at the time, and so many of the people, without knowing it, were practising great Christian forbearance. I didn't think that it was always the best thing that a young minister should automatically go to the rich parish which could afford to have an assistant. I wanted to encourage some of them to go to the industrial areas which perhaps couldn't afford an assistant. I used to come with some of them on holidays, when I was a bachelor, and we'd all enjoy the break. We thought that it would be a good idea to create a fellowship there composed of half a dozen young ministers who were still in training, and the other half of plumbers, masons and carpenters, to start to rebuild the abbey. And that's really how it all started. I then went to the Trustees who held the abbey for the Church of Scotland, and to my amazement they said that we could undertake the rebuilding.'

What had attracted Lord Macleod to Iona? 'Well, I knew the place pretty well, I liked it very much and I was also impressed by the story of Columba – because he was concerned both with politics and theology. Columba knew that these two things were related, as of course they are.' Lord Macleod then told me how, when his party first arrived on the island, they began their enormous task of restoring all the buildings attached to the abbey. They erected huts outside the West Door, and from those huts they began, in the following year, upon their serious work. 'But that was the year that the Second World War broke out, and the work had to be postponed.'

When circumstances allowed, the work was resumed and now the Iona Community has one hundred and forty full members, many of them Church of Scotland ministers working in needy areas in Scotland. Other members work in many other countries around the world. Their rule of life is simple; they all pray for each other, they work towards world peace, and they meet regularly whenever possible. They also give a percentage of their income towards a common fund, most of which is spent in the Third World. None of it goes to Community costs. Friends of the Community number about seven thousand and, in a less formal way, they also strive to uphold the Community Rule. There are several hundred associate members who support the ideals of the Community in the ways that they can. All contribute to Community costs. The work and influence of the Community is expanding all the time. Visitors are averaging 250,000 each year, few of whom can remain unimpressed at what they see and hear on the island. There is a youth centre near to the abbey where young people can stay together and also join in with whatever is going on at the abbey. Every Wednesday evening there is a service in the abbey, where sick people are individually prayed for. The Community firmly believes in the power of prayer as a healing force.

IONA

THE HISTORICAL BACKGROUND

Iona is one of the smaller islands of the Inner Hebrides off the west coast of Scotland, and measures 5.7 by 2.4 km.

In the first centuries AD the population consisted largely of people of Celtic origins, but constant population movement brought people from Ulster to Iona, and so by the sixth century the region had strong political and dynastic ties with Ireland.

In AD 563 Iona was chosen as the base for St Columba's mission to the Picts of the Highlands, although when he founded his monastery on Iona there were definite groups of Christians in southern Scotland. After the death of the saint, Iona remained the centre of the northern Celtic Church and until about 1200 a group of monks who could trace their origin to the mission of St Columba lived on the site of his original settlement.

Roman influence began to spread over Scotland during the late years of the sixth century but touched Iona very little, and for about a century the island and its life remained unchanged. It was not until 803, when the Norse raids first hit Iona, that the religious settlement of the Western Isles was affected at all, but after this time conditions deteriorated, so much so that the Columban mother house had to be moved from Iona to Ireland in the early ninth century. The reform of monasticism in the eleventh century brought a further wave of Roman influence, so that by 1200 a regular Benedictine monastery had been founded on Iona and the Celtic church had all but disappeared. The Reformation, however, did not violently affect Iona. There is no evidence of destruction and in all probability there was merely a slow decline, so that before the mid-seventeenth century the abbey and community had fallen into disrepair.

Before St Columba arrived little of the island was inhabited. The only sign of life was the small hill-fort of Dun Bhuirg on the west coast of the island. Some very interesting remains have been found here which give us an idea of the very primitive and spartan existence of Iona's first inhabitants. The visitor can see the remains of huts with their central hearths. Although they are now roofless it is assumed that originally they had turf or wooden roofs. Situated in an exposed position on a steep hill overlooking a sheer drop of over 100 feet it probably only lasted a short time and had certainly disappeared by the sixth century, when St Columba began his mission.

THE STORY OF ORAN

Oran is held to have been one of St Columba's disciples who accompanied him to Iona, was present at the founding of the first chapel, and was the first of the brethren to die. This is probably true, since not only is it confirmed by most sources which mention his name, but also the name given to the graveyard was Reilig Oran.

Irish sources and two versions of the Gaelic oral tradition attest that it was Oran who offered himself as the sacrifice which in those days was required to accompany the founding of a new sanctuary. Some people, fearing that this idea might cast a slight on early Christianity, have rejected this legend but, in its defence, scholars point out that we must not fail to take into account the strong pagan Celtic heritage into which he was born and in which he grew up.

Strangely enough, we know more about Iona in the sixth and seventh centuries than at any other time. We have extensive material in the writings of the saint's biographer Adamnan and the later writings of Bede. In addition there is the archaeological evidence; we can see the boundaries of the monastic enclosure and the site of St Columba's cell. There is also evidence of a further wooden building and some grave slabs. The remains of the cell stand on the hillock called Tor Abb to the west of the cloisters. Nowadays the visitor can see the low foundation wall of stones placed around a dip, and in the dip can be seen the granite supports for a seat and a rock-cut bed. The cell, as we can see it today, bears exact resemblance to the one described by Adamnan.

Very little that was made by the Columban community has survived, and the little there is, is in the form of stone carving and manuscript illumination. The major crosses are St John's, St Martin's and St Matthew's. These names were not applied to the individual crosses, however, until the last century. These crosses, which stand in front of the abbey, were probably carved about AD 800. St Martin's is farthest away from the abbey door and is made out of a solid block of granite. On the centre of its western face is the Virgin and Child, with Old Testament scenes such as Daniel in the lions' den and David playing for Saul carved down the shaft. At the foot is the now almost indecipherable inscription reading, 'A prayer for the servant of Christ who made the cross'. On its east face is ornamental carving with jewel-like bosses. The cross has stood on this site for almost 1200 years.

In front of the small chapel (where Columba's relics are said to be buried) beside the west door is an exact replica, made from a mould, of St John's cross. St Martin's and St John's, together with the Kildalton cross on Islay, form a group unique in Scotland but closely linked with the high crosses of Ireland. The shaft of St Matthew's cross, a slightly later one, stands beside the well.

MANUSCRIPT ILLUMINATION

The famous Book of Kells, which is now in the library of Trinity College Dublin, is often claimed to have been illuminated by the monks from the Iona community. This is thought to be true, since the style seems to belong to a date around AD 800. It is also the most ambitious surviving manuscript of the whole of Irish illumination, and so to suggest that it might have come from the most important monastery of the community of Iona, of which Kells was subsequently the centre, is not a far-fetched theory.

Kells became the centre of the Iona community because of the Viking raids. In one of the raids of AD 803 Iona was pillaged and burned, and later raids of the ninth century made the situation of the monastery too precarious for settled life, so the monks who survived finally moved to Kells which took over the supremacy of the Columban congregation. They eventually returned in AD 818.

THE REILIG ORAN

The Reilig Oran is a group of scattered graves surrounding a small chapel and encircled by a low stone wall. It is thought to have been one of the most important parts of the island between the years 800 and 1180. Kenneth MacAlpin, the most powerful leader in Scotland in the late ninth century, chose Iona as his burying ground and the low stone wall, mentioned previously, is thought to have been built on his orders. After his death the kings of Scotland were buried there for two centuries and tradition has it that other kings of Ireland, Norway and France were also buried here. This tradition was not broken until Malcolm III established a royal vault at Dunfermline.

There is an interesting processional way called the Street of the Dead which leads from the head of Martyrs' Bay, the original landing place, through the village and up to the graveyard.

The chapel in the graveyard is a small stone structure with a round arched doorway. It is badly worn but you can still recognise the animal and bird heads among its decoration. It is thought that it was not carved before 1140.

THE COLUMBAN MONASTERY

From the hillock of Tor Abb one can see the abbey precincts. The main group of monastery buildings was probably in the east side of the enclosure, roughly where the present buildings are, but the area covered by the Columban monastery is thought to have been a much larger area than the present abbey precinct.

THE BENEDICTINE ABBEY

No one knows the exact date of the founding of the monastery but it is thought to have been between the years 1156 and 1203. It was founded by Reginald, son of Somerled, Lord of Argyll, and built by the Benedictines to serve as a burial place for their founder. Compared with the great religious houses of Scotland it was a small monastery, but its connection with St Columba gave it pre-eminence in the West.

Originally the abbey church was considerably shorter and narrower than the present church. Very little of the twelfth-century church remains; only sections of the tower, the east wall of the north transept and the west section of the north wall of the choir certainly date from this time.

We have historical evidence for at least one major rebuilding at around 1450, but alterations were certainly made at other times. Little stylistic change was made during these rebuildings, and since the new decoration closely followed the twelfth and thirteenth-century designs it makes dating of the church very difficult. Many scholars claim that it was remodelled in the sixteenth century.

The north window of the tower is earlier than the other three windows and some think it could even be from earlier than 1300. The original doorway to the refectory looks as if it, too, should belong to the thirteenth century. An interesting piece of architectural deception is the sacristy doorway, which at first sight appears to be of a date around 1200 with Celtic additions, but is discovered, on closer examination, to bear the distinctive marks of fifteenth- and sixteenth-century building.

The visitor can see the remains of the choir on a lower level than that of the present floor. In view of this confusing array of architectural styles, it is easy to see why experts still argue about the relative merits of their theories of dates for the building and rebuilding of the church and the monastery.

Simply, the main body of opinion asserts that there was originally a Romanesque church built about 1190, an eastern building or addition in the thirteenth-century, a rebuilding and enlarging in about 1420 and a final stylish refurbishing in 1500.

MARTYRS' BAY

A recently excavated burial mound here has yielded surprises. Traditionally the mound was thought to have been burial ground for monks killed in the Viking raids, but the remains discovered there have been only those of women, and the age of the remains is confirmed as being around the year 1300 rather than 800 as was previously supposed. The clue to who these women were is given by the fact that none of them shows any signs of having borne children, and this fact, in addition to their age of around thirty-five to forty, suggests a nuns' burial ground. There is still controversy about this conclusion, but it seems to be a fairly convincing one.

THE MONASTERY BUILDINGS

To the north of the refectory is a building which was probably the abbot's house. Two buildings which lie to the east of the main buildings have been restored from their foundations. There is confusion as to what these two rectangular houses were used for, but it is possible that they were the infirmary and its chapel.

To the south of the refectory is the Michael Chapel, and its added interest is that it was restored by the gifts of South Africans. The roof and the stalls are made of Utile wood from Ghana.

THE IONA COMMUNITY

The Iona Community was founded in 1938 by George Macleod, now Lord Macleod of Fuinary, and is an ecumenical centre, although it is under the jurisdiction of the Church of Scotland. It was set up in the words of George Macleod, to be 'a cradle and a challenge' for the Church in facing the problems of Christianity in the twentieth century.

The Community was originally founded in Govan, part of the city of Glasgow, when George Macleod was the minister there; he felt that the Church in Govan was unconcerned about the needs of the whole community. Their minister wanted to help the Church rediscover how to care for the community and their families, especially in the climate of unemployment which pervaded Glasgow at that time.

Iona was chosen as the centre for this project, first because of its connections with St Columba. In 1773 Dr Johnson found his 'piety grow warmer' there and such has been the experience of many visitors over the years.

When George Macleod thought of going to Iona the church had been rebuilt but the abbey buildings were still in ruins. His idea was to pioneer a rebuilding project which would involve young workers and ministers. By working and worshipping together they would achieve a new perspective on their Christianity which they could take with them back to Scotland.

Joining the community involves a training period, and during this time the trainees stay at the abbey. The idea is not for members to live there, however, but to be scattered throughout the world. Specialising in community development and Church renewal, the members are asked to take on certain undertakings embodied in the Rule of the Community.

The abbey is open for all but four weeks each year as a centre for renewal, education, community and hospitality to anyone who wishes to come, and some 1,600 people come each year to share the Community life and worship. When organised groups are in residence, the Iona Community, through its staff at the abbey, works in partnership with each group in a programme of education and renewal. It is open for people of all persuasions and none. Further information can be obtained from The Warden, The Abbey, Iona PA76 6SN.

Community House in Glasgow is the mainland administration centre. There is an office of the Community in Edinburgh at the Candlemakers Hall, 36 Candlemakers Row, Edinburgh EH1 2QF.

TRAVELLING TO IONA

Iona is an island which lies off the south-west toe of the island of Mull. To reach Iona, then, one must first cross Mull. The principal mainland port for Mull is Oban, though there is a small ferry which plies between Lochaline on the Morvern peninsula and Fishnish on Mull.

PUBLIC TRANSPORT
To Oban

The only way to reach Oban is by bus from Glasgow, Edinburgh or Fort William, or by train from Glasgow.
Edinburgh to Oban by bus: St Andrew's Square Bus Station, Edinburgh
Glasgow to Oban:
by bus: Buchanan Street Bus Station, Glasgow
by train: Queen Street Station, Glasgow

From Oban to Mull and Iona
The steamer to Mull is a passenger/car ferry which sails from the Railway Pier in Oban. Passengers for Iona should alight at Craignure on Mull (a scheduled 45 minute sailing). There is a bus service from Craignure across Mull to Fionnphort, where a small ferry crosses the mile-wide Sound of Iona. The ferry from Fionnphort Jetty to Iona takes about 5 minutes and operates on weekdays between 0810 and 1800 hours (on Sundays April to September, until 1700 hours). The complete journey from Oban to Iona takes between two-and-a-half and three hours but is, of course, subject to weather conditions. Booking is advisable for the bus across Mull, but foot-passengers have no need to book the Oban–Craignure ferry. Cafeteria facilities are usually available on the steamer.

During the tourist season there is the 'Sacred Isle' cruise, a direct sailing from Oban to Iona on Tuesday and Thursday 0915–1200; return sailing same days 1600–1845.

CAR TRAVEL

Visitors cannot take cars onto the Island of Iona, but there is ample parking space for those who would want to drive as far as Fionnphort. In this case, you would take your car on the Oban–Craignure ferry. Vehicles must be booked in advance with Caledonian–MacBrayne Limited, The Pier, Gourock, Renfrewshire PA29 1QP. Tel: Gourock (0475) 33755. Alternatively, there is a car-park at Oban Station near the Railway Pier.

ACCOMMODATION

At Iona Abbey: The accommodation is mostly in rooms with double-tier bunk-beds. There are a few twin-bedded rooms, a few with three or four beds, and a couple of single rooms. Pets cannot be accommodated. A public telephone is available for guests at the Abbey: Iona (06817) 343.
At the Macleod Centre (from Spring 1989): The accommodation is in four-, five- and six-bedded rooms (not bunks).

SHOPS

There are two general stores in the village, a restaurant, two craft shops and a post office. There is no bank on Iona but a travelling bank comes to Fionnphort on the Isle of Mull on Tuesday mornings, but it is awkward to get there and there are usually long queues.

HOURS OF WORSHIP AT THE ABBEY

There is no special seating at the abbey, and people are asked to fill the choir stalls first. Descriptions and explanations of the various services are found in the Abbey Services Leaflet, available in the church and on sale in the bookshop.

Morning Prayers: 0840 hours Mondays to Saturdays.
Sunday Communion: 1030 hours, except

last Sunday in the month, May to September.

Peace and Justice Prayers: 1400 hours, Monday to Saturday, June to September.

Sunday quiet time: 2130 hours, 15 minutes for silent worship and prayer.

Evening prayers: 2100 hours Mondays to Saturdays.

Monday evening is a peace and justice liturgy.

Tuesday evening is prayer for the sick and the ministry of the laying on of hands.

Wednesday evening is led by Abbey guests.

Thursday evening is an Act of Commitment.

Friday evening is an informal Communion service celebrated around a long table down the centre of the choir.

Parish services are normally held in the abbey from June to September at 1200 and 2000 hours. These services are normally conducted by the parish minister, Church of Scotland, and all are welcome. From October to May these services are held in the parish church. The last Sunday of each month from May to September is a celebration of Holy Communion, for which reason the 1030 hours service is not held on these Sundays. Holy Communion is celebrated daily at St Columba's Chapel in Bishop's House at 0800 hours. For those staying at the abbey a late breakfast can be arranged.

HOTEL ACCOMMODATION IN IONA

Note: The telephone numbers as given here assume the caller is within the United Kingdom or Ireland. When ringing from abroad, the 0 at the start of each code must be omitted and the appropriate International Code must be prefixed.

Argyll Hotel, Mr & Mrs Menzies
Tel: Iona (06817) 334

St Columba Hotel, Mr & Mrs A Johnson
Tel: Iona (06817) 304

Bishop's House, Mrs P Roome
(*Retreat Centre of the Episcopal Church in Scotland*)
Tel: Iona (06817) 306

Clachan Cirrach, Mrs J Black
(*Evening meal, if notice given*)
Tel: Iona (06817) 323

Dunara, Mrs A MacDonald
Tel: Iona (06817) 320

Duncraig, Mrs J Wall
(*Evening meal, if notice given*)
Tel: Iona (06817) 346

Finlay Ross Ltd, Miss A Wagstaff
Tel: Iona (06817) 357

Kilona, Mrs G MacCormick
(*No advance bookings*)
Tel: Iona (06817) 362

Seaview, Mrs N Kirkpatrick
(*No advance bookings*)
Tel: Iona (06817) 373

Sithean, Mr & Mrs Clark-Kirchwehn
Tel: Iona (06817) 331

Postal address: Isle of Iona, Argyll PA76, Scotland.

Apart from accommodation at the abbey itself for visitors who wish to live the Community life, the Community also owns a house (Shuna) and a hut (Cul-Cul-Shuna) in the village on Iona and these are sometimes available for letting; further information is obtainable on request.

WALSINGHAM

For close on 1,000 years pilgrims have visited the English shrine of Walsingham in Norfolk to venerate the Virgin Mary. The shrine was founded in Saxon times in the year 1061 when Edward the Confessor was on the throne (1042–1066). Looking at a map of England and Wales of the late Middle Ages, you might be surprised to find just how many national shrines existed in those times, mainly devoted to the Virgin Mary. For example there were Jesmond (1125), York (1050), Lincoln (1196), Walsingham (1061), Ely (1120), Ipswich (1152), Evesham (702), Cardigan (1160), Glastonbury (530) and Canterbury (866). The Walsingham legend has its roots in the Holy Land, and in Nazareth where Mary was told by the angel Gabriel that she had been chosen to be the mother of Jesus. As St Luke in the Gospel tells us:

> God sent the angel Gabriel to a city of Galilee called Nazareth, where a Virgin dwelt, betrothed to a man of David's lineage; his name was Joseph, and the Virgin's name was Mary. Into her presence the angel came, and said, 'Hail, thou who art full of grace; the Lord is with thee; blessed art thou among women."
> (Luke 1:26–28).

About a thousand years after this momentous event in Nazareth, a woman called Richeldis de Faverches also had a vision in the Norfolk village of Walsingham. Richeldis was a widow and Lady of the Manor, and apparently on three occasions the Virgin Mary appeared to her in the setting of the house in which the angel Gabriel appeared to her and gave her the great news. The Virgin instructed Richeldis to note the exact proportions of the house, and to build an exact replica in the village. 'Do all this unto my special praise and honour,' the Virgin told Richeldis, 'and all who are in any way distressed or in need, let them seek me here in that little house you have made at Walsingham. To all that seek me there shall be given succour. And there at Walsingham in this little house shall be held in remembrance the great joy of my salutation when St Gabriel told me I should, through humility, become the mother of God's Son.'

Immediately Richeldis set her carpenters and builders to work. 'Twenty-three and a half feet long and twelve feet ten inches high,' she commanded, as the Virgin had told her. However, things went badly on that day for the workers, and they returned home in the evening downcast and dispirited with their day's work. During the night, Richeldis, unable to sleep and worried about the building, heard singing outside which seemed to be coming from the direction of the unfinished house. The lady rose, dressed and went out to investigate. As she moved close to the site she saw angels leaving the building which now seemed to have moved away from its original place and nearer to her as she approached. On closer examination Richeldis was to discover, to her amazement and subsequently to everybody else's, that the house had been miraculously completed in every particular, and solid as a rock upon its new foundations. A chronicler of the time wrote, '. . . that night the house had been borne two hundred feet and more from the first place by "angels' handys [artificers]" who sette it where it is." The next morning even the workmen had to agree that the quality of the work on the finished house was far beyond their capabilities.

And so became established the 'Holy House', and the reason why Walsingham became known as the 'Little Nazareth' for ten centuries. In fact so important did Walsingham become in the thirteenth century that it ranked equally in importance with Rome, Jerusalem and Santiago de Compostela in Spain. These four shrines were the most important in the Christian world of those times. Walsingham was also the first European shrine to be devoted exclusively to the Virgin Mary. When Richeldis died, her son Geoffrey, who was now Lord of the Manor and Earl of the Marches, took over the responsibility of seeing that the Holy House flourished as a pilgrim centre. Sir Geoffrey himself was anxious to be away to the Crusades in the Holy Land, but before he left he made ample provision for the shrine for its upkeep and also for the upkeep of the parish church of All Saints. Perhaps here lies the clue to Walsingham's subsequent popularity and why pilgrims, almost from the moment the house had been completed, made their way to Walsingham from every corner of Europe throughout the year. It was within the means of Sir Geoffrey and others who shared his high birth and wealth actually to go to Palestine to wrest the Holy Places from the grip of the infidel. However, for the ordinary man such a journey was out of the question. So what better and more practical alternative than to see the next best thing – obviously, the Holy House at Walsingham built on instructions of the Virgin herself. This is one of the major reasons why Walsingham became so extraordinarily popular in the thirteenth century. Henry III (1216–1272) went on pilgrimage to Walsingham in 1248 and was welcomed at the Priory. Henry's son, Edward I (1272–1307), went to Walsingham as a true pilgrim – that is, barefoot from the Slipper Chapel. This could be the reason why the chapel bears the name 'Slipper', where pilgrims would leave their footwear and continue into the village on bare feet as a penance. However, the exact origin of the name is uncertain. Later another English monarch, Edward III (1327–1377), made his way to Walsingham, after which, it is said, he gave protection to Robert Bruce of Scotland who had the leprosy.

Queen Joanna, widow of Henry IV (1399–1413), went to Walsingham in 1427 with her retinue and found accommodation at the Augustinian Priory there, which had been founded in 1153 to cater for the spiritual needs of the pilgrims. During these busy times, naturally the village itself changed considerably, owing to the ever increasing pilgrim traffic which was passing through. Pilgrim hostels were built, as were lodging houses and new markets, and shops sprang up. From all walks of life they came to Walsingham, to venerate the statue in the Holy House of the Virgin, who held the Infant on her left knee. The true origins of the statue have never been discovered, although we do know that in late mediaeval times statues were growing in importance and acceptance as holy objects. For three hundred years Walsingham enjoyed royal patronage, and almost every crowned head of England made the journey at least once in their lifetime.

In mediaeval times, more so than today, places of pilgrimage depended on miracles to sustain people's interest, and certainly

Walsingham provided what was then seen as some miraculous power at work. Richard Pyson's ballad on Walsingham, written in 1465, tells us exactly what the pilgrims were seeking:

> Many sek ben here cured by oure ladys's myghte
> Dede agayne revyved if this is no doubt
> Lame made hole and blynde restored to syghte
> Maryners vexed with tempest safe to port brought
> Defe wounds and lunatyke that hyder have fought
> And also lepers here recovered have be
> By our ladye's grace of their infirmyte.

Perhaps the best description we have of the shrine of the sixteenth century we owe to the Dutch philosopher Erasmus, who during the considerable time he spent in England paid a visit to Walsingham in 1514. 'Within the church . . . there is a small chapel, which admits by a narrow and little door on either side those who come to salute Our Ladye; the light is feeble, in fact scarcely any, excepting from the wax candles, whose most delightful fragrance gladdens one's nose.' Erasmus goes on to mention the fact that surrounding the statue were trinkets and gifts of some value. 'Brilliantly does it shine on all sides with gems, gold and silver.' Erasmus also recorded the fact that Walsingham was the most frequented place in all England, and that a man could not expect to prosper unless he paid an annual visit there.

In 1511 the second Tudor King of England, Henry VIII (1509–1547), visited Walsingham. This was not his first visit; in 1486 he had come to Walsingham as a prince with his father Henry VII (1485–1509). Henry VIII had a great devotion to the Virgin Mary both as a boy and a young king, and on this occasion he came to give thanks for the birth of his son, Prince Edward (later Edward VI), who died at the age of seventeen in 1553, having reigned for only six years. Henry also made a pilgrimage to Canterbury in 1520 'with every sign of devotion'. Only a short time after Henry had been to Walsingham, his Chancellor, Cardinal Wolsey, wrote in 1517, 'I am so vexed with the sweating fever that I intend to start off for the Shrine of Walsingham and from there to Our Lady of Grace, in fulfillment of my vow, which may correct the weakness of my stomach.' The Cardinal probably went and took the waters from the Holy Wells, near the Shrine which were said to have healing powers. When the Reformation came some twenty years or so after Henry's last visit to Walsingham, all shrines were doomed. At the same time as the dissolution of the monasteries in 1536 and 1539, the shrines were also laid waste. Thomas Cromwell, who became Henry's right-hand man on the death of Cardinal Wolsey, had the task of dismantling the monasteries and shrines. In 1538 the statue of Our Lady of Walsingham was removed from Norfolk, along with those from the other shrines, and taken to London for 'burnyinge'. An English author of the time, John Stow, wrote, 'The images of our Lady of Walsingham and Ipswich were brought to London, with all the jewels that hung about them, and divers other images both in England and Wales, whereunto any common pilgrimage was used, for avoiding idolatry, all of which were burned by Thomas Cromwell.'

Although the dissolution of the monasteries and the destruction of the shrines were done in Henry VIII's name, it is arguable that the now Head of the Church probably never intended the spirit of the Reformation to gain such a hold. Overzealous henchmen like Thomas Cromwell, Bishop Hugh Latimer and Archbishop Cramner were the ones who interpreted 'justification by faith alone' in its literal sense. Martin Luther and his German followers taught that good works, penance and pilgrimage were quite useless as effective methods of furthering spiritual aims; a firm faith in Jesus Christ as Saviour of mankind was sufficient. In this light, therefore, the shrines of England were seen as being contrary to the true, cleansing spirit of the Reformation. When Henry died in 1547 it was said that 'on his deathbed, in all the agonies of remorse, he bequeathed his soul to Our Lady of Walsingham'. A poem of the time, called *The Wrecks of Walsingham*, lamented the destruction of this once-celebrated shrine, and in a sense its sentiments reflect the fate of Walsingham over the next three centuries:

> Bitter, bitter, O to behold
> The grass to grow
> Where the walls of Walsingham
> So stately did show.

It was an Anglican lady who started a revival of interest in Walsingham back in the 1890s. In 1863 Miss Charlotte Boyd was attracted to an old, dilapidated chapel to the south of the village. It

Walsingham. The statue of Our Lady of Walsingham being carried in procession

was the old Slipper Chapel. Since Reformation times it had been used for many purposes, including a barn, cottages, a workhouse and even a cow byre. At some point Miss Boyd became a Roman Catholic, and when she finally bought the chapel and restored it she presented it to the Benedictines. This good lady requested that the chapel 'should be used for all time as a place of prayer and penitence for unity in England'. The first modern pilgrimage to Walsingham took place in 1897. Roman Catholics have come to their shrine in greater and greater numbers ever since.

In 1921 the Anglican priest of Walsingham parish, Father Alfred Hope Patten, decided that he, too, wanted Walsingham to become a place of pilgrimage for Anglicans once again. He commissioned a statue to be made according to representations of the original. This statue is now in the Anglican Shrine Chapel, and is of a Virgin sitting on a high-backed chair with a lily in her right hand and the Infant Jesus sitting on her left knee. There is a plaque outside the chapel of St Michael and All Souls which reads:

THIS HOLY HOUSE OF NAZARETH WAS RESTORED PARTLY ON THE ANCIENT SITE IN 1931. TO IT PILGRIMS COME TO SEEK HEALING IN THE ANCIENT HOLY WELL AND TO ASK FOR THE PRAYERS OF BLESSED MARY THE MOTHER OF GOD; FOR THEM-SELVES AND FOR THE WHOLE WORLD. ENTER AND PRAY THAT CHRISTIANS MAY BE ONE IN CHRIST; THAT ENGLAND MAY ONCE MORE ACKNOWLEDGE HIS KINGSHIP AND THAT ALL MEN MAY COME TO HIM IN PEACE. OUR LADY OF WALSINGHAM, PRAY FOR US.

So today, Walsingham is the centre of two national shrines – one Anglican and the other Roman Catholic – a direct result of the Reformation 400 years ago. In the centre of Walsingham you can still see the remains of the east end of the Priory and some of its fine tracery work around the windows. But perhaps the most interesting aspect within the grounds is a small piece of land, not twenty yards from the Priory ruins. It is a slightly raised flat mound, and tradition has it that this is the actual site of the Holy House, where over a thousand years ago Richeldis built her vision. The Anglican tradition has it that their shrine – the New Holy House – is built on the original shrine. The Roman Catholics maintain that the flat mound in the Priory grounds is nearer the truth. In fact in 1961, the Royal Archaeological Society declared that the mound was indeed the original site of the Holy House. Not only did they find the charred remains of a wooden building of the exact proportions of the original, but they also found the remains – identified by a signet ring – of a rich nobleman of Henry III's reign, whose will is in the British Museum in which he asks to be buried in the Holy House at Walsingham.

Just before the gates to the Old Priory were closed, I walked around the ruins with an old Roman Catholic priest I had met. He had served all his priestly life in that diocese. By now the wind had dropped, it was very still and a few pigeons flapped high in the traceries of the ruin which cast long shadows across the spring greensward. My guide pointed out the remaining east arch, a truly beautifully proportioned piece of mediaeval architecture. Opposite the arch, down the building, we saw the remaining pillars at the west end, and over to our left the refectory. Part of the Priory church still stands over to the south side near the banks of the river. As we walked and talked, the priest began to tell me why he thought so many came to Walsingham. 'We revere Our Lady, not as an object in herself,' he said, 'but as a way of showing Christ to the world. We're doing nothing more than Christ himself did, are we? After all, he chose a human being for the greatest possible vocation.' The old man then spoke of pilgrimage in its widest sense. 'Pilgrimage is a pious devotion which has great significance; we are a pilgrim church, a pilgrim people and going to heaven, just as the Hebrew people were on pilgrimage when they came out of bondage in Egypt for forty years. That's a round figure which means a span of life. So, just as they were on pilgrimage to the Promised Land of Canaan, the Church is on a journey to the Promised Land. Each of us has his own way of doing this, but the whole Body of Christ, the whole human family is on pilgrimage. And in a way a pilgrimage is a kind of sacrament; it's a sign of a greater pilgrimage that we have of going to God.'

WALSINGHAM

In the northern part of the East Anglian county of Norfolk there are two villages called Walsingham; Little Walsingham is where the shrines are to be found, and Great Walsingham is a mile farther north. Little Walsingham has the larger population, but Great Walsingham has the larger area of land within the parish boundary.

For many people the pilgrimage to Walsingham starts at the Slipper Chapel, the official Roman Catholic shrine, which is a mile south of Little Walsingham in the village of Houghton St Giles. It is called the Slipper Chapel possibly because it was here that the pilgrims of the Middle Ages used to leave their shoes in order to walk the last penitential mile barefoot. The exterior of the chapel is fourteenth century but is has undergone considerable restoration work, particularly towards the end of the last century. Until that time it had been allowed to fall into

decay, but when the scheme to restore Walsingham as a place of pilgrimage was decided, the Slipper Chapel was renovated.

On 15 August 1934 the Roman Catholic bishop of Northampton celebrated the first public Mass in the Slipper Chapel for 400 years. The chapel stands immediately adjacent to the road that leads to Walsingham, and around it the garden is full of crosses brought by pilgrims. The chapel is so small that there is never enough room to seat all those who come on pilgrimage; however, a new Chapel of Reconciliation has now been built close to the Slipper Chapel, on the site that was once intended to hold an open church designed by the late Donovan Purcell. However, his concept of an open church was considered impractical because it would give little protection from the chilly Norfolk winds. His base has now been used as the foundation of the new chapel, in the form of a Saxon barn. It can now accommodate 7,000 pilgrims and is so designed that one side opens up to allow as many as 10,000 to participate in the service. The chapel was consecrated on 25 March 1981.

On the way to the village of Little Walsingham you will pass the ruined friary, built in 1347 but almost destroyed at the time of the Reformation. Unfortunately it is not open to the public, but it can be seen quite clearly from the road. In the village itself lies the Anglican shrine built between 1931 and 1938. The focal point for most pilgrimages, Anglican and Roman Catholic, is the ruins of the priory built in the fourteenth century. Originally the monastery was built by the Augustinian Canons who, during the Middle Ages, looked after the shrine, but at the Reformation the priory was dissolved and the building and grounds sold to Mr Thomas Sidney for £90! The priory is still privately owned but is open to the public on Wednesdays and frequently on other days during the season. Standing alone in the centre of the grounds are the remains of the east façade of the Priory church with its great arched window and adjacent columns.

Across the road from the priory grounds is the new Anglican shrine church built during the 1930s around the spot where the original Holy House, built by Richeldis de Faverches in 1061, was thought to have been. Recent archaeological evidence has since disproved this theory and has placed the site of the original shrine in the priory grounds opposite.

The Anglican shrine church is built of red brick and granite like many buildings in this part of Norfolk. It has a white plastered west façade, on the apex of which stands a statue of the Virgin Mary. The style of the church is not modern, since it was decided that the shrine should reflect the architecture of the mediaeval age, when Walsingham was a great centre of pilgrimage. As the pilgrims enter the church they will see on their right a window depicting the original founder of the shrine of Walsingham, Richeldis de Faverches; she can be seen kneeling in front of a vision of the Virgin and Child and on her knee the Virgin holds a small model of the Holy House. Inside the shrine church there are numerous small chapels and altars, many dedicated to and named after the important events of Mary's life: there is an Altar of the Annunciation and one dedicated to the Coronation of Mary in Heaven. There is a Chapel of the Nativity and a Chapel of the Visitation of Mary to Elizabeth. In the centre of the church stands the Holy House, a shrine within a shrine. Facing the pilgrim as he enters the Holy House is an elaborately designed altar above which is the famous Walsingham Statue of the Crowned Virgin; her crown and cape are removed during the seasons of Advent and Lent. Below her on the reredos are painted three major incidents in her life, the annunciation of Christ's birth by the angel Gabriel, Mary's visitation to her cousin Elizabeth and in between the coming of the Wise Men after the birth of Christ. For Anglican pilgrims their visit to the Holy House marks the culmination of their pilgrimage. Outside the Holy House, but still within the church itself, there is a High Altar on which stands a set of six tall, elegant candlesticks and a crucifix which are copies of a set made in the seventeenth century. Beyond the High Altar there are a number of small chapels; the one dedicated to the Holy Spirit is of a more modern design than the others. Near this chapel are stairs leading up to a gallery from which the pilgrim gets a fine view of the shrine church below. There are also chapels off this gallery, one of which is an Eastern Orthodox chapel and is designed like a small Greek or Russian Orthodox church. The Orthodox pilgrims come to this chapel to pray and to celebrate their liturgy. Downstairs again there are more chapels to see; one of particular interest to pilgrims is the chapel dedicated to St John Vianney, Curé of Ars.

Leaving the church on the north side the pilgrim enters the Memorial Cloister which is dedicated to the memory of Father Alfred Hope Patten, founder of the Anglican shrine, who died in 1958. Inside this cloister is the Holy Well, the water from which is used for both drinking and blessing and is considered by many to have healing properties.

Adjacent to the Anglican shrine is the Hospice, where pilgrims may stay. There are 150 to 200 beds available and facilities for the disabled. Pilgrims are advised to book well in advance if they wish to stay at the Hospice.

The parish church in Little Walsingham is an interesting building to visit. It is situated in the southern part of the village off the High Street. The interior of the church was almost completely destroyed by fire some twenty years ago, where the scorch marks can be seen on the tomb of Sir Henry Sidney and his wife. The church also has a famous statue of the Risen Christ by the modern sculptor Jacob Epstein. The east window of the church shows some of the history of the village of Walsingham.

VILLAGES AND TOWNS AROUND WALSINGHAM

Since the shrines in and around Walsingham can easily be visited in a day, some pilgrims may wish to see other towns and villages which have interesting churches or historical buildings open to the public. The county of Norfolk as a whole is full of ruins of priories and monasteries destroyed at the time of Henry VIII and the dissolution in the sixteenth century. In the village of *Binham*, which lies about a mile north of Walsingham, there are the ruins of a priory which was once the home of a community of Benedictine monks, whose senior house was at St Albans in Hertfordshire. It was built in about 1100 for the Benedictines by Peter de Valoines. All that remains is the nave of the priory church, cruciform in shape, which is now the parish church of Binham. It is still possible to trace the outline of the rest of the priory because there are still some walls and some mounds enabling you to see the basic shape and form of the old priory. The most notable feature of what is now the parish church is the exterior west façade; built in the early English style, it is said to be one of the oldest of its kind in England, even pre-dating that of Westminster Abbey in London. The rest of the exterior of the church has been spoiled because of the destruction of the surrounding buildings. However, the interior is still, for the most part, intact. Unlike the exterior, the inside of the church is in the style of the Norman period. One of the most interesting features of the church is the Seven Sacrament font. There are a number of these fonts in the parish churches of Norfolk, and this one, built sometime during the fifteenth century, is a well preserved example. A Seven Sacrament font is usually made in an octagonal shape and on each face, carved in stone, are displays of the Roman Catholic sacraments: Baptism (showing a small baby with its parents), Confirmation, Marriage (the bride and groom), Reconciliation, Holy Euchar-

31

ist, Anointing of the Sick and Orders. The eighth side usually shows the Crucifixion scene.

To the west of Walsingham are the two villages of Creake, North Creake and South Creake. In North Creake are the ruins of an abbey, which was, like the Priory of Walsingham, for a community of Augustinian Canons. Founded in 1206, most of the present ruins are from the thirteenth century. The cloister and some parts of the church are part of the neighbouring house and garden. The area open to the public contains beautiful Norman arches and arched windows. The parish church of South Creake contains another example of a Seven Sacrament font, but its condition does not match the one at Binham. Also in this church there is a delicately carved rood screen, which stands at the entrance to the chancel of the church, dividing it from the nave.

Travelling north from the village of Creake you come to the Burnhams. Once there were seven parishes of Burnham, but now there are only five, and the large village of Burnham Market includes three of the old parishes. Each of the remaining villages has a parish church, each with its own interesting features. The village of Burnham Thorpe was the birthplace of the famous English Admiral, Horatio Nelson, and in the church there are various reminders of this, most notable of which is the lectern, made from the wood of Nelson's flagship, *Victory*. It was on the *Victory* that Nelson met his death during the battle of Trafalgar in 1805. Between Burnham Market and Burnham Norton there was once a Carmelite Friary. Only the gatehouse and some other fragments remain, but the gatehouse is of interest because it is said to have had the same designer as the Roman Catholic shrine, the Slipper Chapel at Houghton St Giles. The

church at Burnham Deepdale has a large square Norman font. Along the sides, carved in stone, are scenes showing the labour of the seasons. It is considered to be the most interesting Norman font in the whole of East Anglia.

The nearest major city to Walsingham is Kings Lynn, which stands at the mouth of the Great Ouse river which flows into a part of the sea known as The Wash. The word Lynn comes from a Celtic word meaning pool, an appropriate name for a town standing on a plain which was constantly flooded. People have lived in the area since Saxon times, when The Wash extended further south and the coastline used to be where King's Lynn now stands. Before the Norman Conquest the town was called Bishop's Lynn because it was owned by the bishop of Thetford, a town further south. In 1537 Henry VIII changed the name to Lynn Regis or King's Lynn because the town had remained loyal to the Crown. During the Civil War it was an important Royalist stronghold, when the rest of Norfolk was staunchly Parliamentarian. The modern town still has notable features. Travellers from London by car arrive at the ruins of the old South gate, the only surviving gate of the walled citadel that was the ancient town of Lynn. The first notable church in King's Lynn is that of St Margaret's in the place of the same name. The church is an extraordinary mixture of architectural styles, including twelfth-century Norman and fourteenth-century Decorated, and has fifteenth-century perpendicular windows. The pulpit is Georgian and the lectern is mediaeval. For those interested in brasses the church has two of the largest brasses in England. Each is made from a complete sheet of brass on which the images are engraved. The largest of the two brasses measures 9 feet 10 inches by 5 feet 8 inches and is in memory of Adam de Walsoken who died in 1349. The other brass, which is slightly smaller, commemorates Robert Braunche and his two wives. To the east of the town in a park called The Walks is the Red Mount Chapel. It is a strange building architecturally, for it has eight sides, is made of red brick and stands on a mound. The chapel is unfortunately kept locked, but will be opened on request.

The journey to King's Lynn from London can be done either by road or rail. Trains leave King's Cross regularly throughout the day. The journey by car is also straightforward, leaving London on the M11, passing through Epping and Bishop's Stortford to Cambridge, then changing on to the A10 which goes direct to King's Lynn. Travellers by train are advised to hire a car in King's Lynn, since public transport from King's Lynn to Walsingham is very erratic. It is possible to catch a bus from King's Lynn to Fakenham, but difficult to get from Fakenham to Walsingham. The route by road from King's Lynn to Walsingham is not difficult, leaving King's Lynn on the A14 westward to Fakenham then turning on to the B1105 which eventually arrives at Walsingham.

Since there are few hotels in Walsingham pilgrims may find it easier to stay in King's Lynn overnight and travel on to and from there. King's Lynn has a number of good hotels, including a three-star hotel called the *Duke's Head Hotel* in Tuesday Market Square. A less expensive hotel is the *East Anglian Hotel* in Blackfriars Road near the railway station. However, there are a number of hostels in Walsingham or near the Slipper Chapel for the accommodation of pilgrims, organised by either the Anglican Shrine Office or the Roman

Catholic Pilgrim Bureau. Altogether they can accommodate only about 400 pilgrims, and it is therefore essential to book well in advance. There is also a youth hostel nearby which is open to all.

There are other hotels in other villages around Walsingham. In the small town of Fakenham (five miles south) there are two hotels, and in the town of Wells-next-the-Sea (five miles north) there is one hotel where bed and breakfast is available at a reasonable price.

USEFUL ADDRESSES

Note: The telephone numbers as given here assume the caller is within the United Kingdom or Ireland. When ringing from abroad, the 0 at the start of each code must be omitted and the appropriate International Code must be prefixed.

The Anglican Shrine Office
Walsingham
Norfolk
Tel: Walsingham (032872) 255

The Pilgrim Bureau (R.C.)
Walsingham
Norfolk
Tel: Walsingham (032872) 217

HOTELS AND HOSTELS

Hospice of Our Lady
Walsingham
Norfolk
Tel: Walsingham (032872) 239

KING'S LYNN
Duke's Head Hotel
Tuesday Market Place
King's Lynn
Tel: King's Lynn (0553) 4996

33

East Anglian Hotel
Blackfriars Road
King's Lynn
Tel: King's Lynn (0553) 3074

FAKENHAM
The Crown Hotel
Market Place
Fakenham
Tel: Fakenham (0328) 2010

WELLS-NEXT-THE-SEA
The Crown Hotel
Butterlands
Wells
Tel: Fakenham (0328) 71209

OTHER FACILITIES IN AND AROUND WALSINGHAM

In the village of Little Walsingham adjacent to the Anglican Hospice there is a shrine shop where the pilgrim can buy books, souvenirs and many objects of piety. Opposite the Roman Catholic Slipper Chapel at Houghton St Giles there are also shops which sell souvenirs, and next door there is a tea bar where pilgrims can buy refreshments.

The villages of Walsingham are situated only seven miles from the North Sea coast. If your pilgrimage occurs during the summer months there are plenty of resorts open with all available facilities and plenty of accommodation. Any major shopping should be done on the journey to Walsingham, either in Fakenham or King's Lynn. There is a market every Thursday in Fakenham and early closing day is on Wednesday.

King's Lynn is a much larger town with a big shopping area for all requirements; early closing day is also Wednesday and there are two markets, one on Tuesday and one on Saturday. There is a Tourist Information Centre at the Town Hall in King's Lynn in Saturday Market Place, tel: (0553) 61241. There are also plenty of garages in the town for car-hire services.

CANTERBURY

In the mid-fourteenth century Geoffrey Chaucer's party of pilgrims in his *Canterbury Tales* set out from the Tabard Inn in London to walk to Canterbury. They were going to venerate the remains of 'the Holy Blissful Martyr' St Thomas Becket, who was murdered at Canterbury Cathedral 200 years before in 1170. Doubtless the Chaucerian characters would have prayed at a spot on the cathedral floor which is now marked by a stone, about six inches square. Words carved on the wall nearby tell why this is a sacred place:

THOMAS BECKET

ARCHBISHOP. SAINT. MARTYR.

DIED HERE

TUESDAY 29th DECEMBER

1170

On that dark December day four of the king's men came to Canterbury and murdered the archbishop in his own cathedral. The martyr Thomas was canonised two years and two months after his death. The new saint was to make Canterbury one of the greatest places of pilgrimage in mediaeval Europe.

Canterbury held an important position in Christian Britain many centuries before the death of Thomas. Christians had reached the British Isles two hundred years after the death of Christ in Palestine. In the year 597 the faith truly arrived with St Augustine of Canterbury; he was a missionary sent from Rome by Pope Gregory the Great who had seen Anglo-Saxon slaves in the city and was anxious that they should not be denied the Gospel. Before Augustine arrived there were a few Christians in Britain, mainly confined to the north of Scotland and parts of Wales. There were some in England, and in Canterbury which made Augustine's task of establishing the Roman Church much easier.

Over subsequent years conversion to Christianity came slowly, but eventually the office of Archbishop of Canterbury came to be recognised as the leading bishopric of the Church in Britain. During this period, prior to the Norman Conquest in 1066, Canterbury had shrines established in the cathedral in honour of two Anglo-Saxon saints, Dunstan and Alphege. Later there was great devotion to St Anselm, an Italian who lived in Normandy for many years. Anselm was a distinguished archbishop of Canterbury who died in 1109. Nine years later a boy was born in London to the wife of a prosperous merchant called Gilbert Becket who originally came from Rouen, in France. The infant was baptised Thomas. Because his father was well to do, Thomas received a good education both in London and Paris. In his early twenties he joined the staff of the then-archbishop of Canterbury, Theobald. Like other young men, educated and eager for good employment, Thomas's duties would have been learning how to manage the Church's affairs, including the administration of land of which in those days the Church owned vast acres.

Thomas, a tall and handsome youth, did well in his new employ and impressed his master, the archbishop; he showed a marked aptitude for the law, and consequently he spent more time in France and Italy studying civil and canon law. Like many men of his time, Thomas had become a cleric, taking minor orders and a vow of chastity, but at that stage he probably never intended to become an ordained priest. In 1154 Thomas was made Archdeacon of Canterbury, a position which made him the most important lawyer in the Church in England. It is at this point that Archdeacon Thomas, now in his mid-thirties, met the second protagonist in what was to be a great historical drama. He was the King of England, the young Henry II; he was only twenty-one at his coronation, but already he was well accustomed to governing his large domains across the Channel in France. Henry wanted somebody competent to mastermind the administration of England, and acting on sound advice he chose Thomas to become the

Chancellor of England and Keeper of the Great Seal. Soon, Thomas's reputation as a brilliant administrator began to travel beyond England and into Europe. The king and Thomas quickly became fast friends, and the chancellor grew to be the most influential man in the land. But as history goes on to reveal, this fine friendship was not to last. Instead it was to develop into a bitter and lengthy wrangle which was to result in tragedy.

Both Thomas and the king were proud men, and full of strength of character. They enjoyed each other's company immensely and spent a lot of time together. They often hunted side by side, they dressed in fine clothes (the chancellor more so than the king), and above all they had a great respect for each other. The bond that really held them together was a fierce loyalty to the Kingdom of England. Whilst this friendship was waxing strong, the office of Archbishop of Canterbury fell vacant, and Henry had to find a replacement for this important position.He hit on the idea of making his most trusted servant and friend, Thomas, the new archbishop. Then, as Henry thought, it would be possible for the State to control the affairs of the Church. Everyone approved the idea most enthusiastically, including the Pope. Everyone, that is, except Thomas. However, after much persuasion, Thomas conceded and he became the premier bishop of the Church of England in 1162, having first been ordained priest. What no one but Thomas seemed to realise at this point was that, as Primate of all England, his loyalty was divided between Church and State. Soon after becoming archbishop, Thomas resigned as chancellor, much to the king's annoyance. The new archbishop immediately set about returning to the Church its lands and properties, which Thomas considered to have been misappropriated by the State. This behaviour further alienated Thomas from the king, and later things really came to a head between the two over a matter of clerical immunity. In those days many men were termed 'clerics', as was Thomas himself in his early days, since the more educated classes took minor orders as a matter of course and often found work in the Church's employ. If a cleric fell foul of the law he could not be tried in a civil court. His case had to be tried by an ecclesiastical court, which probably dealt far too leniently with offenders. To redress this balance, Henry wanted all clerics to be tried by the civil court, or at least for the ecclesiastical courts to

Canterbury. The cathedral cloisters

hand out appropriate sentences to miscreants. But Thomas, possessive and unrelenting with regard to the Church and its privileges, would have none of it. A great and protracted argument then ensued over the matter; meetings were arranged between the two and cancelled, oaths were taken and broken and any reconciliation was almost immediately destroyed soon after friendship seemed to have been restored. Thomas and the king would meet, have huge, shouting arguments, and neither would give way. Relations between the two eventually became so strained that Thomas had to flee for his life to France disguised as a lay brother.

During his student days, and later as chancellor, Thomas had spent a lot of time in France, so he had friends and contacts there. French was his mother tongue from his French parents, so he was quite at home in this foreign land. For six years he roamed France in self-imposed exile. He maintained contact with Henry through letter and messenger, but their differences were not resolved; both remained beyond reconciliation. Nevertheless, Thomas did eventually return to Canterbury, probably realising, deep in his heart, what was in store for him. King Henry was in France at the time, celebrating Christmas. He was informed, quite erroneously by Thomas's enemies, that the archbishop was turning public opinion against him back in England and recruiting an army to march against his men. At this false news, Henry finally reached the end of his tether, and he now uttered the infamous phrase: 'Who will rid me of this turbulent priest?' Henry's rage transmitted itself to four of his knights who immediately set out for England and Canterbury, bent on settling the matter once and for all. Eyewitness accounts exist of what happened when the knights arrived at the cathedral on the fourth day of Christmas 1170.

The four knights first met the archbishop, unarmed, in the early afternoon, and they had a violent argument with him, accusing him of being a traitor. In his usual manner Thomas would not give an inch, and the knights left the palace in an even greater frenzy than when they had first arrived. Fearing the worst, the monks forced Thomas into the cathedral, through the cloister, assuming that he would be safe within the sanctuary and protection of consecrated ground. The monks were so terrified that they attempted to lock the entrance to the cathedral through which they had come, but Thomas forbade this. 'This is not a castle, this is the house of God. Open the doors,' he commanded. Moments later the four knights, now armed, rushed in to the cathedral to where Thomas was standing and hacked him to death. The first blow was deflected from Thomas by one of his clerks, Edward Grim, who later wrote a detailed account of the murder. Grim's arm was almost severed in his attempt to ward off the blow, and for a moment Thomas remained unharmed except for a slight graze to his head. Grim and another monk fled to the shadows, leaving Thomas alone facing the knights. Another blow now came, directed at Thomas's head, the force of which killed him outright. The tall and proud archbishop crashed down and lay full-length on the floor of his own cathedral. Not content with that, yet another knight swung his heavy sword at the head of the prostrate figure and took off the scalp, breaking the point of his weapon as he did so. The final act of another assassin was to plunge his sword into the now open skull, and scatter the brains on to the ground about the body. The knights then rushed out of the church, hastily plundered the palace of treasure and made off on horseback into the descending darkness. Some time after the assassins had quit the cathedral, the stunned and frightened monks rushed to the dead body and laid it out before the High Altar for the night. The next day the remains were taken down into the crypt and placed behind the altar of Our Lady Undercroft in a tomb. And it was at this tomb that, later, a repentant Henry was to do public penance for the death of his great friend.

During the rebuilding of the cathedral after the great fire of 1174 (only the crypt remained intact and the only part of the present-day cathedral that Thomas would now recognise) an eastern chapel was added and Thomas's remains were moved yet again into the new chapel. But so popular had the cult of St Thomas become to pilgrims in subsequent years that in 1220 the famous Golden Shrine was erected behind the High Altar in the cathedral itself above the crypt. According to historical accounts, this final resting place for the bones of the martyr was a wonderful affair, as Erasmus, the great scholar of Reformation times, testified when he visited Canterbury almost 300 years after Thomas's death:

> The wooden receptacle encloses a golden one, and when it is drawn up by a pulley, it displays wealth beyond valuation . . . The prior showed the jewels one after the other, touching them with a white wand and adding the French name, and what it was worth and who gave it.

An Italian visitor came to Canterbury in the year 1500 and described the shrine:

> But the magnificience of the tomb of St Thomas the Martyr, Archbishop of Canterbury, is that which surpasses all belief. This, notwithstanding its great size, is entirely covered over with plates of pure gold, but the gold is scarcely visible from the variety of precious stones with which it is studded, such as sapphires, diamonds, rubies, balas rubies and emeralds; and on every side that the eye turns something more beautiful than the other appears. And these beauties of nature are enhanced by human skill, for the gold is carved and engraved in beautiful designs, both large and small, and agates, jaspers, and cornelians set in relief, some of the cameos being of such a size that I dare

not mention it; but everything is left far behind by a ruby not larger than a man's thumbnail, which is set to the right of the altar. The church is rather dark, and particularly where the shrine is placed, and when we went to see it the sun was nearly down, and the weather was cloudy; yet I saw that ruby as well as if I had it in my hand.

It is said that this particular ruby is now part of the Crown Jewels, on public display at the Tower of London.

I stood near to where the Great Shrine used to be, and as I did so I had an uninterrupted view down the vast cathedral, descending on three levels towards the west door. I imagined those mediaeval pilgrims as they filed up the Pilgrim Steps on one side, past the shrine, and down the steps at the other side. Through the years they came, hundreds and thousands of them from many parts of Britain and Europe. The last great pilgrimage to Canterbury was made around 1520, when Henry VIII, 'with every sign of devotion', in company of Cardinal Wolsey and Emperor Charles V of Spain, made the journey to Thomas's shrine. Ten years later Henry gave orders for this shrine, and all other shrines in England, to be destroyed. Naturally, therefore, this period of the Reformation marks the virtual end of pilgrimages in England. Since the very beginning of the Reformation many shrines had been in decline and few pilgrims were actually visiting them.

A little over two years after his death Thomas was canonised by the Church. Almost immediately after his martyrdom scores of miracles began to be attributed to Thomas through his intercession, seen by many as a vindication of his case against Henry II. Pilgrims began coming to Canterbury because of the miracles, and many of them are recorded in the beautiful miracle windows which can be seen today in the cathedral. Not only do these windows illustrate important details of history, including a probable likeness of Thomas, but they are also some of the finest examples of mediaeval stained glass in existence.

At the eastern end of Canterbury Cathedral, near the spot where the Great Shrine stood, there is the eastern chapel, once the resting place of the piece of skull, or crown, which had been sliced from the head of Thomas at his murder. This chapel is now the chapel of the saints and martyrs of our own time, bringing

Canterbury into the twentieth century. There is a list of present-day saints and martyrs posted up at the chapel, including: Charles de Foucauld, died in December 1916, Frenchman, priest and monk who founded the Little Brothers of Jesus, shot in his home in the Sahara by raiding tribesmen; Metropolitan Vladimir of Kiev, died 1917, murdered in the early months of the Revolution; Maximilian Kolbe, Polish Franciscan friar, died in Auschwitz Concentration Camp in August 1941, taking the place of another prisoner condemned to death; Edith Stein, died 1942, theologian and philosopher – from a Jewish family she became a Carmelite nun and died in a gas chamber in Poland; Dietrich Bonhoeffer, died 1945, German Lutheran, theologian and teacher – arrested for his part in the resistance to Hitler – hanged in Flossenburg Concentration Camp on 9 April 1945; Martin Luther King, died 1968 – Baptist minister and civil rights leader – murdered in Memphis, Tennessee; Archbishop Janani Luwum of Uganda, distinguished church leader, murdered in Uganda in February 1977 defending the rights of his people; Archbishop Oscar Romero, died 1980 – courageous champion of human rights – murdered in San Salvador in March 1980. Also, at the eastern chapel, there is a quote from T S Eliot's *Murder in the Cathedral*:

A Christian martyrdom is never an accident, for saints are not made by accident. Still less is a Christian martyrdom the effect of a man called to become a saint, as a man by willing and continuing may become a ruler of men. A martyrdom is always the design of God, for his love of men, to warn them and to lead them, to bring them back to his ways.

CANTERBURY

Long before the Romans came to Britain in the year AD 43, there were people living on the site which is now called Canterbury. When the Romans arrived across the Channel from France (Gaul) they settled at Canterbury and called it Durovernum Cantiacorum. Under its new masters the town prospered, a fact which came to light during the air raids of the Second World War; a bomb fell on the centre of the town and blasted away buildings to reveal the ruins of the largest Roman theatre ever to be found in Britain.

After the Romans left Britain, the country became divided into small kingdoms, and Canterbury was the main town of the kingdom of Kent. During the reign of King Ethelbert of Kent, Pope Gregory the Great (540–604) sent St Augustine and forty monks to England to re-establish Christianity. In the year AD 597, Augustine and his small band of monks landed on the south coast and made their way to Canterbury. They chose to come to Canterbury because King Ethelbert's wife, Queen Bertha, was herself a Christian and the daughter of Charibert, the Christian king of Paris. It was Queen Bertha who persuaded her husband to allow Augustine and his followers to settle in Canterbury and build their first monastery there. From here the faith was taken to all parts of Anglo-Saxon England. Ethelburga, the daughter of King Ethelbert, married Edwin the King of York, and after her marriage she took a monk called Paulinus with her to the north of England. Paulinus became the first Bishop of York and brought Roman Christianity to that part of the world.

In 1066 William the Conqueror, the Duke of Normandy, defeated the Anglo-Saxon King Harold at the Battle of Hastings, about 50 miles to the southwest of Canterbury. Soon after his coronation as the new King of England, William removed almost all the Anglo-Saxon Bishops and Archbishops from office and replaced them with Normans. The new Archbishop of Canterbury was a 65-year-old Norman of Italian birth called Lanfranc. He is important to the development of Canterbury because he rebuilt the cathedral and secured the supremacy of the Archdiocese of Canterbury over that of York in 1072. From that year onward Canterbury became the centre of religious power in the land, a power that was eventually to cause the conflict between King Henry II and his

archbishop, Thomas Becket, whose death led to the great era of pilgrimages to Canterbury.

MEDIAEVAL CHURCHES IN CANTERBURY

ST DUNSTAN'S

The parish church of St Dunstan's is situated on the old road from London, and was probably the first indication to the mediaeval pilgrims that they were nearing their destination. It is an old church dedicated to the tenth-century Anglo-Saxon saint from Glastonbury. Dunstan was born in AD 909 and became Archbishop of Canterbury in AD 959. He is famous for re-establishing the monastic life in England, restoring the abbeys at Westminster, Bath and Exeter. These monasteries followed the Rule of St Benedict but with some features peculiar to Britain. Dunstan is also known to have written part of the present Coronation Rite which was first used when he crowned Edgar King of All England in AD 973. The church was probably built and dedicated soon after the saint's death in AD 988.

In 1170, after the murder of Thomas Becket, King Henry II came to Canterbury to do penance at the tomb of the newly-made martyr. He rode to Canterbury from London, and stopped at the church of St Dunstan's where he took off his royal garments, his jewellery, his sword, and put on a ragged monk's habit. From the church of St Dunstan's he walked the one and a half miles to the cathedral. His example was followed by countless pilgrims who came after him, making St Dunstan's an important church in the years of pilgrimage to Canterbury.

Later in the fifteenth century the church of St Dunstan's itself became a place of pilgrimage. In 1535 Sir Thomas More, once Lord Chancellor of England, was beheaded on Tower Hill in London. He had been tried and found guilty of treason against King Henry VIII, since he had refused to swear the Oath of Supremacy and thereby declare the king Supreme Head of the Church of England in place of the Pope. More's eldest and favourite daughter, Margaret Roper, lived with her husband's family in Canterbury. After the execution her father's head was impaled above Westminster Bridge. Secretly, at night, Margaret had the head removed from its pike and taken back to Canterbury, where it was placed in the Roper family tomb in the church of St Dunstan's. For some years after, Roman Catholics from all over England and Europe came to pray and pay homage at the tomb inside the church.

St Dunstan's, which stands on a mound slightly back from the road, is still used as a parish church today. Inside, the atmosphere is quiet and restful, and thick mediaeval walls insulate the church from the noise of the traffic outside. It is a simple uncluttered church, light and airy, with a very few stained-glass windows. The interior is comparatively small, seating about 500 people. To the right of the altar is the Roper tomb. A brass slab on the floor gives the precise position and the names of those members of the family whose remains are in the tomb. At the turn of the century the tomb was reopened and a photograph was taken of what was thought to be the skull of Sir Thomas More; a reproduction of the photograph can be seen in the church.

ST MARTIN'S CHURCH

If pilgrims coming from London stopped at St Dunstan's church, then the pilgrims coming from the Continent probably stopped at the church of St Martin's which is situated on the south side of Canterbury near the old Dover Road. St Martin's is the oldest church in Canterbury, and it is thought to have been a place of Christian worship since Saxon times and perhaps as far back as Roman Britain. The Church is mentioned in that famous source of early English history, *The Ecclesiastical History of the English People,* completed about AD 731 by the Venerable Bede. In AD 562 King Ethelbert's new wife Bertha arrived in Kent from France, and the King gave her the church of St Martin's, so that she could continue to live as a Christian. The Venerable Bede writes 'There was on the east side of the city a church dedicated to St Martin which had been used by the Roman Christians in Britain. To this church the Queen, accompanied by Bishop Luidhard, came to worship.' Luidhard was also from France and had come to England with the queen to act as her personal chaplain. For 35 years they were the only Christians in this part of England until St Augustine and his monks arrived in AD 597, and it was at the church of St Martin's that the first converts came to be baptised. Probably the most eminent of the new Christians to be baptised at the Saxon font was King Ethelbert. It is thought that the font, which is still in use, was built especially for the occasion of the royal baptism.

The church stands on a hill about half a mile outside the old walls of the city. On arrival the visitor passes through the lychgate into the churchyard, which is surrounded by old and gnarled yew trees, making the churchyard appear rather dark and sombre. There is a path that leads from the lychgate to the church porch. Inside, the church is dark, small and narrow. There is not much left of the original building except possibly the foundations under the nave and the west wall. This wall is the most beautiful feature of the church, and is thought to be one of the oldest walls in England. Its beauty lies in the different shades of colour to be found in the old stones. The wall appears to have been made with thousands of small pebble-like stones of varied shapes and shades, which gives it an unusual texture and feel.

Outside again, and walking round the church away from the lychgate towards the opposite end of the churchyard, the visitor turning to face west has a magnificent view of the cathedral.

ST MILDRED'S CHURCH

St Mildred's church is situated in the southwest part of the city, just inside the old city walls. Like St Dunstan's it is a mediaeval church named after a local mediaeval saint, Mildred; she was a direct descendant of King Ethelbert's and became abbess of a convent at Minster on the Isle of Thanet, a convent which her mother had founded. The date on which the church of St Mildred's in Canterbury was built is not known exactly but it is certainly of the Saxon period. The architecture as well as the name confirms this view. Soon after the Norman Conquest, when William had appointed Lanfranc Archbishop of Canterbury, the archbishop came into conflict with St Augustine's Saxon monks who refused to accept their new Norman abbot appointed by Lanfranc. The archbishop retaliated by locking the monks out of their abbey. The dissident monks sought refuge in St Mildred's, hoping that the archbishop might be forced to change his mind. He did not and the monks had to accept the abbot's appointment before

they were allowed to return to their monastery.

St Mildred's is also historically known as a 'sanctuary church'. In the Middle Ages, an escaped criminal could claim sanctuary from the Church if in his flight he could manage to reach a church and cling to the large iron handle. Afterwards, instead of receiving the usual punishment for his crime, which would be either imprisonment or execution, he would be declared an outlaw, allowed to go free but banished from his home. St Mildred's church stands near the old Norman castle which used to be a gaol and, therefore, was the nearest church for those who escaped and sought sanctuary.

There are two other mediaeval churches still in use in Canterbury: St Peter's on the High Street and St Alphege's just outside the cathedral precincts.

EASTBRIDGE OR ST THOMAS' HOSPITAL

Almost opposite St Peter's church is another of Canterbury's oldest buildings, Eastbridge Hospital. It was built soon after Becket's murder and was used to house the poorest pilgrims who came to Canterbury to pray at St Thomas's tomb. It is very conveniently situated, standing as it does on the High Street, on the main route from London to the cathedral. The hospital consists of a crypt where the pilgrims slept, a refectory and a chapel. Entering from the street the visitors find themselves in a small hall; on the left is a doorway and two steps lead down into the crypt. The temperature, even on a warm sunny day, is icy, since the walls are thick and let in little warmth; just outside, below the window, the River Stour runs directly past the hospital which also adds to the chill. The toughness and perseverance of the

45

mediaeval pilgrims comes to mind when standing in the crypt. Many of them would have walked hundreds of miles to get to Canterbury and then sleep on pallets on the cold stone floor. Upstairs in the refectory the temperature is much warmer, but the furnishing is still sparse and merely functional. At the top of the house is the small and intimate chapel, which seats about 20 people. The roof is well worth a look – it is made of a magnificent collection of old beams. From the hospital the pilgrim only had about half a mile to walk, to reach the cathedral and his destination.

MODERN CANTERBURY

Modern Canterbury has become a thriving shopping centre and university city; the campus of the new University of Kent is about a mile outside the city. For visitors from the Continent, Canterbury has become easily accessible by road and rail. Channel ferries sail into Dover and Folkestone from Calais, Dunkirk and Boulogne regularly every day. There is a regular train service from Dover into Canterbury East Station.

Those who travel by road have an alternative route; they can either drive straight up the main road into Canterbury, or they can take a more circuitous route through some of the most beautiful country in Kent. Once in Canterbury, the motorist will find sufficient parking facilities for his car.

The journey south from London is equally straightforward. The train journey from London Victoria Station or London Charing Cross takes about an hour and a half, and the traveller can choose whether to arrive at Canterbury East Station, which is best for the Cathedral, or Canterbury West which is nearest the northern end of the city. The journey by train gives the traveller

the chance to see the finest view of the towers of Christ Church Cathedral, high above the skyline, as the train draws into the station. Driving from London to Canterbury, a distance of 55 miles, is relatively easy. It is motorway almost all the way. From the centre of London the motorist takes any road leading to the South Circular road which they follow until they reach the turning on to the M2 motorway which takes them all the way to Canterbury.

ACCOMMODATION IN CANTERBURY

Accommodation for the visitor in Canterbury is varied, from hotels to bed and breakfast. Many of the hotels are of significant historic interest: the *Cathedral Gate Hotel* is situated at the very centre of the city, immediately adjacent to the Christ Church Gate of the cathedral. The site has been used by pilgrims and travellers to Canterbury, since the time of Chaucer; it is quite a small hotel, accommodating about 50 people, and some of the bedrooms at the back of the hotel have a magnificent view of the cathedral. Also in the centre of the city is the *County Hotel*, larger than the Cathedral Gate, but with a pleasant mixture of the modern and historic; it has been a hotel since the seventeenth century and is a striking old-timbered building; it has accommodation for about 70 people. Just outside the old city wall is the *Abbey Gate Guest House*, a sixteenth-century coaching inn; it is smaller than the others, having rooms for about ten people. Further up the High Street, through the west gate into St Dunstan's Street, there is the *House of Agnes Hotel*, named after the heroine of Charles Dickens in his novel *David Copperfield;* it is thought that Dickens stayed at this house on his frequent visits to Canterbury and used it as a

model to describe the house of Agnes
Wickfield, in which David Copperfield
stayed as a child. On the whole, accommodation is very good in Canterbury
and caters for all tastes.

Note: The telephone numbers as
given here assume the caller is within
the United Kingdom or Ireland. When
ringing from abroad, the 0 at the start
of each code must be omitted and the
appropriate International Code must be
prefixed.

HOTELS
Cathedral Gate Hotel
Christchurch Gate Way
Canterbury
Tel: Canterbury (0227) 64381

Abbey Gate Guest House
7 North Lane
Canterbury
Tel: Canterbury (0227) 68770

County Hotel
High Street
Canterbury
Tel: Canterbury (0227) 66266

The House of Agnes Hotel
71 St Dunstan's Street
Canterbury
Tel: Canterbury (0227) 65077

FOR INFORMATION ON ACCOMMODATION
South East England Tourist Board

Dept K
Cheviot House
Tunbridge Wells
Kent TN1 1NH
Tel: Tunbridge Wells (0892) 40766

Tourist Information Centre
22 St Peter's Street
Canterbury
Tel: Canterbury (0227) 66567

OTHER FACILITIES
The cathedral. It was the custom of
mediaeval pilgrims to return home with
a souvenir of the pilgrimage; modern
visitors to the cathedral can also buy
reminders of their stay. There are a
number of shops inside the cathedral
precincts, selling anything from post-
cards to glassware.

There are guides always available
giving tours around the cathedral.

The shops. Canterbury has a large modern shopping centre with all the major
trade names represented; it is in the
middle of Canterbury, near the cathedral. Some of the streets are prohibited
to traffic and are for the pedestrian
only, which makes the shopping much
easier. The city also has two cinemas
and two theatres, and many interesting
restaurants, some of which are very
old.

There are bus and coach services in
and out of Canterbury and a number of
car-hire firms.

CROAGH PATRICK

Croagh Patrick, or St Patrick's Mountain, is a few miles to the southwest of the town of Westport overlooking Clew Bay. This is Ireland's holy mountain in County Mayo, where St Patrick spent 40 days and nights of Lent in the year AD 441.

To climb Croagh Patrick is to be a pilgrim, for that is the penance, and before I set out to make that climb I was warned of two things: make sure you are wearing sturdy footwear as the going can be rough, particularly near to the summit, and secondly, do not attempt the climb if weather conditions are bad. I took the first piece of advice, which turned out to be very sound. As for the second warning, the day was fine so the problem did not arise. However, I had heard that people have been lost on the mountain in the cold and swirling mists which gather in from the Atlantic with great and unexpected speed. Had there been any hint of a mist or fog I would not have attempted the climb, particularly since I was alone. In fact as it turned out, I was not completely alone on the mountain; late in the season as it was, there were still quite a few pilgrims toiling up and down the steep slopes of the penitential 'Reek'. There were half a dozen of us gathered around the large statue of St Patrick at Murrisk, the starting point. The Irish patron gazes out across the bay with his back to the mountain, dressed in his traditional bishop's vestments with a crook and a piece of shamrock in his hand. Ever since St Patrick spent his Lent on the inhospitable mountain top in the fifth century, praying and fasting as Jesus had done in the desert, pilgrims have been coming here in an unbroken line to follow in his footsteps.

It is said Patrick was a Scot by birth and lived from about 385 to 461. In his famous *Confession* he writes of his early life and some of his adventures:

48

My father was Calpirnius a deacon, a son of Potitus a presbyter, who belonged to the village of Bannavem Taberniae. He had a farmhouse near at hand where I was taken captive. I was at that time sixteen years of age. I paid no heed to the true God; and I was brought captive to Ireland with so many thousands of persons according to our deserts, because we turned away from God and kept not his commandments, and we were not obedient to our priests, who admonished us about our salvation. And the Lord sent upon us the indignation of his wrath and scattered us amongst many nations even unto the ends of the earth, where now my littleness may be seen amongst strangers.

It was Irish pirates who took Patrick into slavery where he remained for six years. He was probably held in County Antrim, where he was given the task of tending sheep and cattle. On his own admittance, Patrick had not taken his faith very seriously – even though it seems he came from a devout Christian family. However, as his seemingly endless captivity wore on, Patrick's thoughts turned more and more to God.

The love of God and the fear of Him increased more and more, and my faith grew and my spirit was stirred up, so that in a single day I prayed as often as a hundred times, and by night as frequently, even while I was in the woods and on the mountain. Before daybreak I used to be awakened to pray in snow, frost and rain, and I felt no hurt, and there was no sloth in me, as I now perceive, because the spirit then was fervent within me.

For Patrick, as for many other saints, the hard times concentrated the mind wonderfully on to higher spiritual values. So gradually Patrick was transformed into a devout Christian, praying to God incessantly. After his six years in captivity he either escaped or was set free. According to his writings, Patrick had a dream in which he was promised liberty and reunion with his family. He travelled to either County Mayo, in the west, or due south to Wicklow, where he begged begrudging sailors to take him with them. After many adventures, some possibly in France, Patrick was eventually reunited with his family. Once he was back in his homeland he received some form of training to the priesthood, although he never became a learned man. Naturally, Patrick's family hoped that he would now stay with them and settle in Britain, but the call to return to Ireland was too strong. Patrick had a dream which pointed the way for him and mapped out his future.

And once more, after a few years I was in Britain with my kindred, who received me as a son, and earnestly besought me that now, at least, after such great tribulation as I had endured, I should not leave them anymore. And there, indeed, I beheld a vision in the night a man whose name was Victorious coming as it were from Ireland with letters innumerable. And he gave me one of them, and I read the beginning of the letter, which contained 'The Voice of the Irish'; and while I was reading the beginning of the letter methought that at that very moment I heard the voice of those who lived beside the Wood of Foclut, which is near the Western Sea. And as with one voice they thus cried aloud: 'We beseech thee, O holy youth, to come and walk once more amongst us.' And I felt quite broken in heart and could read no more. And so I awoke. Thanks be to God, that after many years the Lord granted to them according to their earnest cry.

Before returning to Ireland in 435 Patrick may have spent some time in France at various monasteries. He succeeded Palladius as a bishop in Ireland and concentrated his evangelical activity mainly in the north of the country in Armagh. Patrick was first and foremost a shepherd to his flock and totally devoted to bringing Christ to those who did not know him. He stamped out idolatory and sun-worship and all other forms of paganism in existence at the time. Patrick's fame as a missionary spread across the water to many parts of England and Wales and to some parts of the Continent. (There is a tradition which connects Patrick with Glastonbury in the west of England. It is believed that the Irish from the eighth century thought that the Irish patron was buried there. Streams of pilgrims would make the journey across the water and visit a place which they believed to be his tomb. In fact, a little way out of Glastonbury is a place called Beckery, which means 'Little Ireland' in Gaelic which is spoken in the Scottish Highlands. The Irish pilgrims had their headquarters here, and it was certainly a holy spot where Irish people came in those times.) This tradition, however – like many others connected with St Patrick – is hard to substantiate. His feast is celebrated in the Christian world on 17

March; his statue depicts him holding the shamrock, the triple-leafed plant, which it is said he used to attempt a simple explanation of the Holy Trinity and the three Persons in one God. Nevertheless, in spite of scant evidence about the details of St Patrick's life, belief in him and the traditions connected with him are still very much a part of Irish Roman Catholic life. In Ireland, Patrick is a religious and a folk hero rolled into one.

In relation to Croagh Patrick, Patrick has been called the Moses of Croagh Patrick, and the tradition goes that he spent forty days and nights atop the lonely mountain. When Patrick came to the west of Ireland, preaching the word of God and baptising people, he came under considerable pressure from his colleagues to resign his bishopric. It seems that thirty years earlier, as a youth, he had been guilty of some indiscretion which he had confided in someone. Spitefully, this confidence was broken, and Patrick was accused of being an unfit person to hold the office of bishop. In the depth of his depression and sorrow, Patrick took to the mountain as Christ had taken to the desert, to pray and fast and seek guidance. He wrote in his *Confession*: 'Christ knoweth that fully and exceedingly did I desire, and was ready, that he should grant me to drink of his chalice, as he had permitted also to others who loved him.'

At the base of Croagh Patrick I enjoyed the view which the statue of Patrick looks out upon; the ground drops away to marshes and deep natural lochs and rugged land and out to the Atlantic. I then turned towards the mountain and commenced a climb of two hours straight up. Just like Patrick, I was ascending the holy mountain, the royal mountain of St Patrick. It has a good cone shape which means that the first half is the easiest. Halfway up the ground levels for a short while, which means a chance to catch the breath and perhaps turn around and marvel at the view which grows grander with each foot of increased height. From there on the going gets tougher by the step. A reasonably fit person can expect to make the climb in less than two hours at a steady pace, including short stops along the way for breath and good views. The last few hundred yards prove to be the real test of the true pilgrim; the angle of the incline looks, at first, so steep as to be impossible to scale. Added to that is the hazard of sharp, shale-like rocks which spill down the Reek side and act as a natural barrier to dissuade anyone from venturing farther. But take heart and keep going and don't look down! The scramble to the summit itself, once clear of the loose shale, is much easier, and with what relief I finally felt the ground level out on the mountain top. There was a timeless quality I felt about being up the mountain, for the view I was seeing was exactly the same as Patrick must have seen when he made the climb over 1,500 years earlier.

There is an old story that on a clear day you can see the streets of New York across the Atlantic. I looked hard in the face of a constant and strong wind, but not one skyscraper did I spy! However, I was not disappointed; to my right I was looking northwards across County Mayo, through Clew Bay and into Sligo; to my left I was looking south, across Connemara and into the Twelve Bens. I was more than 2,500 feet above sea level, and on a

Croagh Patrick

good day you can see through a 180-degree sweep, a distance of over 300 miles. I saw it. By a simple turn of my head I was able to see most of the west coast of Ireland.

On the summit there is a chapel which somehow manages to withstand the constant ravages of the wind and the rain which sweep across Croagh Patrick, regardless of the time of year. The parish priest of the nearby church had kindly lent me the key and so I let myself in. There is a simple altar where Mass is said for the pilgrims in the summer time. To the side there is a confessional, and opposite, at the other side, is the sacristy. Dominating the chapel is a large statue of St Patrick which has been placed above the altar at the rear. The inscription above him reads 'UT CHRISTIANI ITA ET ROMANI SITIS' (that you may be Christians as well as Romans). It is a small chapel, with comfortable accommodation for about 40 people, although there is no furniture of any kind. From the outside the building is whitewashed and plain. It was built 2,500 feet above sea level and each stone, each piece of timber and mortar had to be dragged up that steep mountainside by hand. (I later met a man who has been largely responsible for the present sound state of the chapel, and he thought nothing of making that climb dozens of times in the summer season.)

It is likely that some sort of chapel has existed here on the top of Croagh Patrick for many centuries, although it is difficult to say if anything existed here at the time of St Patrick. It was only at the beginning of this century, in 1903, that Croagh Patrick took on an important significance as a place of annual pilgrimage, which became a national event in Ireland. A year later, on the last Sunday in July 1904, thousands of people from all over Ireland and other countries made the ascent up the holy mountain. The following year the present chapel was completed, and it was opened on 30 July 1905. On that day there were 1,000 people there to see the chapel first used as a place of worship. Today, up to 80,000 pilgrims make the climb, the young and the old alike. Until very recently people started the journey in the early hours of the morning so as to arrive at the summit at daybreak. Many accidents used to occur – particularly towards the top where the loose stones are – so now the pilgrimage begins at dawn on the last Sunday in July. On that day Mass starts on the top at six, and continues for most of the day. On the way up there are prescribed prayers which are said at three penitential stations.

First station: This is at the base of the cone, Leacht Benain. Walking around the Leacht seven times the pilgrim says seven Our Fathers, seven Hail Marys and the Creed.

Second station: This is on the summit, near the oratory at Leabah Phadraig (St Patrick's Bed). This is said kneeling and consists of seven Our Fathers, seven Hail Marys and the Creed. Then in front of the altar are said fifteen Our Fathers, fifteen Hail Marys and the Creed. After this prayers are said as one walks fifteen times around the mound on the summit. Next seven Our Fathers and Hail Marys and one Creed, kneeling at Leabah Phadraig, and finally seven circuits of the Leabha, praying.

Third station: This is the Roiligh Muire, which is some distance down from the top on the west side of the mountain. At each of the circles forming this station, seven Our Fathers, seven Hail Marys and the Creed are said while walking seven times round each circle. Then the Carrdha Mor, in which Roiligh Muire is situated, is circled seven times praying. This completes the traditional stations of the Reek.

Contrary to my expectations, the descent to the base of the mountain was almost as difficult as the ascent; the legs have to work hard in reverse and act as brakes to control the descent. However, after much pounding I at last reached my destination which was the roadside and the public house where I had left my car. About a mile up the road I went to visit the old man who built and preserved the oratory on the top. He is over 70 now, and as he sat before his peat fire in his little cottage he told me of the days when he spent whole weekends up there so that he could complete the work that much more quickly. He told me that he was very disappointed that he did not feel quite well enough to make the journey that year – but that he would certainly be going up next year! He gave me a tiny medal, on one side of which is a picture of St Patrick, and on the reverse a picture of the mountain and the dates 461–1961. I could see in the old man's eyes that he thought a great deal about St Patrick's mountain.

LOUGH DERG

If you want a true taste of Celtic Christianity, then go to Lough Derg, 80 miles to the north of Knock on the Donegal–Fermanagh border with Northern Ireland. It is a place of pilgrimage which goes back many centuries, and its whole emphasis has always been on penance. Pilgrims both high- and low-born came from all corners of Europe to shrive themselves of their sins at St Patrick's Purgatory, a lonely island in the centre of the Lough. As I travelled northwards towards Donegal, I was following a trail which many generations of Irish pilgrims had travelled, since the time of St Patrick. They had wished to undergo an experience of prayer and fasting unlike anything else in Christendom. The weather was fine as I left Knock, and I made good progress on the lonely roads as I passed through Sligo, Ballyshannon and Donegal. When I reached the County Town I headed southeast a few miles to the village of Pettigo, where I booked in at a small hotel on the main street. Only yards from the hotel there is a customs post for those wishing to cross into Ulster. Pettigo is only a couple of miles from Lough Derg, a vast lake four miles wide and six miles long. The water is dotted with many small islands, the main one being St Patrick's Purgatory or Station Island. It is not a place for the faint-hearted, and only those of serious intent need apply. It's a place where the world is left behind, where no radios, no cameras, and no extra food or clothing is allowed. You have to be physically fit and over fourteen before your application will be considered to undergo the rigours of a three-day round of prayer and fasting. What little sleep you are allowed will be taken on a hard bunk bed in a large cut stone building, with no privacy and few facilities.

St Patrick's Purgatory was always the principal landmark on mediaeval maps of Ireland, and indeed the only place in the whole of Ireland mentioned on a world map of 1492. From the twelfth to the fifteenth century pilgrims came from France, Hungary, Spain, England and Holland as well as from Ireland itself. Not surprisingly, there are strong legendary connections between St Patrick and Lough Derg, and it seems quite probable that he knew of the island, since he spent thirty years in the general area evangelising in the fifth century. Actual records of Irish history are scant for this period, and it is only tradition which tells us that St Patrick set foot on the island. At Templecarne there is a church said to have been founded by St Patrick himself. In the graveyard there are the ruins of a church, and if St Patrick did lay its foundations, then he would have spent several months in the area. As he went about Ireland, preaching and converting the pagans to Christianity, he travelled slowly, spending many months at each location, so it is likely that he was aware of the island on the Lough. As in the case of Croagh Patrick, the Irish saint had a predilection for isolated places, and fromTemplecarne, Station Island would have been perfect. Before St Patrick was able to interest the pagan Irish in his Christianity he had to destroy the hold the Druid priests had over them. One account describes the dispossessed Druid gods, fleeing before St Patrick as he marched over the countryside with his retinue. Some of these spirits took up their abode on Station Island, and to prove that his God was greater than all Druid gods, St Patrick set out alone for the island. The people tried to dissuade him from this, because they feared that they would never see him again. Undaunted, he crossed the water, and after twenty-four hours of fierce fighting with the evil spirits St Patrick emerged victorious. He returned to the mainland and dedicated the island as a place of penance. There is another legend which explains the famous 'cave' on the island, which existed there until it was destroyed during the Reformation. In order to convince the people of the horrors of hell and purgatory, St Patrick is said to have drawn a circle on the ground with his staff, whereupon the ground opened up to reveal a glimpse of what was in store for the lost souls in the afterlife. That cave became the most outstanding feature of St Patrick's Purgatory for over 1,000 years. To some historians the whole style and manner which seems to have pervaded the island bore the stamp of St Patrick's Celtic Christianity. In his *Confession* he constantly refers to penance, constant praying and being alone. St Patrick was

Lough Derg

filled with a desire to be 'chastened' for his sins in order to make way for an increased spiritual awareness. Certainly those who came to Station Island after St Patrick knew that this was the sort of experience they would have there; it would be hard, purifying and concentrated on the 'cave'. There are many accounts of what the cave was like, and although they differ in some of the details, they all share the common theme that it was an experience quite out of the ordinary.

Unlike the three-day pilgrimage of today, which includes plenty of hardship, in mediaeval days the pilgrim would go to Station Island prepared to spend fifteen days on bread and water, during which time he or she would attempt to cleanse the soul of sin through confession and prayers. The climax was then a twenty-four-hour-long vigil in the cave, having fasted completely the day before. No food was taken during the vigil in the cave, and nothing during the succeeding day. A Florentine merchant called Antonio Mannini wrote the following description of the cave which he visited in 1411:

57

The place is three feet wide, nine feet long and high enough for a man to kneel but not to stand upright. It is exactly like a sepulchre, for it is vaulted overhead and lies towards the south, that is, there is a niche about three feet long in the direction of the chapel, in which the prior had told me to remain and wait, saying my prayers the while.

For centuries the cave was a symbol of the complete renunciation of the world, and one of the most chilling accounts of the way the pilgrimage was conducted by a Hungarian knight called Georgius who came to the island in 1353:

After these fifteen days of fast, the Office of the Dead is said for him morning and evening during five days as though he were dead and as though for a dead man in this manner, a bier covered with a black cloth is placed in the midst of the choir of the church of St Patrick and there the pilgrim, who is going to enter the Purgatory, is laid like a corpse. Priest and deacon, sub-deacon and acolytes are vested as they were wont to be vested for one dead. The full Office of the Dead is then sung aloud with cross, thurible and holy water. After this has been sung in the morning the Mass of Requiem is promptly said for him and what was said in the morning must be said and done later except for the Mass. When Mass has been said, the pilgrim is absolved as though he were to be taken to the grave with bells sounded as is the custom for the dead. And the same method of singing Mass and Office of the Dead is observed during the four subsequent days.

The fifteen-day fast was later reduced to nine days in the sixteenth century, and since the early nineteenth century the three-day fast has been the norm at Lough Derg.

It was not until the year 1147, about fifteen years after the Canons Regular of St Augustine took possession of the island, that the penance of the cave became widely known beyond the shores of Ireland. An Irish-born soldier of fortune called Knight Owen had a profound experience in the vigil cave, in which he said that he caught a glimpse of heaven after fighting with the devil. Later, whilst in England, he recounted his story to a monk. The story was then written down as a poem and soon became a very popular tale. In modern times it could be called a 'best-seller' since it caught the imagination of mediaeval man who loved a good yarn – especially one with a moral tale to it where good triumphs over evil. The poem also has the attraction of putting beyond doubt to the mediaeval mind the reality of an afterlife. The poem is a long one, but to give a flavour of the monk's interpretation of Knight Owen's strange experience, here is the part where he enters purgatory:

> Such was his light when it was best
> As it is in winter at the sun's rest.
> When he had the light, forth went he
> Till he came in a great country.
> It seemed well for to be wilderness,
> For there was neither tree nor grass;
> But as he beheld him on his right hand,
> A well fair hall he saw there stand.
> It was high, both long and wide,
> And it was open on every side;
> Single pillars thereon were,
> That meetly the walls were bare,
> It was made of such guise
> Like a cloister on all wise.

The poem was copied and recopied and many writers of the next four centuries incorporated Owen's story into their own writings. It is thought that Dante used part of the recounted experience in his *Inferno*. As the poem spread throughout Europe, the publicity given to Lough Derg through its popularity had a curious effect on the image of the island; it came to be considered as the only place where the really wicked could gain forgiveness and salvation. It became the sort of 'San Quentin' of mediaeval times, at least in the minds of non-Irish pilgrims. So streams of people from Europe began to come to St Patrick's Purgatory, and many of them probably for the wrong reasons. Things became so acute that all non-Irish visitors had to have a signed permit from the local bishop to say that they were *bona fide* pilgrims. This practice of permits led to the closure of the cave in 1497, when a monk from Holland found access to the island difficult without substantial payment – almost a bribe to the authorities. Outraged, the monk took his complaint to Rome and to Pope Alexander VI, who issued a Papal Order to have the cave filled in. Later, by popular request, the pilgrimage started up again in the early sixteenth century, and still they flocked to do penance. Amongst them was the Jesuit Edmund Campion, the English saint and martyr, who visited Lough Derg in 1570, eleven years before his death.

The year 1632 marked the end of St Patrick's Purgatory as a place of mediaeval pilgrimage. The Canons Regular had already given up their stewardship of the island to the Franciscan Friars, who existed under an order of suppression from the Government, issued in 1629. So popular had the island become over the centuries that the Government, which wanted to see an end to Catholicism in Ireland, made Lough Derg a prime target. It was seen as a rallying point for those who wished to remain Roman Catholic, and for that reason it had to be destroyed: 'that monster of fame called St Patrick's Purgatory with St Patrick's Bed and all the vaults and other houses and buildings' read the order issued by the Lord Chancellor to destroy the place of pilgrimage and raze it to the ground. In that year the order was carried out and St Patrick's Purgatory was finished. It is not certain whether the cave was ever filled in at the time, although its original site has never been found. There is a theory that the real cave was preserved and that another cave was destroyed in its place. It is very interesting to note that almost 70 years after the pilgrimage site had been destroyed and made illegal, an Act of Queen Anne in 1701 imposed heavy penalties on those who still dared to visit Station Island, indicating that substantial numbers still went there.

During the time of persecution the pilgrims received help and advice from the Franciscans, who lived in farms in the area and made themselves available whenever the pilgrims needed help. Not until 1760 were the Friars allowed to return to Station Island, nearly 100 years after it had been destroyed. Now the climate was a more tolerant one, and interest in the island was revived on an official level. So depleted had the numbers of Friars become by 1781 that the Franciscans had to leave, and the running of the pilgrimage was taken over by the diocese, where it still remains.

The law forbidding people to visit the island was not removed from the Statutes until 1871, but of course the pilgrimage had never really ceased – even in the darkest days of the first part of the seventeenth century. In 1795 a great tragedy occurred at Lough Derg when 90 pilgrims were drowned in less than ten feet of water only yards from the island shore. Some of those victims, all Irish, were buried in a mass grave on nearby Friars Island and others at Templecarne graveyard. However, this did not deter other pilgrims from coming to Lough Derg, and in 1846, when Ireland was suffering because of the great famine, 30,000 visited Lough Derg during that season, and on one occasion 1,300 landed on the same day. When you have seen the size of the island (it measures roughly one acre), you realise what a feat of organisation that must have been! In the late nineteenth century there was a decline in the number who came to the island to make a pilgrimage, but in 1909 another revival took place and that momentum has been maintained ever since. A peak year was 1952 when over 34,000 set foot on the island for a three-day period of prayer and fasting.

I had made arrangements to meet the parish priest of Pettigo, and Prior of the island, Father Gerard McSorley. Together we drove the couple of miles to the edge of the Lough. As we travelled the rain came lashing down, the wind blew and the low, grey clouds glowered at us as we made our way. A boatman was waiting for us at the mainland jetty, and after sailing for about ten minutes in fairly choppy water we arrived on the island at St Patrick's Purgatory. As we were crossing the water I could see the outline of several buildings, all of which were dominated by the eight-sided Basilica of St Patrick, which was consecrated in 1931 and holds 1,200 people. I had come to the island out of season, so the question of spending three days 'hard' did not arise. Out of courtesy I did ask permission to bring along a camera and a tape recorder, things which under normal circumstances would be banned. As I walked round the island with the priest, the wind blew harder and the rain never ceased. I saw the comfortless huts where the pilgrims sleep in their hard and narrow bunks with no privacy; I saw the 'beds' (the remains of the hermit cells dating from the time of St Patrick) around which the barefoot pilgrims turn, time after time, to the rhythm of their rosaries.

I wanted to know in greater detail exactly how the three-day pilgrimage is spent on the island, and as Father McSorley and I took shelter from the driving rain in the chapel dedicated to Our Lady of the Angels, I was told in some detail the programme the pilgrim can expect. Having fasted since midnight on the day of setting out to the island, the pilgrim must arrive by three in the afternoon of the first day of penance. The first task is for everybody to take off their shoes and begin the first penitential exercise. This is called a 'station' which takes place in the open air. It is a mixture of silent and vocal prayer with continuous walking, standing and kneeling around two crosses, the basilica and the six penitential rings near to the water's edge. The pilgrim must complete three stations before 9.20 that evening of the first day, each one taking about three-quarters of an hour. At any time after the first station the pilgrim may eat some dry bread and black tea with sugar, but this meal must be taken only once per day. At 10.15 the pilgrims all assemble in the basilica to begin the vigil, which lasts for twenty-four hours and is the most difficult part of the whole programme. This vigil begins with a holy hour of preparation in common for confession, followed by the saying of the rosary. Through the night the congregation is conducted through four stations, using the interior of the basilica to walk around. At dawn Mass is said along with communal morning prayers. Emerging from the basilica to face the second day, the pilgrim must complete another station, and the same on the third day. On the second night the pilgrim is allowed to sleep, but throughout the fasting regulations apply. On the third and last day a station must be completed, and some time during the afternoon of that day the pilgrims leave St Patrick's Purgatory.

I knew that Father McSorley had been doing the pilgrimage himself since he was a boy of fourteen, and so I asked him what were the benefits to someone coming here to the island and putting themselves through three hard days and nights of prayer and fasting. To what purpose?

'It is part of Christ's own message that penance has a place in our lives,' he replied as the rain ran off our coats and on to the chapel floor, 'not simply for suffering's sake, but because it is through self-denial that we have a chance to confront the basics of life. Through the penances of the Lough Derg pilgrimages the important aspects of life thus become clear, and so too does the desire to embrace those things which lead to true happiness. In this way, a renewal or conversion of one's life takes place and happily the pilgrim leaves Lough Derg feeling closer to God.'

As we made our way back to the island ferry our patient boatman was there waiting for us. The weather was now even wilder, and the motor at the boat's stern laboured hard to push us through waves and spray and on to the mainland shore.

KNOCK

It was Pope John Paul II who put Knock on the map and showed it to an international audience when, on Sunday 30 September 1979, before a record crowd of 450,000, the first Pope to set foot on Irish soil said these words: 'Since I first learned of the centenary of this shrine, which is being celebrated this year, I have felt a strong desire to come here to make yet another pilgrimage to the shrine of the mother of Christ, the mother of the Church, the Queen of Peace.'

What occurred here in 1879 made Knock one of Ireland's national pilgrimage shrines. On a wet August evening of that year, a group of twenty villagers saw an apparition which appeared on the parish church wall and remained there for two hours. Seven weeks later the Archbishop of Tuam appointed an ecclesiastical commission to examine the phenomenon. Those who saw the vision were a good cross-section of village life of the time, and they included men, women, teenagers and young children: Bridget Trench was 75, Mary Byrne 26, Patrick Walsh 65, Dominick Byrne 20, Patrick Hill 14, Patrick Byrne 16, Margaret Byrne 15, Catherine Murray 8½, and John Curry, the youngest, was 6.

This is the story of what the villagers said they saw at Knock just over 100 years ago. The day of 21 August 1879 started with fine weather in County Mayo; as the day wore on a light rain started, and by the afternoon it was raining heavily. Margaret Byrne, who was sister to the church sacristan, left her house at about seven o'clock to lock up the church for the day. As she made her return journey she noticed an unusual brightness over the church, but she thought no more about it and went home. Some time later the parish priest's housekeeper went to visit the Byrne family, some of whom had just returned from holiday. To get to the

Byrne cottage she had to pass the south side of the church and the gable wall. As she passed she noticed some figures up against the wall, but thinking that they were statues which the priest must have bought and had placed them there prior to putting them inside the church, she thought nothing odd. The housekeeper did not mention what she had seen to any of the Byrne family when she arrived at their cottage. An hour later her visit came to an end and, in the company of Mary Byrne, she left for home. As they passed the gable wall, Mary remarked on the statues and asked the housekeeper why they had been put there; the two women came closer to the wall, whereupon Mary exclaimed with some excitement that what they were seeing could not be statues because they were actually moving!

Immediately Mary ran back home to tell her mother and the rest of the family. On hearing this startling news, the whole Byrne family, and a niece who was staying with them, hurried down to the church to see for themselves what Mary had been telling them. Whilst all this was going on, Mary was rushing about the village telling everyone she met about the vision on the church wall. Soon a small crowd of villagers had gathered at the wall, gazing at the sight before them. As all the witnesses reported later in their depositions, they saw three figures up against the gable wall, all hovering about two feet off the ground. One of the figures they identified as the Virgin Mary, one St Joseph and the third that of St John the Evangelist. To the left of St John was an altar with a lamb and a cross upon it. The figures said nothing, but they appeared 'full and round as if they had a body and life'. When those in the small crowd attempted to approach the figures, they receded towards the wall. An old lady, Bridget Trench, tried to kiss the Virgin's feet, but found nothing there but the wall. The figures were surrounded by a soft and brilliant light which covered the whole of the gable wall. The apparition lasted a full two hours and was seen by about twenty people, fifteen of whom later submitted statements to an official enquiry. Apparently at no time were the figures touched by the rain, although it rained hard throughout the whole time that the apparition remained. All the onlookers were thoroughly drenched. At one point, Bridget Trench tested the ground underneath the figures and she said that she found it to be bone dry – even though the wind was driving the heavy rain towards the wall. At the actual point of seeing the figures, many naturally thought for a while that they were indeed statues bought by the parish priest, the Rev Archdeacon Bartholomew Cavanagh. They did not believe it for long. About six months after the apparition occurred, a reporter from the *Weekly News*, an Irish newspaper, paid a visit to Knock and went to see Mary Byrne who was in her mid-twenties. The reporter describes Miss Byrne as a tall person, thin and with black hair and an oval face with an olive complexion; she had regular features, and even more pleasing from a journalist's point of view she 'never delays to reply, except when a question calls for a special effort of memory', observed the reporter. Mary Byrne was interviewed at length and in great detail by the journalist, the substance of which is contained in her deposition, given to the Ecclesiastical Commission of Enquiry in the late autumn of 1879:

> I live in the village of Knock. Mary McLoughlin came on the evening of the 21 August to my house at about half past seven o'clock. She remained some little time. I came back with her as she was returning homewards. It was either eight o'clock or quarter to eight at the time. It was still bright. I had never heard from Miss McLoughlin about the vision which she had seen just before that. The first I learned of it was on coming at the time just named from my mother's house in company with Miss Mary McLoughlin, and at the distance of three hundred yards or so from the church. I beheld all at once, standing out from the gable, and rather to the west of it, three figures which, on more attentive inspection, appeared to be that of the Blessed Virgin, St Joseph and St John. That of the Blessed Virgin was life-size, the others apparently either not so big or not so high as her figure. They stood a little distance outside the gable wall and, as well as I could judge, a foot and a half or two feet from the ground. The Virgin stood erect, with eyes raised to heaven, her hands elevated to the shoulders or a little higher, the palms inclined slightly towards the shoulders or bosom. She wore a large cloak of a white colour, hanging in full folds and somewhat loosely around her shoulders, and fastened to the neck. She wore a crown on the head, rather a large crown and it appeared to me somewhat yellower than the dress or robes worn by Our Blessed Lady. In the figure of St Joseph the head was slightly bent, and inclined

towards the Blessed Virgin, as if paying her respect. It represented the saint as somewhat aged, with grey whiskers and greyish hair. The third figure appeared to be that of St John the Evangelist. I do not know, only thought so, except the fact that at one time I saw a statue at the chapel of Lecanvey, near Westport, County Mayo, very much resembling the figure which stood now before me in group with St Joseph and Our Blessed Lady, which I beheld on this occasion. He held the Book of Gospels, or the Mass Book, open in his left hand, while he stood slightly turned on the left side towards the altar that was a little over him. I must remark that the statue I had formerly seen at Lecanvey chapel had no mitre on its head, while the figure which I now beheld had one, not a high mitre, but a short-set kind of one. The statue at Lecanvey had a book in the left hand, and the finger of the right hand raised. The figure before me on this

Knock. Montage of the apparition

present occasion of which I am speaking had a book in the left hand, as I have stated, and the index finger and the middle finger of the right hand raised, as if he were speaking and impressing some point forcibly on an audience. It was this coincidence of figure and pose that made me surmise, for it is only an opinion, that the third figure was that of St John, the beloved disciple of Our Lord, but I am not in any way sure what saint or character the figures represented. I said, as I now express, that it was St John the Evangelist, and then all the others present said the same – said what I said. The altar was under the window, which is in the gable and a little to the west and near the centre, or a little beyond it. Towards this altar St John, as I shall call the figure, was looking, while he stood at the Gospel side of the said altar, with his right arm inclined to an angle outwardly, towards the Blessed Virgin. The altar appeared to me to be like the altars in use in the Catholic Church, large and full-sized. It had no linens, no candles, nor any special ornamentations; it was only a plain altar. Above the altar and resting on it, was a lamb, standing with the face towards St John, thus fronting the western sky. I saw no cross or crucifix. On the body of the lamb, and around it, I saw golden stars, or small brilliant lights, glittering like jets or glass balls, reflecting the light of some luminous body. I remained from a quarter past eight to half past nine o'clock. At the time it was raining.

In 1936 another Commission of Enquiry was set up, and three of the witnesses who were still living were further questioned. The three were Mary Byrne (now Mrs Mary O'Connell), Patrick Byrne and John Curry. As in the first enquiry in 1879, the verdict of the second investigation was that all depositions were trustworthy and satisfactory. Shortly before Mary Byrne died she affirmed, 'I am quite clear about everything I have said, and I make this statement knowing that in a very short time I am going before my God.' Catherine Murray was eight and a half at the time of the apparition, having been drawn to the spot by the wild enthusiasm of the other villagers: 'I followed my aunt and uncle to the chapel. I then saw the likeness of the Blessed Virgin and that of St Joseph and St John, and I learned from those that were round about where I was. I saw them full twenty or thirty minutes.' The youngest witness was John Curry, who was six and a half, and of his deposition the records simply state, 'The child says he saw the images, the beautiful images and the Blessed Virgin and St John. He could state no more than that he saw the fine images and the light, and heard the people talk, and went up to the wall to see the nice things and the lights.'

In the Church there is what is known as a Canonical Process which must be followed when claims are made that an apparition has taken place. This entails the setting up of a Commission of Enquiry by the local bishop to examine all the evidence in great detail. The bishop can then either accept or reject those findings according to his own judgement. In the case of Knock two Commissions were established, one in 1880 and the second in 1936. The verdict of the bishop, Archbishop John MacHale, on the findings of the first Commission, was very important to Knock because if he had rejected them then pilgrims would have been discouraged from the start from visiting the shrine. In March 1880 the Archbishop received at his residence in Tuam the first organised pilgimage ever to visit Knock. It was organised by the Archconfraternity of the Holy Family attached to the Redemptorist Church at Limerick. As part of his address to the pilgrims, and to the press who were also there, Mgr MacHale said these words: 'It is a great blessing for the poor people in the west of Ireland, in their wretchedness and misery and suffering, that the Blessed Virgin, Mother of God, has appeared among them.' It was clear that the archbishop had accepted the Commission's findings, and thus he laid the way open for pilgrims to visit Knock Shrine with full ecclesiastical approval. The second Commission, of 1936, endorsed the archbishop's conclusion when it said that 'the evidence of the witnesses was upright and trustworthy'.

As at many places of pilgrimage, what happened at Knock after the apparition was as important as the apparition itself in establishing it as a shrine. By all accounts, the parish priest, Archdeacon Cavanagh, was a very holy and charitable man. He was born in Annaghdown, County Galway, and he was one of thirteen children. For twenty-one years he worked as curate at nearby Westport, and in 1867 he came to Knock where he remained until his death eighteen years after the apparition. He lived in a house which is now the Knock Folk Museum, a little way down the hill from the parish church. The archdeacon soon realised what would ensue within his parish as a direct result of the apparition, and he immediately began to record all the details of the miracles which people began to claim had come about through their devotion to Knock. Thousands of pilgrims began to converge on Knock soon after news of the apparition became known; they came from all parts of Ireland, from England, America and the Continent. A pious tradition of carrying away cement from the church soon arose, and many began to claim that they had been cured simply by laying the cement on parts of the body which needed to be made whole. Some very distinguished pilgrims made their way to the tiny Irish village, including Archbishop Lynch of Toronto, in thanksgiving for a favour; Archbishop Murphy of Tasmania travelled 16,000 miles to Knock because his sight was returned through applying the cement to his eyes. Archbishop Clune of Perth said that he had been cured of an infirmity through prayers to Knock, for which he presented an oil painting to the church. These and other cures the archdeacon recorded in his diary. The very first cure associated with the shrine, according to the archdeacon, involved a twelve-year-old deaf girl, Delia Gordon, who was cured on 31 August 1879, only ten days after the apparition had been seen. While she was attending Mass at the shrine, her deafness left her completely. Later in life Delia emigrated to the United States, and in 1930, when she died, her little piece of Knock cement was buried with her. The archdeacon's diary records hundreds of cures of blindness, cancer, epilepsy, heart disease and mental disorders. An American who came to Knock with a short and shrivelled arm is said to have left the village with both arms the correct length. In fact, so bad did the cement collecting become that an iron railing had to be erected a few feet from the wall to prevent too much demolition taking place, which was beginning to threaten the very church building itself. This protective railing can be seen in old photographs – reprinted in the many books about Knock – as can many of the crutches of those who found a cure there and left their redundant aids hanging on the gable wall. This practice is very reminiscent of Lourdes, where crutches at one time practically obscured the whole of the Grotto wall.

In the *Tuam News* of 1880, when the favours granted at Knock were very numerous, a report appeared, describing what was happening there:

The Catholic world has heard of the name and fame of Lourdes, once a wild spot, but now frequented by all the world, far away in the mountainous region to the south of France. A second Lourdes is arising at Knock, a small village surrounded by little hills, from which, as expressive of the natural character of the locality, it is known to the natives as the 'village of the hills'. It is distant about six miles from Claremorris, which is favourably situated on the Great North Western Railway. . . . The multitudes who, on today, Thursday, are flocking to the chapel or Catholic Church, at Knock, from the surrounding districts are quite as numerous as those from the monster meetings of the Land League which for some weeks are being held in the counties Mayo, Galway and Sligo. . . . A vast gathering of people from all the border towns within a circuit of twenty miles are assembling on today, Thursday, at this unpretending village. Some of the pilgrim travellers start before the day, guided by the light of the stars alone, and urged onward by the fervour of their own faith. Some are seen wending their way on foot, others on horseback, while whole families of peasants proceed on their pilgrimage, journeying on the ordinary country vehicle known as a cart, the better class indulging in the luxury of sidecars or as they are known in Dublin by the name 'outsiders'. . . . Here one can behold the blind, the lame, the crippled and the deformed, the deaf, the paralytic and epileptic – all seeking to be cured like those whom the Redeemer found at the Pool near Jerusalem. Accounts without number are coming to our ears of cures effected here on the holy ground. On this very day, in this blessed place, two remarkable miracles have just been performed on two persons who for years have, from the result of accidental causes, been unable to walk. The man finds himself so greatly cured that he has left his crutches and is bounding home like the lame man cured before the golden gate of the Temple of Jerusalem by St Peter and St John the Evangelist – walking and bounding along, and all the while giving thanks to God and blessing God's holy name. . . . The fame of these miracles, and the story of the apparition too, are going abroad and creating an immense amount of conjecture and discussion amongst the people relative to the Natural and the Supernatural world.

71

One of the most prominent figures at Knock in recent times was the late Mgr James Horan, who died at Lourdes on pilgrimage in 1986. He came to the village as a curate in 1963, and later became the parish priest and director of the shrine. Mgr Horan was a man full of energy and enthusiasm for Knock Shrine, and was also anxious to pass on any information about the shrine to those with a genuine interest. During his time at Knock, Mgr Horan transformed the shrine from something parochial into something which now commands international recognition. Behind the little parish church is a vast, lawn-laid area on which stands the great Basilica of Our Lady Queen of Ireland, which was built in record time once Mgr Horan had launched his appeal. This man also built two hostels for the sick, St Joseph's House for residential invalids and St John's Rest-and-Care Centre, the new confessional chapel at the shrine, as well as the ingenious glass-covered shrine at the gable wall. He also opened the Knock Folk Museum which graphically portrays the desperate plight of the Irish people of the district at the time of the apparition. One of the things of which the Monsignor was most proud was that the Pope went to Knock in its centenary year of 1979. It was largely through the efforts of the Monsignor that Pope John Paul came to Ireland in the first place. The Papal visit was one man's lifetime ambition realised. Mgr Horan recounted for me what it was like on that day.

'It was extraordinary that in our centenary year we had about 2,500,000 people here, and on the day the Holy Father visited there were about 450,000 here. They were spread out all over the hills. It really was a sight to see so many people in such a small Irish village.' It was well known at the time immediately before the Pope's visit to Ireland that such a visit might have a marked effect for the better on the spirituality of the Irish people. In effect, it was hoped that the visit would give the national faith a great boost.

'There are people coming here to Knock now who had never been before – simply because the Holy Father came. After all, he made Knock the centre of his visit; he prayed at the shrine, and because of that others wanted to follow in his footsteps and come on pilgrimage also. It has given a new standing to Knock Shrine. It was always a major Marian shrine, but since the Holy Father came more and more people are coming. In fact we're hoping for an airport in the very near future, and that would make it truly international because it will make it easier for overseas visitors to get here. This year already we have had Germans, French, Spanish and Italians on pilgrimage; there is much more interest in Knock from overseas than there ever was before.'

An international airport was completed at Knock just before Mgr Horan died.

To understand Knock fully it is necessary to visit the Folk Museum opposite the shrine. The museum describes the social and economic life of the Irish peasant in that part of Ireland 100 years ago. Certainly the people were oppressed by cruel landlords who exacted impossible rents and tithes from those who worked the land. Many families were evicted under the 'no work, no credit' principle, and often their only resort was to construct mud hovels as best they could for shelter. Many lived a subhuman existence and added to that, the crops failed repeatedly, so that those who relied on the land gained little from it. The dreadful name 'greenmouth' was coined at this time, which described many of those unfortunate people who were reduced to eating grass, leaves and wild herbs – or indeed anything – to stave off the gnawing hunger pains. For obvious reasons this was a time of mass emigration to America and to Britain. The museum tells in pictures, words, documents and newspaper accounts (both Irish and foreign) exactly what conditions were like, and to add a realism to the atmosphere there are charming and accurately constructed room scenes of typical Irish homes of the period.

At many of the places of pilgrimage there is often a message attached to the apparition, as in the case of Lourdes, Fatima, Walsingham and to some extent at Assisi where the crucifix spoke to St Francis. However, at Knock there seemed to be no message – at least not a verbal one. To those who saw the apparition they heard no words, the figures did not speak to them, but according to Mgr Horan there is a message at Knock.

'It may seem strange that there were no words spoken during this apparition and no word was ever attributed to Our Lady by the witnesses. However, God can communicate with us in many ways and is not confined to words. The message of Knock is found in the very rich symbolism of the apparition itself. After all, words are only symbols – sound symbols – and these can change from place to place and nation to nation. The language of the Knock Shrine apparition is the language of the Crib that has spoken to the hearts of Christians down the ages. It is a liturgical language and transcends all language barriers and all frontiers. Our Lady visited Knock at the time the Irish people were hungry, miserable, oppressed and without hope. The potato crop had failed and hunger and famine stalked the land. They had no security on their little farms and evictions were the order of the day. They were suffering because of their religion, and in these circumstances Our Lady came to console them, to encourage them and to give them new hope. The apparition was a heavenly vision and she wanted them to know that she was praying for them before the throne of God. She wore a crown and appeared as Queen of Heaven. The Knock apparition therefore anticipated the decision of the Church in 1950 to define the dogma of the Assumption. This dogma declared that Our Lady was assumed body and soul into heaven through a special privilege of Almighty God. St John the Evangelist appeared as a bishop wearing an Eastern-type mitre. He had a book in his left hand and the index finger and the middle finger on his right hand were raised as if in preaching. He seemed to be drawing attention to the altar, the lamb and the cross on the one hand, and to Our Lady on the other hand. He seemed to be saying that in spite of all their difficulties they should remain loyal to their faith and to the sacrifice of the Mass. He also implied that they should listen to the teaching of the Church and have confidence in their prayers and in the intercession of Our Lady. In this way they could resolve their many problems in a peaceful manner at a time when people were tempted to resort to violence and agitation. St Joseph was there as a layman who had been appointed Guardian of the Church in 1882. His presence seemed to indicate the important role of the layman in the church, and especially the layman's role in defending the Church. In the apparition the Church seemed to be represented by St John the Evangelist and St Joseph, and Our Lady was there as the mother of the Church. In her role as mother she was showing her concern and praying for them. It is interesting to note that Vatican II declared Our Lady to be mother of the Church. It can truly be said that the Knock apparition truly represents all the basic dogmas of the Roman Catholic faith.'

Although the Pope's visit to Knock was truly a great event and a milestone in the shrine's short history, there were in fact other papal honours granted to the shrine since the 1950s. On 1 November in the Marian Year of 1954, on the occasion of the new feast of the Queenship of Mary, His Holiness Pope Pius XII blessed the banner of Knock in St Peter's Basilica and decorated it with a special medal. By kind permission of the Vatican Chapter, the statue of Our Lady was solemnly crowned on the feast of the Immaculate Conception in 1954. The crowning ceremony followed the general lines of the ceremonial used in Rome when Pius XII crowned the picture of Our Lady – *Salus Populi Romani*. The Knock Crown is also similar in design to that of the crown used in the Rome ceremony on 1 November.

In 1957 the Church of the Apparition of Knock became an affiliated church of the Basilica of St Mary Major in Rome and special indulgences were granted to the stewards and handmaids of Knock, and to pilgrims, by the Sacred Apostolic Penitentiary. The indulgences were renewed in 1967 when Pope Paul VI promulgated a revision of indulgences.

Knock is first and foremost a place of prayer. The apparition itself was born out of the suffering and hardship of the people whose whole way of life was geared to prayer. The Irish people take their religion seriously, and to some extent it continues to be an austere and an intense experience. Knock is not for the casual nor the merely inquisitive; pilgrims go to Knock to get down on their knees and to pray hard either in a mood of hope or gratitude. However, there is nothing long-faced about the Irish and their religion – they enjoy it immensely – and those who visit Knock Shrine from foreign parts can always be assured of 'a hundred thousand welcomes' (Céad míle Fáilte). Should the pilgrim be a returning exile, then as Mgr Horan used to say, 'Fáilte Romhaibh Abhaile' – you are welcome home.

IRELAND

Ireland holds a unique place in the history of Europe, since it was one of the few countries of Western Europe not to be occupied or in any way influenced by the Romans. During the Dark Ages, after the collapse of Rome and the Barbarian invasions, Ireland was cut off from the centres of the Christian Church in the Mediterranean and developed its own Celtic Christianity. In the later Dark Ages, through its monks, Ireland became a centre of great intellectual and spiritual life and it was from there that missionaries went out to reconvert Europe to Christianity. There were saints like Columba of Iona who took Christianity to Scotland, and Columban, who established monasteries in parts of France in the late sixth century. Because of his strict, Celtic type of Christianity, he was forced to leave France, and with some of his monks fled to Italy where he started the monastery of Bobbio. The first monastery to be established in Ireland is attributed to St Enda who began a community on the island of Aranmore in Galway Bay. It is thought that he had learned monastic life from St David of Wales in his community in Pembrokeshire.

Because Ireland was so cut off from the Roman Catholic Church, its art and architecture developed along different lines from other parts of Europe. The famous illustrated Bible, the Book of Kells, which is at Trinity College Dublin, shows the unique quality of Hibernian art at this time. The architecture of its churches and monasteries also developed independently of that in other parts of Europe. Many of these buildings can still be visited, and although many are in ruins, they are in good enough condition to show what life was like for the sixth-century Irish monk.

The Celtic Church continued to develop independently, spreading northwards into western Scotland and then south into northern England. The most famous Celtic community in northern England was Lindisfarne in Northumbria. By the seventh century southern England had come under the influence of Roman Christianity which met with Celtic Christianity and made conflict inevitable. The main areas of disagreement were, mainly, the dating of Easter and the kind of tonsure to be worn by Christian monks. At the Synod of Whitby in AD 663 the Roman adherents defeated the Celtic supporters and thereby brought the Church in Britain under Rome. Many of the Celtic monks went to Ireland and set up monasteries there. The influence of Rome did not really reach Ireland until the eleventh and twelfth centuries, which saw the introduction into Ireland of such orders as the Augustinian Canons Regular and the Franciscan and Dominican Friars. A number of Church buildings in Ireland are architecturally interesting because they combine early Celtic with later Norman and Decorated styles.

CROAGH PATRICK

Pilgrims travelling west by car from Dublin to Croagh Patrick may wish to visit the great sixth-century monastery of Clonmacnois. In order to reach it, turn off the N4 on to the N6 towards Athlone. Before reaching Athlone, fork left towards Shannonbridge to reach the monastery. It was second in importance only to Armagh, and second to none in its art and literature. It was founded by St Ciaran in AD 545, but the saint died only a few months later and did not live to see it in its greatness. The ruins include eight churches, two Round Towers, three High Crosses and over four hundred gravestones. The graves include many of the kings of Tara and Connacht. Legend has it that no less than Diarmit the First, King of Tara, helped Ciaran the saint to build his first church, and when Diarmit was murdered in AD 565 his head was brought to Clonmacnois for burial. Anyone in the least interested in early Irish history, arts or architecture should visit Clonmacnois.

Farther west from Clonmacnois, still

on the way to Croagh Patrick, on the eastern border of County Galway, stand the ruins of St Brendan's Cathedral at Clonfert. This cathedral is said to be the best example of Irish Romanesque architecture in the whole of Ireland.

In AD 558 St Brendan founded a monastery on this site. It was the same Brendan, called the Voyager, whose story is told in the tenth-century tale 'Brendan Voyage', which tells of how Brendan sailed with some of his monks to a place they called 'The Land of Promise' which is thought to have been the Canary Islands. Whether the story is true is not known, but it is certain that Brendan travelled to western Scotland, parts of England and France during his lifetime. The monastery itself has had a chequered career, for it was severely damaged in AD 844 by a Viking raiding party, and was destroyed by fire no less than four times in the tenth and eleventh centuries. During the twelfth century it became a priory for Augustinian Canons Regular and at the same time Clonfert became the See of a newly-founded diocese. What can be seen today is the skeleton of the small cathedral. It is the design and style of the west door that attracts most visitors, with its continuous arches intricately carved. Above the arches is a triangle carved into the stone within which can be seen the faces of many saints looking down upon the visitor as he enters through the door. Originally the cathedral was only a single-chamber church, but a thirteenth-century chancel has been added. In this chancel the east window is worthy of attention both from inside and outside.

From Brendan's cathedral the pilgrim should then travel on to Westport which is the nearest major town to the sacred mountain of Croagh Patrick near Clew Bay. Westport is a small market town and seaport conveniently placed for pilgrim and tourist alike, for south of Westport is some of the most beautiful country scenery in all Ireland. Here on the ancient Pilgrim's Way is the road to Croagh Patrick which passes through the small village of Aghagower where it is said Patrick founded a church and later a monastery was built. There is still on the site a restored Round Tower and the ruins of a thirteenth-century church. Near the church are two wells, now dried up, which are said to have been used by St Patrick to draw water for the baptism of converts.

A few miles from here the pilgrim can visit Ballintubber Abbey which is Ireland's last remaining Royal Abbey. In it Mass has been said continuously for more than 700 years. It was founded in AD 1216 by Cathal of the Wine Red Hand, King of Connacht, for a community of Augustinians. During the Reformation and the rule of Cromwell the Order was suppressed and most of the buildings burned down, but fortunately a great part of the vaulted chancel of the church remained intact and here the monks continued to say Mass. In 1966 the church was restored and it is interesting for its varied architectural designs. The ruined abbey was excavated and among the buildings discovered was an early guest house used by pilgrims on their way to the annual pilgrimage, climbing the mountain of Croagh Patrick.

Organised pilgrimages to Croagh Patrick occur throughout the summer months, June to September, and Pilgrim Sunday is always the last Sunday in July. On this day thousands of pilgrims climb the mountain in remembrance of St Patrick's Lenten fast in AD 441. There is a special train service from Westport to Croagh Patrick on this pilgrimage Sunday and details can be obtained from any C.I.E. (Irish Railways) office.

KNOCK

The next place of pilgrimage in Ireland is the now famous Marian shrine at Knock, County Mayo. The best route from Croagh Patrick to Knock is via Westport and Claremorris. Pilgrims can travel by either car or train between Westport and Claremorris and then catch a bus or drive on to Knock.

On the way to Knock from Westport, pilgrims will cross the Plain of Mayo, Maigh Eo – The Plain of Yew, from which the county gets its name. In the seventh century, after the Synod of Whitby had declared in favour of Roman Christianity, rebellious monks who preferred the Celtic way came from Lindisfarne and set up a monastery here to carry on their Celtic traditions. Some of the ruins of the monastery can still be seen.

The shrine at Knock is the most important place of pilgrimage in Ireland, and like Lourdes in France it is a special place for the sick and disabled. From May to October the last Thursday in every month is the special day for the disabled pilgrim, and during the season there is a daily service of communal Anointing of the Sick.

The new Basilica of Our Lady Queen of Knock is so designed as to allow those in wheelchairs easy access. During the Masses the disabled pilgrims have a position of honour around the altar in the sanctuary area. This new church is built in the round and can hold as many as 15,000 pilgrims at one time. The altar and the sanctuary are in the centre so that all pilgrims can see them from wherever they are in the building. The basilica is divided into five chapels with four radiating walls joining them; in each of the four walls there is a replica of a mediaeval church

window, copied from a church in each of the four provinces in Ireland, one of them a copy of the beautiful east window of the Cistercian Abbey, Holy Cross, County Tipperary. Around the outside of the basilica is a sort of cloister or ambulator with 32 pillars representing the 32 counties in all Ireland, and each of the counties has provided special stone to decorate their particular pillar. There is also an outside altar used daily at 1830 hours for a Mass, after which there is the ceremony of the Anointing of the Sick.

The old parish church at Knock is the centre and focal point of any pilgrimage for the shrine, since it was here that the villagers saw the vision of Mary on 21 August 1879. The most important part of the church, now called the 'Apparition Gable', is protected by glass. Replicas of Mary with Joseph and John the Evangelist can be seen where the villagers saw them 100 years ago.

The season for organised pilgrimages begins on the last Sunday in April and ends on the last Sunday in October. During this period, on all Sundays and holydays, there are Masses in the parish church at 0800, 0930, 1100, 1200, 1530 and 1800 hours. The public ceremonies begin at 1500 with the Stations of the Cross. Then there is a Mass at the outdoor altar at 1530 followed by the ceremony of the Anointing of the Sick, and then the Solemn Blessing of the Sick. After Benediction a hymn brings the public ceremonies to a close. On weekdays from 1 July to 30 September public ceremonies begin at 1615 with a Mass at 1700. On all weekdays from May until the end of October Masses are also celebrated at 0800, 0900, 1200 and 1500 hours. During the closed season from November to May there are Masses said in the parish church at Knock each day at 0900, 1000, 1200,

1500 and 1700 hours including Sundays.

There is a Folk Museum at Knock which is well worth a visit, as the visitor can see what it was like in the village of Knock 100 years ago at the time of the apparition. The museum also gives the visitor a good idea of what life was like, economically and socially, throughout Ireland at this time. It also shows how the shrine itself developed over the next hundred years.

Knock is now an extremely popular place of pilgrimage, and therefore it is advisable to book well in advance. All bookings should be addressed to Mrs J C Coyne, Honorary Secretary, Knock Shrine Society, Castlebar.

LOUGH DERG

The last place of pilgrimage in Ireland is at Lough Derg in County Donegal. It is important not to confuse it with the larger Lough Derg which lies further south in County Clare. On the way, those pilgrims travelling by car may like to take a short detour to the west and visit the ruins of Strade Abbey, a thirteenth-century Franciscan Friary which later became the home of a Dominican community. It is the church connected to the Friary which is the most interesting, particularly its beautiful delicate stone carvings. The most outstanding examples are the decorations around a mediaeval tomb said to be of the founder of the monastery. These decorations were obviously carved in a later period. The tomb is found in an arched recess in the north wall, and above it in the arch are patterns of interlacing stone ribs resembling the branches and leaves of a tree. Underneath the tomb in the wall are the figures of various saints recognisable by the symbolic objects they carry; St Peter carries the keys to heaven.

From Strade Abbey the pilgrim must travel through the county of Sligo north into County Donegal where the shrine at Lough Derg is situated. Southwest of Lough Derg lies the town of Ballyshannon, a seaport and market town at the head of the Erne estuary. Just northwest of the town are the remains of the Cistercian abbey of Assore. The ruins that are left are from the twelfth century, and nearby there is a cave where Mass was said in secret during the years when Roman Catholicism was banned throughout Ireland.

The nearest town to Lough Derg is the county town of Donegal. The word Donegal comes from the Gaelic name Dunnan Gall which means Fort of the Foreigners, because for a long time it was a Viking stronghold. A quarter of a mile south are the ruins of Donegal 'Abbey', a Franciscan Friary founded by Red Hugh O'Donnell in AD 1474. All that is left are parts of the church and the cloister. There are many ruins of churches and friaries in and around Donegal.

TRAVELLING ABOUT IRELAND

Those pilgrims coming from Britain have a choice of transport. They can fly into Dublin or take a ferry from Liverpool, then hire a car or take a train to Westport, and from there a bus or special train to the first place of pilgrimage, the sacred mountain of Croagh Patrick. Travellers from America fly into Shannon Airport on the southwest coast of Ireland where they can hire a car to drive north, or take an express bus to Westport. Those who wish to go by train take a bus into Limerick and from there catch a train to Kildare. At Kildare change trains for a westbound to Westport. The Irish Railways C.I.E. offer a ramblers' ticket lasting eight days with which the visitor can travel anywhere on train or bus. Because of the distance and isolation of both Croagh Patrick and Lough Derg it would be better to travel to the nearest large town and hire a car for the day there. Westport is the nearest town to Croagh Patrick and there is either Donegal or Ballyshannon near Lough Derg. There is an express bus from Ballyshannon to Lough Derg which operates in the summer months only. The best route between shrines would be to take a train from Dublin to Westport and there hire a car to drive to Croagh Patrick. On Pilgrim Sunday, the last Sunday in July, pilgrims can catch a specially organised train which will take them to the foot of the mountain.

Returning to Westport, the pilgrim should take a train east to Claremorris and then take a bus to Knock. There may be special buses available for pilgrims during the season May to October.

From Knock to Lough Derg is easiest by car or bus. There is a bus that goes from Knock to the town of Sligo and from there another bus goes to Ballyshannon and on to Lough Derg. It is important to remember that there are very few buses and trains which run on Sundays or major feast days, and therefore it would be best to arrange pilgrimages to any of the shrines accordingly. Travellers by car from Dublin should leave the city on the N4 going as far as Longford, and then turn left on to the N5 which will take them all the way to Castlebar, eleven miles from Westport, the nearest major town to Croagh Patrick. The journey from Croagh Patrick to Knock is comparatively easy. Returning to Westport the pilgrim should take the N60 to Claremorris and from Claremorris turn left on to the N17 which will take them directly to the shrine at Knock. From Knock the journey to Lough Derg lies northward

through Sligo and from Sligo on the N15 to Ballyshannon; forking right just past the town the pilgrim will find the direct road to Lough Derg. Because of the distances involved it is advisable to arrange your pilgrimage so that a whole day is allowed for the journey to each place of pilgrimage. To see all three places, a stay in Ireland of six days is recommended.

ACCOMMODATION

Since all three of the Irish shrines are still small, accommodation is difficult. The pilgrim is therefore advised to stay in the larger towns nearby: for Croagh Patrick in either Westport or Castlebar; for Knock in either Claremorris or Ballyhaunis; for Lough Derg in Donegal. The price of accommodation throughout Ireland is very reasonable.

USEFUL ADDRESSES

Note: The telephone numbers as given here assume the caller is within Ireland or the United Kingdom. When ringing from abroad, the 0 at the start of each code must be omitted and the appropriate International Code must be prefixed.

KNOCK

There are a few hostels in Knock.
St Mary's Hostel
Knock
Co Mayo
Tel: (094) 88119

PILGRIMAGE GROUPS
Rev Parish Priest
Knock Shrine
Co Mayo
Tel: (094) 88100

Knock Shrine Bureau
29 South Anne Street
Dublin 2
Tel: (0001) 775965

Mrs J C Coyne
Hon Sec Knock Shrine Society
Bridgemount
Castlebar
Co Mayo
Tel: Belcarra 3

HOTELS
The Central Hotel
Claremorris
Co Mayo
Tel: (094) 71305

Western Hotel
Claremorris
Co Mayo
Tel: (094) 71050

CROAGH PATRICK

HOTELS
River Bank House
Lousburgh Road
Westport
Co Mayo

Clew Bay Hotel
Westport
Co Mayo
Tel: Westport (098) 173

The Westport Hotel
Westport

Co Mayo
Tel: Westport (098) 351

Breaffy House
Castlebar
Co Mayo
Tel: (094) 22033

LOUGH DERG

HOTELS
The Central Hotel
The Diamond
Donegal
Tel: (0907) 30030

The Abbey Hotel
Donegal
Tel: (073) 21014

OTHER ADDRESSES

Coras Iompair Eireann (C.I.E.)
Travel Enquiry Bureau
35 Lower Abbey Street
Dublin 1
Tel: (0001) 787777 or 300777

Central Reservations Service
Irish Tourist Board
P O Box 273
Dublin 8
Tel: (0001) 781200

LISIEUX

When Pope John Paul II visited France in 1980 he revived an old ecclesiastical name when he described the country as 'the Eldest Daughter of the Church'. To realise just what that title means you only have to scan a map of France to see those names of places which tell of some of the oldest and richest Christian heritage in existence. There is the city of Tours, for example, where St Martin, an early Christian convert, was bishop (c.316–397). To the southwest of Paris there is the wonderful Chartres Cathedral with its matchless stained-glass windows. At Clairvaux lived the great Cistercian monk and reformer St Bernard (1090–1153), under whose guidance the Order flourished throughout Europe. Not far from Clairvaux are the two towns of Sens and Pontigny, both places closely connected with St Thomas Becket, who sought protection there during his self-imposed French exile in the twelfth century. The Benedictine abbey of Fleury on the banks of the River Loire became famous for its claim to have the relics of St Benedict, translated there in the seventh century. Fifteen miles to the north of Grenoble is the seventeenth century monastery of La Grande Chartreuse, founded by St Bruno in 1084. One great pilgrim centre in France of the early Middle Ages was Rocamadour, a shrine built into a hillside. It was named after St Almadour, a hermit who settled there; and there are many more such places throughout the whole of France, waiting to be visited. I was obliged to reduce my choice to three places of pilgrimage which are relatively modern, and which enjoy increasing popularity as each year goes by. My journey included Lisieux in Normandy, where St Thérèse of the Child Jesus lived in the Carmelite convent. I next went south to Nevers and to another convent where St Bernadette of Lourdes spent her life as a religious; I then went to Lourdes in the foothills of the Pyrenees, where millions visit every year. Finally, I cut across the country to a small village north of Lyon called Ars. It was here that a simple parish priest of the eighteenth century, Jean Marie Vianney, showed France and countries beyond, the true meaning of prayer and piety.

The story of Thérèse Martin starts not in Lisieux, but in the town of Alençon, about 100 kilometres south of Lisieux in the Departement of Orne. At number 50 Rue Saint-Blaise on 2 January 1873, the youngest of nine children was born into the Martin family. The baby girl was christened Marie-Françoise Thérèse. The Martin family was devoutly Catholic and much attached to family devotion and the life in their own parish church. Louis Martin, the head of the family, was a watchmaker and jeweller by trade. He made a comfortable living for his wife and daughters. Madame Zélie Martin made Alençon lace which supplemented the family income. To the great sadness and distress of the Martins, four of their nine children, two boys and two girls, died at an early age. This meant that Thérèse was the youngest of five surviving daughters; Marie-Louise was the eldest and was born in1860; she entered the Carmelite convent in 1886, two years before Thérèse. Next came Marie-Pauline, born in 1861, who also became a Carmelite nun in 1882. Then came Marie-Léonie who was born in 1863, and later became a nun in the Order of the Visitation at Caen. Marie-Céline was born in 1869 and entered Carmel in 1894. There can be no doubt that the early life of Thérèse at Alençon was a happy one, lived in complete harmony with her parents and her sisters. 'God has seen fit to surround me,' wrote Thérèse later, 'with love at every moment of my life. All my earliest impressions are of smiles and endearments. And if he planted love about me, he planted it in my childish heart too.'

Thérèse turned out to be a very loving and open child. Her mother said of her that she had a good brain but that she was very stubborn, and whenever little Thérèse had uttered the word 'No!', then nothing would ever change her mind! But even in her very tender years Thérèse showed signs of self-sacrifice and an unwillingness to complain. In childish tiffs about ownership of certain toys Thérèse became increasingly the one to make her will predominant, but eventually she would give in without a word of complaint. As it turned out, this was fine training for Thérèse as a nun, whose patience and willingness to bear suffering uncomplainingly became necessary. But this idyllic state of affairs was not to last. When Thérèse was still only four years old Madame Zélie died of cancer after a long illness. Naturally, this event had a devastating effect on the whole family. Thérèse felt this cruel blow so severely that the event changed her character and made her introverted and shy; she had lost much of her gay, outgoing nature, and instead became serious and reserved. These characteristics were to stay with Thérèse for at least ten years, until a new spiritual awakening was to turn her back into her old self once more.

Because Thérèse had lost her mother, she immediately adopted her second sister Pauline as her new mother, her 'little mother' as she would refer to her. It was both right and natural that a little girl of four years old should insist on having a mother figure, and Pauline was the chosen one. The significance of this choice turned out to be a far-reaching one; it was Pauline, as Sister Agnes of Jesus and Thérèse's superior at one time, who ordered Thérèse to start writing her childhood memories. Soon after her death Thérèse's diaries were published under the title *The Story of a Soul*. The book caused an immediate sensation and remains a best seller today. Without Pauline's influence *The Story of a Soul* would not exist. One can now wonder whether Pauline saw in her young sister nun something very special which made her different from the rest of the community. As a young nun we know that Thérèse was in the habit of charming the others with tales of her childhood. But who would have thought that such stories would also have fascinated the world at large? Perhaps Pauline did, instinctively. There now exists a unique document which we can read and know the precise workings of the innermost soul of St Thérèse – a step-by-step account of a saint in the making.

When the stricken family were about to lay their mother to rest, there is an incident which gives us a clue about the nature of Thérèse, and it shows us how different she was from her sisters. As Thérèse was giving her mother a farewell embrace as she lay dead, 'she did so without uttering a word, or shedding a tear'. Another incident, years later, recalls a similar incident where Thérèse's reaction is not what one would expect in the circumstances; on the day she finally entered the convent at Carmel to become an enclosed nun, her family were in tears – but not Thérèse: 'she herself shed no tears'. What is to be made of these two, seemingly unemotional reactions? It could not be construed as a hardness of heart, for Thérèse demonstrates continually that she was by nature quite the opposite of that. Perhaps such reactions only come from a spiritual nature which sees things in a different way from others. Thérèse did not regard either of these incidents as 'losses'; on the contrary, she viewed them as positive 'gains'. Her mother had gone to her eternal rest, and her own entry into the convent was most certainly a time for much rejoicing in her heart. For Thérèse neither occasion was a time for weeping.

To try to start afresh, and to escape the place which once held such happy memories for him and his family, M. Martin decided that they would all move to Lisieux; his late wife's brother, M. Guérin, lived at Lisieux, and he thought it would be a good thing for his daughters to be near their uncle. The Martins settled in their new home at Lisieux which was called 'Les Buissonnets', a house which still remains near the railway station. With her sisters around her, and especially her 'little mother' Pauline, Thérèse was happy in their loving care. When she was eight, Thérèse attended the Benedictine Abbey School of du Pré. Here she proved to be a pupil of above average intelligence, but this did present certain difficulties for a sensitive child like Thérèse. Praise from teachers only served to promote jealousy amongst the other pupils, and as Thérèse later tells us, she suffered greatly from their taunts and jibes. An essential part of Thérèse's make-up was her ingenuous nature and her enormous capacity for loving and giving. Thérèse would be cut to the quick if her love were not returned – yet she had the reserve to go on giving that love. In fact she was capable of loving a person more, precisely because they did not return any feeling towards her. Not long after Thérèse had begun her schooling, Pauline left the family home and entered the Carmelite convent. 'Pauline is lost to me,' wrote Thérèse, for the loss of her second mother was almost more than she could bear.

It was around this period that Thérèse became very seriously ill. The doctors were mystified as to the cause of the illness. The symptoms were violent trembling and recurring bad dreams. Thérèse was certainly very ill and confined much of the time to her bed. Her family were naturally very worried, particularly when

Thérèse seemed to make no improvement. It was decided that a novena should be made, whereby prayers over nine successive days would be said for the invalid's recovery. Thérèse was later to divulge that, during this novena, she had a vision of the Virgin Mary. There was a statue of the Virgin in the sick-room, and this is how Thérèse recalls the incident as she looked one day towards the figure in her state of complete helplessness: 'All at once she [the Virgin] let me see her in her beauty, a beauty which surpassed all my experience. Her face wore such a look of kindness and pity that I can't describe it. But what pierced me to the heart was her smile.' And from that very moment, it seems, Thérèse began to make a speedy recovery.

It was Christmas 1886, and the family was returning from Midnight Mass, early in the morning. The custom in the Martin house had always been for the children to have their presents placed in their shoes on the hearth. Thérèse, being the youngest, was the only child to find presents in her shoes that year because the other girls had grown out of the custom. As she was preparing to see her presents, she overheard her father saying, in a rather disapproving manner, that Thérèse was now too old for this custom to continue. At that precise moment, Thérèse tells us, she came of age. She wrote in her journal, 'On this night of grace, in one instant Our Lord, satisfied with my goodwill, accomplished the work I had not been able to do all these years.' This moment marked Thérèse's true conversion and her decision to follow the religious life. By now, both Pauline and Marie-Louise had become nuns at the convent at Lisieux.

Even though Thérèse was only fourteen, she summoned up the courage to break the news to her father that she, too, wanted to enter the convent as soon as she was fifteen. Thérèse knew full well that such an age was far too young to be considered by the authorities. Twenty-one was more the age when a person would be considered mature enough to take such a big decision. Life at the Carmel convent was both physically and spiritually very rigorous. When the Mother Superior of the convent, and also Marie-Louise, heard of Thérèse's plans, they both said that she was far too young. Only Pauline encouraged her to persevere. But the odds were formidable; the Church authorities were very much against the idea, as was the bishop of the diocese, with whom Thérèse had

Lisieux. The basilica; in the foreground, statue of Thérèse

pleaded on more than one occasion. But Thérèse was not to be put off; she went straight to the top. M. Martin decided to take both Thérèse and Céline on a pilgrimage to Rome. Thérèse decided that, should she get the chance, she would appeal directly to the Holy Father himself, Pope Leo XIII.

The small party from Lisieux was ushered into the room where they were granted a private audience. Would this slip of a girl dare to speak directly to the Pontiff? Yes, she would – and she did! As the line shuffled past the Pope's throne, Thérèse grasped Pope Leo's hand and spoke up. 'Most Holy Father, I have a great favour to ask. In honour of your jubilee, permit me to enter Carmel at fifteen.' Pope Leo, slightly nonplussed, turned to a priest who was in charge of the French party for some sort of explanation. A rather flustered and equally nonplussed priest hurriedly explained that the

87

matter was in hand at home in Lisieux. 'All's well, all's well; if God wants you to enter then you will,' replied the Pope.

The somewhat amusing conclusion to this rather unusual story is recalled by Thérèse in her writings. Apparently two of the Noble Guard had to be summoned to take Thérèse out of the audience chamber, such was her tenacity and her reluctance to leave the Pope's presence until she felt she had received a satisfactory reply! Although Thérèse had not received the answer she wanted from the Pope, nevertheless she somehow felt that what Pope Leo had said to her gave her some scope for hope. She returned to Lisieux more optimistic than when she had left with regard to her plans coming to fruition. However, immediately upon her return home, Thérèse wrote once more to the bishop, begging him to look into her case again and to allow her to enter the convent. After a long and depressing wait, when hope had begun to fade, Thérèse received from the bishop the answer she had wanted; he gave his consent for Thérèse to enter when she became fifteen. The constant and unwavering barrage against the gates of the convent had finally borne fruit. Thérèse had won!

So, within a year of revealing to her father that she wished to become a Carmelite nun like her two elder sisters, Thérèse entered the convent of Carmel on 9 April 1888. The family, including aunts and uncles, were there to see the youngest daughter begin her new life as a religious. It was a great and very emotional occasion. Everyone was in tears – except, of course, Thérèse. 'My heart beat so violently,' she wrote, 'that I asked myself whether I was not about to die.' The fifteen-year-old French girl rejoiced as those gates closed behind her and shut her in from the world outside. She had fought long and hard for this day; she had overcome obstructions which seemed, at one time, to be conspiring to prevent her from entering the convent. The newest and most certainly the youngest postulant was warmly received by the Carmelite community, which included her two sisters, Pauline and Marie-Louise. Pauline was now known as Sister Agnes of Jesus, and Marie-Louise as Sister Marie of the Sacred Heart. This was now to be Thérèse's new family, including Pauline, her 'little mother'. The precise status of Thérèse was that of postulant; she had a certain period of time to adjust to convent life to see if she could adapt to it. The convent, for its part, was naturally eager to see if the newcomer was suited to the life from their point of view. It was a testing period and Thérèse threw herself into it with enthusiasm. It was revealed, only much later, that the life did not suit Thérèse at all; she found it irksome and downright difficult. But all during her life not a hint of this was made known to anyone. It is not clear if Thérèse ever imagined she would like the life in the convent, and whether the reality of the routine was either a shock or a real disappointment to her.

However, disagreeable Thérèse found life at Carmel, she turned it to her own advantage. It was a contemplative life devoted to prayer, penance, hard physical work and a good deal of silence. The idea was that, through unceasing prayer, the enclosed religious grows closer to God and away from the distractions of the world. The main burden of their work was to pray for mankind. St Teresa of Avila (1515–1582), the great Spanish mystic and reformer of the Carmelite Order, wrote, 'A Carmelite nun, who does not by her prayers and penance gain souls for heaven, must consider her life wasted.' By examining the daily routine in a Carmelite convent, it is not difficult to picture the sort of life which Thérèse led for over nine years until her death in 1897. From her tiny, sparsely furnished cell, Thérèse of the Child Jesus would be summoned from her bed to the cold chapel at about five o'clock, perhaps a little later in winter time. The Divine Office, the official prayer of the Roman Catholic Church, would then be sung or chanted by the community, followed by an hour's prayer and then Mass. After this period in chapel each nun would go about her job within the convent to ensure its smooth running. As a postulant, Thérèse was allotted many of the more menial tasks, which she found disagreeable. This is not surprising when in the Martin family there was always outside help for the household chores, in the form of paid domestics. The scrubbing of floors, the sweeping of the cloisters and the heavy laundry work, therefore, came as an uncomfortable shock to this middle-class girl. The fact that Thérèse was so young tended to count against her rather than in her favour. The Mother Superior of the time was well aware that the vocation in one so young had to be put fairly and squarely to the test. On one occasion Thérèse was roundly scolded in front of all the other nuns for doing a less than perfect job of cleaning the cloisters. 'The cloisters are obviously being swept by a fifteen-year-

old,' boomed Reverend Mother. 'It's a disgrace. Now, Thérèse, go
and sweep that cobweb away, and in future be more careful.' We
know that Thérèse was more careful.

At eleven o'clock the community would again gather in the
chapel for more prayers, and then dinner would follow. A simple,
strictly vegetarian meal was served, after which the nuns had an
hour's recreation when they could talk to one another. Most of their
day was spent in silence. After recreation there was more prayer
and more work. At six o'clock there was a light supper followed by
another period for recreation. More chapel after that, and by eleven
o'clock Thérèse and the other nuns would all be back in their cells.
The bed was small and made of wood with a straw mattress, on top
of which was a woollen blanket but no sheets. The convent had no
heating, which always proved of particular trial to Thérèse, who felt
the cold very much. The dress of a nun was a brown tunic, with a
white cloak and wimple with a black veil and open sandals. (In the
chapel of Carmel there is a statue of Thérèse as she reclines on her
own tomb; she is dressed in the habit of the day, which has changed
little since Thérèse wore it.)

A few days after her sixteenth birthday, on 10 January 1889,
Thérèse, at her clothing ceremony, became Sister Thérèse of the
Child Jesus. She was now a full member of the Carmelite Order.
This was now her new life officially starting; the old life was at an
end. She, like other postulants, was offering her life completely to
God. Supported by the daily, rigorous routine of convent life,
Thérèse began to climb the long spiritual ladder which was to lead
her to sanctity and ultimately to sainthood. On 8 September 1890,
two and a half years after she had entered the convent, Thérèse
made her solemn profession – she became a Bride of Christ. But
even at this time, when the apprenticeship had been most loyally
served, Thérèse was not to know complete happiness and confidence in what she was doing. Until the eve of her 'wedding day' she
was plagued by doubts about her true vocation. Throughout her
religious life, Thérèse suffered a spiritual darkness which she not
only had the strength to cope with but actually managed to grow
from. 'I am grateful to Jesus,' she wrote during the last year of her
life, 'for making me walk in darkness. I am in profound peace.
Willingly I consent to remain during the whole of my religious life
in this sombre tunnel, into which he has made me enter.' However,

on the very morning of Thérèse's profession she felt that her spiritual life had taken a turn for the better. 'Rivers of peace inundated my soul, and in that peace which passeth all understanding I make my Holy Vows . . . I felt that time would never take me from my joy.'

By April 1896 Thérèse knew that she was very ill. She coughed blood and from then on her condition became worse, and eventually she developed intestinal tuberculosis. She received treatment from the doctor, but all to no avail; Thérèse was going to die. All through her illness, which lasted a painful eighteen months, Thérèse was still plagued by doubts about her faith and her love for God. In August 1897, two months before her death, Thérèse made a remarkable prediction. When she was told that her manuscript would be published after her death, Thérèse replied. 'After my death, my manuscript should not be spoken of to anyone until it is published. If you do otherwise or delay publication, the devil will set man snares in order to hinder God's good work – a work that is very important.' Several weeks later, on her deathbed, Thérèse made the following observation about her journal: 'These pages will do a great deal of good. Through them God's gentleness and sweetness will become better known. . . . Everyone will love me.' So, clearly, Thérèse was fully aware of the importance of her writings, for as early as July 1896 she is quoted as saying, 'Everyone will see that it all comes from the good God, and whatever fame I may have will be a gratuitous gift which will not belong to me; this will be quite clear to all.' Thérèse died on 30 September 1897, and at the moment of death she fixed her gaze on a crucifix and exclaimed, 'I love him. My God, I love you.'

The authorities were not slow in dealing with Thérèse's manuscript. A book appeared exactly a year after her death. At first it was eagerly read by Carmelite nuns in convents throughout France, and later throughout the world. Soon the book was being read by the general public, and it caused a spiritual sensation. *The Story of a Soul* is now published in dozens of languages, and its print runs into millions.

When Pope Pius XI canonised Thérèse in 1925, he called her 'the star of his pontificate'. When Thérèse died, letters had poured in to Lisieux from every corner of the globe, extolling the virtues of this young Carmelite nun, made plain through her own writings.

Peoples' lives had been changed by her, miracles worked through her intercession so that, almost spontaneously, pilgrims began to flock to Lisieux soon after Thérèse's death. When her body was exhumed in 1923, a strong scent of roses came from the coffin as the remains were translated from the cemetery to the convent, where they now lie. As the procession from the cemetery to the chapel was on its way, two pilgrims were instantly cured of their physical disabilities. The public pressure to have Thérèse made a saint mounted, to such an extent that certain canonical rules were suspended so that the process could be speeded up. A quarter of a million people, to the accompaniment of bells and trumpets, applauded Pope Pius XI's pronouncement in St Peter's Square, as he said the words, 'We declare Blessed Thérèse of the Child Jesus to be a saint, in the name of the Father and of the Son and of the Holy Spirit, Amen.'

The convent of Carmel in Lisieux is a little way down the Avenue Saint Thérèse, and back towards the town itself. The chapel is open to the public, where Mass is said at various times of the day. The nuns are still enclosed, but they can be heard singing their daily prayers from a side chapel, which looks on to the main altar. Down towards the front of the chapel, on the opposite side to the community chapel, you may be able to catch a glimpse of a modern-day enclosed Carmelite nun. About halfway down the chapel on the right-hand side is the side altar containing the remains of St Thérèse. Above the tomb, and reclining on it, is a life-size statue of Thérèse in her brown Carmelite habit. Above the statue is the inscription which, translated from the French, reads, 'I shall spend my life in heaven doing good on earth.'

LISIEUX

The northern French town of Lisieux lies about 60 m from the coast of Normandy. For centuries it was a small market town, but since the death and canonisation of the town's most famous daughter, the Carmelite nun, Thérèse of the Child Jesus, Lisieux is now the focus for pilgrims from all over the world. All the places of pilgrimage in and around the town have some connection with the young saint. The town is dominated by the great basilica, towering above the valley, perched high on the hillside. The money to build it came entirely from donations sent by people from many nations who had benefited in some way from the life and work of St Thérèse.

Any pilgrimage to the tomb of St Thérèse should, ideally, start not in the town of Lisieux, but in Alençon, some 90 km south of Lisieux where Thérèse Martin was born. The house where she was born originally belonged to her maternal grandparents, and Thérèse's parents moved in there when they were first married. Thérèse's mother, Zélie, was a lacemaker of some renown, and in the front room of the house in Alençon she would sit and do the fine lace work. Above the kitchen is the room where Thérèse was born, and where, four years later, Zélie Martin died. Some of the original furniture and clothing of Thérèse and her family are in the house and it is open to the public. In order to get to Alençon the pilgrim can either go directly by car, taking the road to Le Mans, or by train, changing at Mezidon and on to Tours. If the pilgrim is intending to go on to Lourdes or Nevers from Lisieux it would be better to leave a visit to Alençon till last, because the town is on the route to those two places of pilgrimage.

In Lisieux the first place to visit is the house where the Martin family lived after their move from Alençon. Grief-stricken at the death of his wife, Louis Martin could no longer bear to live in the house in Alençon and so he moved his family to Lisieux, to the house on the north side of the town, called Les Buissonnets. Thérèse lived in this house with her father until she entered the Carmelite convent at the age of fifteen. The house, now a museum, is quite a walk from the centre of the town but well worth a visit. It stands in its own grounds, back from the busy road, and the garden is surrounded by a high hedge which helps to protect it from the dust and noise of the traffic outside. It also gives it an atmosphere of quiet solitude and peace. The house itself has been scupulously kept just as it was when Thérèse and her family lived there. There are usually at least two nuns on duty in the house who are very helpful. In slow and careful French (for the sake of the pilgrims who speak only a little French), the nuns will explain each room and why the various pieces of furniture, ornaments, toys or clothing are on display. Entering through the front door the visitor is invited to look through a glass panel into the dining room. It is full of the dark, heavy furniture fashionable at the end of the nineteenth century. There is a large open fireplace with the hearth where the Martin children placed their shoes at Christmas for their presents. It was in the dining room that Thérèse ate her last meal before entering the Carmel. Upstairs her bedroom has been left exactly as she knew it and on the bed are some of her clothes. In the bedroom is a small replica of the famous statue of the 'Virgin with a smile' which was said to have been in Thérèse's room at a time when she was very ill. She said, later, that during the worst part of the illness she had seen the Virgin Mary who smiled at her and helped her recover. In the garden at the back of the house, there is a life-sized statue of Thérèse with her father. She is obviously pleading with him to allow her to enter the Carmel.

Leaving Les Buissonnets the pilgrims must retrace their steps back into the centre of town in order to reach the Carmel, the convent where Thérèse spent the rest of her short life. From Les Buissonnets the visitor must walk in the direction of the railway station past the church of St Jacques to the bus station. Diagonally across the square from the bus station is the Rue de Carmel named after the convent itself. The convent is not open to the public because it is still occupied by the enclosed nuns of the Carmelite Order, but the chapel is public and so is the exhibition next door.

The chapel of the Carmel is a bright, surprisingly uncluttered church, with very few ornaments or stained glass. Standing in the north aisle are three small altars. The first is dedicated to St Michael, the second to the Carmelite friar, St John of the Cross, and the third is dedicated to the foundress of St Thérèse's order of Carmelites, the Spanish mystic, St Teresa of Avila. Directly opposite these altars, to the right of the nave, is the chapel containing the shrine of the saint, which is the most elaborately decorated part of the church. What immediately catches the eye is the extremely life-like statue of the saint dressed in her habit, encased and lying on top of the tomb. There are some relics which are kept either locked away in a silver casket under the shrine or are part of the reliquary in the great basilica on the hill. Also in the shrine is the original statue of the 'Virgin with a smile' that did so much to help Thérèse through her near-fatal childhood illness. Visitors to the chapel of the Carmel are asked to remember that it is still in use as a convent chapel and therefore is a place of prayer. At certain times of the day the nuns from the Carmel enter the chapel and sit behind a grille in the enclosed part of the church. Members of the public are allowed to take part in the public seats in the nave. The offices are sung at 0715, 1330 and 1715 hours. There are also three Masses said every day at 0800, 0900 and 1130 hours.

Outside the chapel of the Carmel, on the right as you come out, there is a hall and exhibition depicting Thérèse's life inside the convent. The last of the Martin relatives to enter the convent was Thérèse's cousin Céline, who was given permission to take in a small camera. These contemporary photographs show us something of the life Thérèse led within the convent walls. In the exhibition in the hall of the Carmel the photographs have been enlarged to almost life-size. The visitor can see Thérèse at work in the laundry and at leisure with her sister nuns. Also on show in this exhibition is the Carmelite habit and the head-dress Thérèse wore, together with her white bridelike gown in which she dressed at her entry into the convent as a postulant.

From the Carmel convent the pilgrim must climb up the steep Avenue de St Thérèse to reach the great basilica. As you walk up the hill, the thing that first catches your eye is the huge dome at the end over the altar. But as you draw nearer, you are dwarfed by the great façade with its arched entrance between two enormous pillars. It is said that the basilica is the largest church to have been built in the twentieth century, and standing just outside the west door you can well believe it. In order to enter the basilica, you must climb the flight of stone steps, pass under the arches and enter through the west door. If there is no service in progress the interior is sombre and the vastness of the building can only be sensed, not seen. In the far left-hand corner hundreds of lights from small candles flicker in the darkness around the reliquary that contains two bones from the right arm of the saint. Along the side aisles are small chapels, each bearing the name of a country whose people donated sums of money to build the basilica. In all, there are nineteen of these small chapels.

When the lights of the basilica are switched on, the whole interior of the building is transformed. The eye is immediately drawn to the enormous mosaic above the High Altar. The colours are not the usual dull, faded ones, but the bright dazzling blues and greens of a modern church. The mosaic depicts God the Father with his arms outstretched as if to gather up all beneath him. Below him in the lower arch is Jesus Christ, with Mary his mother on his right, and on his left, kneeling as if in prayer, is St Thérèse herself, dressed in her Carmelite habit. The entire ceiling of the basilica is made up of large arches joined at either side by pillars stretching from floor to ceiling. Each pillar and each arch is decorated with mosaics depicting various saints, or with words from the story of St Thérèse. The altar itself is quite plain, with steps leading to it made out of pale marble in contrast to the mosaics above.

Mass is said in the basilica every Sunday at 1000 hours and on special feast days.

Underneath the basilica is the crypt, the ceiling of which is rounded and supported by pillars on either side. Like the basilica above, the crypt is decorated with brightly-coloured mosaics of both patterns and pictures. The altar is quite elaborate, with a large statue of the Virgin Mary above. Behind her the mosaic shows both saints and angels paying homage to Mary as the Queen of Heaven. The colours are as bright and vivid as those above.

Mass is said more frequently in the crypt than in the basilica; there is at least one Mass every day at 1000 hours and often at 1700 hours. There is also a service for pilgrims at 1530 hours every afternoon.

Another place of interest for the visitor is the Cathedral of St Pierre in the centre of Lisieux. For those interested in church architecture the cathedral is worth a visit, because it is considered to be a fine example of Norman Gothic. In the old cathedral of Lisieux King Henry II of England married his equally strong-willed wife Eleanor of Aquitaine, the mother of Richard the Lionheart and King John of England. The present cathedral was begun in 1180. A large dark building, it has perhaps been neglected in favour of the modern basilica. In contrast to the white stone of the more modern building, the cathedral stone is dark brown with age and wear. The interior is very plain, even austere, and the atmosphere is very still and hushed. The cathedral does have a specific connection with St Thérèse, for it was here that she and her family came to hear Mass every day from Les Buissonnets. In the cathedral there is a small shrine dedicated to the saint. Altogether the cathedral is an interesting contrast to the more flamboyant building on the hill.

OTHER PLACES OF INTEREST IN LISIEUX

Church of St Jacques, a beautiful fifteenth-century church on the Boulevard Jeanne d'Arc, near the bus station.

The Ancient Episcopal Palace, with its famous Gilded Hall and Louis XIII furniture.

The Museum of Old Lisieux, on the Boulevard Pasteur: opening time 1400-1800 hours.

THE JOURNEY TO AND FROM LISIEUX

The town of Lisieux is on the main road from Paris to Caen and is therefore easily accessible by car. Pilgrims coming from Britain are advised to cross the Channel from Southampton to Le Havre. Those travelling by car leave Le Havre on the N182, crossing the mouth of the Seine at Pont de Tancarville, and should then head for Pont l'Évêque on the N815. Just befor reaching the town, turn left on to the N179 which goes all the way to Lisieux. By car the journey is approximately two hours.

The journey by train from Le Havre is not as straightforward because there is no direct rail link between Le Havre and Lisieux. The best way is to go to the bus station in Le Havre situated on the Rue Charles Lafitte and catch the coach to Caen via Honfleur. There are four coaches each day, two in the morning and two in the afternoon. Buy a ticket to Honfleur and then at Honfleur bus station take the S.N.C.F. coach which goes direct to the railway station at Lisieux. Rail travellers from Paris have a direct journey to Lisieux and it is possible to make a day trip to Lisieux from Paris. The trains in the afternoon returning to Paris are very infrequent and therefore should be checked for times. It is possible to make a day trip to Lisieux from Britain; many pilgrims do this during the last week in September when the big celebrations in Lisieux take place. However, there is really not enough time to visit all the places of interest in Lisieux in the limited time of a day trip. Pilgrims who are travelling on to Lourdes can catch a train to Mezidon, change there and catch a train to St Pierre des Corps. Change again on to the main Paris to Lourdes Express, making sure to board the right part of the train because it divides at Dax and part of the train goes on to Biarritz.

ACCOMMODATION IN LISIEUX

There are many hotels in Lisieux and it is usually unnecessary to book in advance, except during the last week in September. During that week pilgrims flock to Lisieux for the anniversary of the saint's death and the town is always very full. In order to get accommodation during that week you will have to book well in advance. The price range for the hotels is varied and many are

renowned for their restaurants. Some hotels have one star for their accommodation, but two stars for their restaurant. For a very reasonable sum the visitor can get full board and eat extremely well. At the top end of the price range is the *Hôtel de la Place* in the centre of the town, which has a very good restaurant attached and plenty of parking facilities. Nearer the railway station is the *Grand Hôtel de l'Espérance* which is a two-star hotel and has 110 rooms. A smaller hotel nearer the station is the *Hôtel de Lisieux*, which gives special prices for block bookings and would therefore be suitable for church parties. Finally, the *Maris Stella Hotel* has good accommodation with a superb two-star restaurant; it is conveniently situated between the station and the basilica.

USEFUL ADDRESSES

Note: The telephone numbers as given here assume the caller is within France. When ringing from abroad, the appropriate International Code must be prefixed.

HOTELS
Hôtel de la Place
Place Thiers 67 Rue H-Cheron
14100 Lisieux
Tel: 31311744

Grand Hôtel de l'Espérance
16 Bd Ste Anne
14101 Lisieux
Tel: 31621753

Hôtel de Lisieux
27 Rue du Dr Lesigne
14100 Lisieux
Tel: 31620637

Maris Stella Hotel
56 bis Rue d'Orbec
14101 Lisieux
Tel: 31620105

RAILWAY STATION

Gare S.N.C.F.,
Place de la Gare
Tel: 31621452

BUS STATION

Gare Routiers,
Place Boudin-Desverge
Tel: 31621108

TOURIST OFFICE

Bureaux de l'Office Municipal de Tourisme de Lisieux
11 Rue d'Alençon
14103 Lisieux
Tel: 31620841 and 31620298

OTHER FACILITIES

Since Lisieux is still a thriving market town, there are plenty of shops for both food and clothes and good restaurants. There are four garages which hire cars in and around the centre of Lisieux and a wide range of shops selling souvenirs. For quality souvenirs the best place to go would be the Office Central de Lisieux on the Rue du Carmel selling all kinds of souvenirs at reasonable prices and in reasonable taste. Also try the Diorama just a little way beyond the Carmel convent, on the same side of the road.

ARS

Jean Marie Vianney was born on 8 May 1786 in the village of Dardilly, near Lyons. His father, Matthieu, was a farmer whose family had worked the same land for generations. Although the storming of the Bastille took place only three years after Jean's birth, much of the old social order in France was already fast disappearing, and the new revolutionary spirit was already evident. Religious belief and education was in decline, and those who tried to cling to the old ways were actively persecuted. Luckily for Jean Marie, and others like him who lived in the country, the storm of religious scepticism raged all around them in nearby Lyons and far-away Paris, but left them untouched. The life of the French peasant went on much as before; the crops had to be harvested; the grapes had to be pressed and the cattle still had to be taken to market. Young Jean was instructed in his Christian faith by his mother, Marie; she patiently taught Jean and her other children their prayers and the truths of the Roman Catholic faith. Perhaps the main difference in the way Jean's mother had been raised in the faith, and the way she had to raise Jean, was that going to Mass was somewhat different. Many of the faithful priests had been driven into exile, with the result that many churches were without a pastor. This was the case at Dardilly so that Marie and her children would have to go to different houses to attend Mass. This would be celebrated by a priest who was in disguise. Often, the Vianneys' own farmhouse on the outskirts of the village was used as a venue. The outlaw priest would quickly say Mass for those who dared to attend, hear a few confessions and depart before the authorities could find him and arrest him. Jean developed into a strong boy, and he became a great asset on the farm. He was intelligent – and probably would have become a good average pupil in later life but for two main reasons: life on the farm made little demand on his awakening intellectual capabilities, and his schooling was badly neglected at a crucial age. During the time when Jean was nine and ten he only attended school during the winter months. There was much to do on the farm when there was plenty of light, and farm work took priority. By the time he reached the age of 10 Jean could barely read and write. However, by some miracle, and by his mother's efforts, his religious education seemed to be intact. When he was thirteen Jean made his first communion. 'I shall always remember it,' he later remarked, 'it took place in our house under the big clock.'

It became apparent to those who knew him that Jean became more and more devout as he grew into his teens. He was much given to prayer and religious things, which probably explains why he was as well informed as could be expected. He read the lives of the saints slowly, and *The Imitation of Christ* was amongst his favourite books. As the late eighteenth century turned into the early nineteenth century, and Jean had reached his mid-teens, religious observance in France became more tolerated. This meant that the young farmer's son could go to church much more frequently. He often went to Mass before his work on the farm began, early each morning. It was at this time that he felt he had a vocation to the priesthood, although he must have realised that great difficulties lay in his path. He was intelligent enough to know that even if his father could afford his priestly education – which he could not – his level of learning fell abysmally short of the elementary require-ments. Further, Jean's sister Catherine was soon to be married and her substantial dowry had to be found. Added to all this, the family's eldest son was approaching military age, and should he be conscripted, that would leave the farm seriously short of labour. Jean's immediate ally, his mother, was delighted with the news that her son wanted to be a priest, and determined to overcome any obstacles which lay in his path. Choosing her moment carefully, she managed to convince her husband that Jean Marie should be allowed to study for the priesthood.

Now a stroke of luck came Jean's way; in 1804 a new parish priest, Abbé Charles Balley, was appointed to nearby Ecully. He was a saintly man and someone who was to affect Jean's life greatly in the future. As the Curé of Ars Jean would often refer to the Abbé

Balley as the man who had most influenced his whole life. Always anxious to see that any early signs of a religious vocation were carefully nurtured, Abbé Balley agreed to take Jean Marie into his junior seminary. Here, Latin and other subjects were taught to enable the students to graduate to a major seminary within a couple of years. Jean, almost a grown man amidst much younger pupils, found application to books and learning very trying, so much so that his progress after a time was almost nil. The down-hearted Jean Marie now had to wonder if he really had a vocation at all. To put it to the test, and with the blessing of his mentor, Abbé Balley, Jean set off on a pilgrimage to the shrine of St John Regis at La Louvesc. The round trip was a distance of 130 miles, which Jean walked, begging his bread as he went along. He returned to Ecully exhausted, but refreshed in his determination to pursue his studies in spite of the difficulties.

Then came a strange episode in the life of a man who was eventually to become a saint. Jean Marie reached the age when he was eligible to be conscripted into the French Army, and to fight for the hugely successful Napoleon in his European campaigns. In 1803 an agreement had been signed between General Bonaparte and Pope Pius VII to the effect that all students for the priesthood should be exempted from military service. By some unfortunate oversight it seems that the name of Jean Marie Vianney had been omitted from Abbé Balley's seminary list. Whatever the reason, call-up papers were duly served in 1809 at Dardilly in the name of Jean Marie Vianney. What a blow! Such a disaster could well have ended forever any hope of ordination. At best, service in the army for an unspecified length of time could postpone any notion of becoming a priest for many years. But like thousands of others, Jean Marie had to respond to the call, however reluctantly, and on 26 October 1809 he reported to the military barracks at Lyons. Such was the cultural shock of army life for this young man, who had hitherto led a very sheltered and protected life, that he became ill with a fever almost immediately. It took him many weeks to recover from the malady which no one seemed to be able to diagnose, and by this time Jean Marie's company had left for Spain. When he was fit enough, the young recruit was ordered to catch up with his draft in Spain, a command which he made a very half-hearted attempt to fulfil. In fact, what happened was that Jean

Marie became a deserter; he sought refuge in a remote village where he worked on a farm, thankful to forget that he should have been a fighting soldier. As a result of this action, when it was discovered that Jean Marie had not joined his unit, his father Matthieu was heavily fined. It should be said here that the French population at the time was heartily sick of conscription simply to satisfy the ambitions of Napoleon Bonaparte. So in this sense desertion was considered to be a praiseworthy act rather than something to be ashamed of. The system of the time was that if a person did not wish to be conscripted, then he could pay someone else to go in his place. The solution to the problem came in 1810 when Napoleon married Marie Louise of Austria. A general amnesty was declared and Jean Marie was at liberty to return to a delighted family at Dardilly. However, a substitute had to be found, and Jean Marie's younger brother, François, agreed to go to war for the sum of 3,000 francs, which was paid out of what was to be Jean Marie's inheritance. As the Curé of Ars Jean Marie often referred to this episode in his life with no sense of shame or embarrassment.

Returning to his studies under the watchful eye of the Abbé Balley, Jean Marie was eventually sent to the major seminary at Lyons. Again, through lack of aptitude he was told that he could not continue to the priesthood, and again Abbé Balley came to the rescue. After a good deal of string-pulling, Jean Marie was reinstated at the seminary. Such were conditions in France at the time that students were ordained within two years, instead of the usual four years. It is interesting to discover that one of Jean's classmates at the major seminary was Marcellin Champagnat, founder of the Marist Brothers, who now in their thousands dedicate their lives to orphanages throughout the world. Marcellin Champagnat was beatified in 1955. On 14 August 1815 – just a few months after Napoleon had been defeated by Nelson at the Battle of Waterloo – Jean Marie Baptiste Vianney was ordained priest at Grenoble. Although the new priest could celebrate Mass, he was as yet not allowed to hear confessions. He was considered by the authorities not quite competent to carry out this function. In later years he was to become an extraordinary confessor, helping people to unburden their sins upon him. Happily for Abbé Vianney, he was first assigned to be curate to his friend and mentor the Abbé Balley. The two spent a joyous time together at the parish of Ecully in close and mutual understanding. This partnership came to an end two years later when Abbé Balley died on 17 December 1817.

The short time Abbé Vianney spent with Abbé Balley was a very important one in the formation of the young man's priestly character. There is no doubt that Abbé Balley was an extremely holy man, remaining faithful to the Roman Catholic Church through all the vicissitudes of the French Revolution and the accompanying persecution of the Church. It was from Abbé Balley that his curate learned to eat barely enough to live on; to wear a hair-shirt and to use the whip liberally on himself in an effort to subjugate the physical to give room to the spiritual. Considered today, these measures would be thought of as exceptional, but in those times they were not. Certainly for many of his early years as a priest, Abbé Vianney waged an unceasing and ferocious war against the flesh, and although he lived to the ripe old age of 73, he had ruined his health by the time he was 45 in his quest for perfection. Only by order of his bishop did he eventually agree to eat enough to keep body and soul together.

Whilst the foundations of Abbé Vianney's spiritual life were laid at Ecully under Abbé Balley, their actual application was put into practice at his first and only parish at Ars. After Abbé Balley's death Abbé Vianney was appointed parish priest to Ars-sur-Formans. He was now 32 and, in February 1818, Abbé Vianney arrived at Ars with a few sticks of furniture left to him by Abbé Balley. Ars was considered to be a dull backwater by the diocese, and exactly the sort of place to send a rather dull and unintelligent priest: the 'Siberia' of the diocese. At that time the inhabitants of Ars numbered 370. The people of Ars had long since forsaken any serious religious practice, because of neglect by the church authorities who had long despaired of bringing any real Christianity back to Ars, and also because of the secular attitude which existed in France at the time. 'How small it is,' commented the new parish priest when he caught sight of his church as he came down the main street with his belongings. From this moment the name Abbé Vianney disappears. To his death over 40 years later he was always known as the Curé of Ars. He has been known as that ever since.

For the young Curé his task at Ars was a formidable one. Prior to his coming the Vicar General had remarked that the Curé would not find much love of God there, and he was right. Few villagers went near the church, except for a few children and older women. The children's religious education was badly neglected, a fact which the Curé discovered as he set about visiting each house as soon as he could. Sunday at Ars was just another weekday to the peasants who worked out in their fields. Before the Curé felt that he could start asking the people to come back to their faith, he felt that two things had to be sorted out first: dancing and drinking. Even by the standards of his own day, it could be said that the Curé was rather old-fashioned. He firmly believed that dancing particularly was an occasion of sin, and he determined to stamp it out. There was also great drinking and drunkenness in the village, a thing the Curé was also against. Little by little, with great patience and his own good example, the people at Ars gradually began to listen to their parish priest, and they began to realise that here was someone out of the ordinary. The Curé began to teach the children the rudiments of their faith soon after he arrived at Ars. It took ten years of back-breaking work before he could safely say that God had come back to Ars and to his parish. The Curé founded an orphanage within the parish called the Providence; its doors were flung open to destitute children, and the fortunes of the institution – and they were varied – were always close to the heart of the Curé. The Providence continued for many years after his death.

The village church the Curé knew is still at Ars; it is dingy and the paint is peeling from the walls. To the left is a side chapel dedicated to St Philomena. Although little is known about this girl martyr-saint, the Curé had a great devotion to her. In fact it seems open to doubt whether St Philomena really did exist; all that is known about her is that in 1802 an inscription was discovered in the catacombs in Rome which read, 'LUMENA PAXTE CUM FI.' It was speculated that the inscription – on tiles – was wrongly spelt and that it should have read, 'PAX TECUM FILUMENA' – 'Peace be with you, Philomena.' Behind the inscription were found the remains of a young girl aged about thirteen years. It seems the Church thought this enough to authorise devotion to Philomena as a saint, and the Curé adopted her as someone quite special to himself. Throughout his life he would call upon the Virgin Martyr to help him when help was most needed. Many miracles, both physical and spiritual, were attributed to the Curé during his life and after his death. When confronted with the fact that a person had been cured from a disease for which the Curé had prayed, he would often 'blame' St Philomena for the miracle. To the right of the entrance to the church is the sacristy, still as it was in the Curé's time. In an ante-room through which you must pass to get into the sacristy there is on the left-hand side the very seat from which the Curé heard the men's confessions. This seat is best described as a box, with high sides and a back. In this dark and depressing place the Curé made his reputation as a highly gifted confessor. If we consider the daily routine of the Curé of Ars, we gain some insight into how this man set about his task. As soon as he arrived at the presbytery at Ars, the Curé gave most of what he had of value away. The food he ate would have appalled anyone who knew what constituted a healthy diet; he lived for years on potatoes, which he cooked on a Monday and ate sparingly throughout the week. He

Ars. Statue of Jean Marie Vianney, the Curé of Ars

drank only water and occasionally ate unappetising flour cakes. He once even tried unsuccessfully to live on grass. By the 1830s the Curé's reputation as a confessor had grown so widespread that thousands of pilgrims were pressing him to hear their confessions. The following routine – incredible as it seems – continued for no less than thirty years. At one in the morning the Curé would emerge from the presbytery; even the short journey he had to make from there to the church would be constantly interrupted by pilgrims pulling at him and asking him for favours. He never turned anyone away without some word of advice or comfort. Women's confessions would then be heard until six o'clock, followed by an hour's preparation for Mass, and Mass at seven. The Curé would then hear the men's confessions in the ante-room to the sacristy seated on his high wooden seat, with the penitent kneeling to the side, resting against a large press used for vestments. By mid-morning the Curé would take a break in the chapel to pray some of his office, after which he would reture to the chapel of St John the Baptist to listen to a never-ending stream of women who wished him to hear their confessions. Around midday the Curé would drag himself back to the presbytery for a cold potato and perhaps a drink of water, and then back to the confessional until the early evening. For all those years the Curé spent upwards of nineteen hours every day listening to people's faults, peccadilloes, serious sins and scruples. Such a routine would have killed an ordinary man in a very short time, not to mention the mental state it would have brought about. Someone once remarked to the Curé about this punishing routine, to which he replied 'The sinners will end up killing the sinner.' And eventually they did. As the years rolled by the Curé's reputation for the skilful handling of even the most difficult issues began to spread. He must have often smiled inwardly, when even the bishop – who once considered him to be incompetent – sent along to him difficult cases which he could not solve.

In spite of the Curé's great powers of stamina and dedication, it must not be forgotten that there was a human side to him as well. Although his daily routine was of his own making, it does not mean that he did not try to escape from it and shrug off the responsibility. On no less than three occasions the Curé made an attempt to leave Ars, which was becoming too much for him. He longed for solitude and, as he often said, time to 'weep for my sins'. He thought that the only way to do this was to go off to a monastery to be alone. In 1840, feeling very depressed with an overwhelming sense of failure – although quite the reverse was true – he set out from the village with the intention of leaving for ever. His parishioners got wind of this and managed to stop him as he was leaving. Three years later he tried to leave again and failed. In 1853, when he was 67, he tried to leave Ars for the last time to join the Trappist monks. Again he was persuaded to return, and then resigned himself to spending the rest of his days as the Curé of Ars.

There was a period in the Curé's life when he was not only assailed by those who constantly demanded his attention, but he always maintained he was tormented from another, more sinister source. From the mid-1820s until around 1845 the Curé was convinced that the devil himelf was troubling him; he would refer to this evil as the *grappin*, which meant a hook or a 'grabber', because he believed the devil was trying to wrest him away from goodness. The devil came to the Curé in many different guises, including strange noises both inside and outside his house. Filth was discovered to be plastered over holy objects, furniture and other things were constantly hurled around the house and smashed to pieces, and on one occasion the Curé's bed was set alight whilst he lay on it. Some of these phenomena were both seen and heard by others, and not confined solely to the Curé's imagination. When the period of devil-persecution had passed, the Curé once remarked to the bishop, 'I believe it was the devil because I was afraid, and God does not make people afraid.'

Unfortunately there are no photographs of the Curé, who always resisted any attempts to be photographed by cameras which were just being introduced at the time. What we do have, however, is a detailed description of the Curé as written by an English bishop, Mgr Bernard Ullathorne, who was bishop of the diocese of Birmingham. In 1854, when the Curé was 68, Bishop Ullathorne went to Ars on a pilgrimage to see the man whose fame was fast spreading. The bishop caught sight of the old parish priest as he was praying his office in the chapel, after hearing yet more confessions. This is Mgr Ullathorne's description:

His face was small, wasted and sallow; many expressive traces were marked around his mouth. His thin hair was as white as snow, his expansive forehead pale, smooth and clear, whilst his eyes were remarkably deep in shadow and covered with thin lids.

Later the bishop heard the Curé preach as he stood by a church pillar, supporting himself with a walking stick.

His voice soft, yet shrill, rose into heights of anguish as he spoke of 'sin', his contracted hand was placed between his eyes, his brow shrank together and his tears began to fall. . . . He opened his eyes and those shaded recesses became full of light. He spoke for twenty minutes and with a simplicity, a self-abandonment, an energy and a variety of tone and action as his subject varied, all spontaneous from the heart. It was as if an angel spoke through a body wasted even to death.

Later the Curé heard the bishop's confession, which was a remarkable experience for the Englishman, so clear and to the point did the Curé deftly treat the bishop's spiritual problems.

Five years after Bishop Ullathorne's visit to Ars the Curé was dead. After three weeks' illness during a hot July the old and worn parish priest died on 4 August 1859. Two days later, on the Saturday, over 6,000 people attended the Curé's funeral. The bishop of the diocese, Mgr de Langalerie, lost no time in organising the process which would eventually lead to the Curé's canonisation. The Curé was declared Venerable in 1872 and beatified on 8 January 1905. Twenty years later he was canonised by Pope Pius XI on 31 May 1925, before a congregation of over 70,000 in St Peter's Square. In 1929 the same Pope consecrated the Curé as patron saint of parish priests throughout the world. During the process leading to canonisation the Curé's body was exhumed in 1904, and it now lies at rest for all to see in a side chapel in the church at Ars. The head is shrunken and covered in wax, and the hands and feet are exposed and blackened with age.

The presbytery has been preserved exactly as it was when the Curé lived there, and many of the things he actually used, as well as personal effects, remain. This was the house in which he ate little, slept little, prayed a lot and was tormented by the devil. The kitchen is crude and comfortless, his study lined with the stern-looking tomes from which he managed to read. Perhaps realising his inadequate learning, he was a perpetual and conscientious student. In the bedroom even his old and ugly shoes are neatly placed just under the bed, and his old soup-plate hat (which he never wore) is there on a chair. Propped up against the wall is the Curé's umbrella which saved him from the rain as he made the short walk from house to church.

Towards the end of my stay at Ars I met up with a priest who has had a great affection for the Curé for many years. He is Father Louis Genton who lectures at the Catholic Faculty of the University of Lyons. In the past Father Genton has raised thousands of pounds in the United States for the building of the crypt, which is now able to accommodate many pilgrims who come to Ars and wish to worship together. Father Genton and I walked around many places at Ars, and I was grateful for his explanations and his deep knowledge and understanding of the Curé of Ars. When I asked Father Genton to sum up the Curé and his life, he replied, 'He firmly believed that there was no limitation to performing one's duty. He lost his name to the benefit of his function, which means that he was through and through a pastor. Then, as now, he's not known as St John Vianney, but the Curé of Ars.'

The Curé of Ars was, and still is, often quoted on the things he had to say on prayer and the spiritual life. On being a good priest he said, 'A good pastor, a pastor according to God's heart, is the greatest treasure which God can bestow on a parish, and one of the most precious gifts of divine mercy.'

To his own bishop the Curé would say, 'If you want the conversion of your diocese, you must make saints of all your parish priests.'

Commenting on his hard life at Ars he said, 'Even though I should have to stay at Ars till the end of the world, leave bed at midnight and suffer as much as I do, still I would be glad to stay in order to go on with my work for the conversion of the sinner.'

Although it is true to say that the Curé didn't know a great deal of theology, he was a master at the art of prayer. 'What pleases God in prayer is not the length of it nor the beauty in the words – but the heart in it.' And, 'Private prayer is like wisps of straw scattered here and there. If they are set on fire the flame is small. But if the straws are put together, the flame rises high. And so it is with public prayer'.

Perhaps the most famous story attached to the Curé is the one which involved an old parishioner who used to spend just a few moments in church every day. 'What do you say to the good Lord?' the Curé enquired one day. 'I say nothing,' came the answer, 'I look at him and he looks at me.' The Curé would often tell this story and add, 'How wonderful my children, how wonderful!'

ARS

The church at Ars has been preserved much as it was in the Curé's day. There is now a basilica, which includes two churches: the old church built by the Curé himself, and the new church with its three domes, constructed after his death. In the old church there are two pulpits: the high one from which the Curé preached on Sundays, the other, on the opposite side of the church, was used for his famous eleven-o'clock talks to the crowds which gradually increased as his fame for holiness spread. Inside the basilica the body of the saint is preserved intact. Only the face has been covered with wax. Not to be missed is the sacristy and the confessional box where the Curé spent endless hours hearing men's confessions. The huge crypt behind the church is the latest addition to the complex. It is used mainly for large pilgrimages, the most important of which gathers at Ars each year on 4 August, the day the Curé died in 1859.

Part of any visit to Ars must include at least a cursory tour of Lyons, one of the great cities of France. Ruins of the old Roman city, called Lugdunum, can still be seen in that part of the city called Fourvière, situated high on a hill on the west side of the city. Because of its elevated position, on a clear day you can see as far as the French Alps which made it a natural place for a fort. In AD 177 the famous Christian martyrs of Lyons were put to death for alleged crimes of cannibalism. The Roman officials had wrongly understood the words 'Take, eat, this is my body which is given for you,' which they had interpreted literally. Some of the Christians were fortunate to die in prisons; those who were Roman citizens were beheaded. The less fortunate were taken to the amphitheatre and sent into the arena to be killed by wild beasts. The ruins of the amphitheatre and the arena remain and are open to the public. The opening hours in winter (November to April) are 1400–1700 Monday to Friday, closed on Saturday and Sunday. In summer (April to November) it is open 0800–1200 and 1400–1800 on Monday to Friday, and 0900–1145 and 1500–1745 on Saturday. On Sundays and feast days it is only open 1500–1745.

If you climb higher from the Roman ruins following the Rue de Roger Radisson, you will come to the great basilica of Notre Dame de Fourvière. It was built at the end of the nineteenth century in order to fulfil a vow made in 1870 by the citizens of Lyons. At the time the whole city was threatened with invasion and the citizens vowed that if they were saved from the siege they would build a church and dedicate it to the Virgin Mary in thanksgiving for their deliverance. On the left-hand side of the door into the basilica there is a plaque which reads, '8 October 1870, the people of Lyons made a vow to build a church to the Virgin if the siege was lifted.' The plaque on the right-hand side of the door reads, 'Near the ancient sanctuary where popes, kings and people used to come to pray, the town of Lyons, faithful to its vow of 1870, has set up this church.' The large basilica stands in a prominent position on the hillside. Particularly outstanding is a golden statue of the Virgin Mary – Our Lady of Fourvière – which stands on top of the southeast tower, gleaming brightly in the sun; it can be seen from anywhere in Lyons. The basilica has a magnificently carved west façade, consisting of two towers on each side with four pillars in between which rise up to form three arches over the door. Above each of the four pillars is carved one of the four symbols of the Gospel, the Winged Man, the Winged Lion, the Winged Ox and the Eagle. Standing in a row above them are eight hand-maidens and at the very top of the building is a marble statue of the Virgin and Child. They in turn are surrounded by the eleven apostles. The west façade is a beautiful example of skilled workmanship.

The interior of the basilica is not perhaps as impressive as its exterior. It is large and square with very few stained glass windows. Along the two side aisles are six large mosaics, three on each side, which depict important events in French history and various incidents in the development of the cult of Mary. The first mosaic shows the arrival of St Pothinus in Lyons, to become its bishop and to lead a mission to convert the tribes of Gaul. Later, at the age of 90, he was among the martyrs of Lyons killed in AD 177. The

next mosaic shows various episodes in the life of St Joan of Arc: hearing the voices that called her to save France; her victorious entry into Rheims and finally her death at the stake at Rouen. The third mosaic on that side shows the saintly king Louis XIII declaring the Virgin Mary protectress of France. This is, of course, a direct reference to the reason for the building of the basilica. On the other side of the church three mosaics depict three important incidents directly connected with Mary herself. The first shows the Council of Ephesus in AD 451 which declared that Mary the mother of Christ was truly the mother of God. The second mosaic is a marvellous display showing the Battle of Lepanto in 1571, when the Turkish fleet was completely defeated by a joint force from Venice and the Papal States. The mosaic shows Pope Pius V with his rosary in his hand, praying to Mary for victory in battle. The third and last mosaic shows Pope Pius IX, sur-rounded by clergy and people, pro-claiming the dogma of the Immaculate Conception in 1854. In between these mosaics are white marble statues each representing important incidents in either the life of Christ or that of his mother Mary. At the east end of the basilica, above the altar, there is a beautiful carved figure of the Virgin and Child.

The basilica is open every day, 0800–1300 and 1400–1800 in winter, and 0630–1300 and 1400–1900 in summer. There are four Masses said daily, at 0630, 0900, 1100 and 1700 hours. There is also a High Mass on Sundays at 1000 hours.

The basilica is built on the very edge of the scarp of Fourvière; beyond the church the land drops away suddenly for 200 feet, where it levels off slowly down to the river Saône. Because of the height and sudden drop the outlook from the edge is magnificent. There is a great panoramic view of the city of Lyons below, reaching across to Mont Blanc beyond.

In order to return to the centre of the city you can either walk down the winding road (a distance of about a mile) or take the funicular, a type of underground cable-car. The bottom leads out on to the Avenue Doyenne, and turning left into the Place de St Jean you see the cathedral of the same name.

The cathedral was built in the eleventh century. Although not very large it is architecturally interesting, with its rectangular shape and prominent tower or spire. There are two square Norman towers on either side of the west façade and a similar one, the bell tower, at the cathedral's east end. The west frontage has three arched entrances and above the middle entrance is a small but attractive rose window. The interior of the building, if there is no service in progress, is dark and quiet. The most notable features inside are the beautiful stained-glass windows, particularly the rose window above the west door, which is a tight flower formation in blues and reds that casts purple shadows across the cathedral floor when the sun streams through. The larger, more elaborate window above the altar is also circular and in its centre shows the Dove descending. In a circle around it are the faces of various saints, around whom are bigger circles depicting Biblical New Testament scenes. In the outer circle of the window are brightly coloured floral patterns. One can sit in the cathedral looking at this window for a long time and yet not appreciate it fully because of the intricate mass of colour. There are also a number of small roundels, little windows high up in the cathedral wall, each with a different colour scheme. The cathedral is worth visiting just for the windows, but the building also has a very old astronomical clock. Situated in the east end of the north aisle, the clock stands about ten feet high. It is square with three faces; on the left side the face tells the hour, on the right it tells the minute, and the principal clock face is carved like the face of the sun. Under the main face is a calendar dated from the twelfth to the twenty-first centuries. It is not known exactly when the clock was built but it is mentioned in a manuscript dated 1383. It is still in good working condition and chimes at 1300, 1400 and 1500, so if possible try to time your visit to coincide with the chimes. The calendar is very elaborate, giving all the Saints' Days and showing the important Roman Catholic feast days in red. Above the sun face the clock is carved like a church tower with the chiming bells inside.

BASILICA OF ST MARTIN D'AINAY

Another interesting church in Lyons is the small basilica of St Martin d'Ainay, on the Rue d'Abbé d'Ainay. One of the oldest churches in Lyons and built in the Romanesque style it is very plain, with square towers and rounded buttresses. The windows are very small, but since they have clear glass the interior of the church is not too dark. The interior is simply decorated and the thick walls give it an atmosphere of stillness and silence. There are no specific opening hours so it is possible to visit the church any time during the day.

THE CHURCH OF ST BONAVENTURE

This church is situated in the north-central part of Lyons, near the Metro station of Cordelier. The building is large, the most notable features of which are its stained-glass windows. The glass is bright and modern in beautiful shades of blue, purple, dazzling reds and greens. The window over the altar shows Mary, Joseph and the baby Jesus on the way to Egypt to escape the wrath of Herod. The chapel in the south aisle has an intricately carved stone reredos, and on the altar beneath are equally skilled carvings of Biblical figures. Unfortunately the church is not always open, the best times are before or after a service. There is a daily Mass said at 1000 hours.

MODERN LYONS

Lyons is ranked as the third largest city in France with a population of over one million. The centre of the city is situated between the two major rivers of Saône and Rhône. In this part of the city the visitor will find all the large shops, the hotels and the mainline railway station, Lyon-Perrache. The residential area and the educational institutions are to the north and west. It is a major university city, particularly renowned for the study of sciences. There are no less than twenty-four museums in the city, notably the Natural History Museum, the Museum of Roman Gaul and a Museum of Puppets or Marionettes; this museum includes some of the famous French puppets as well as some brought from Turkey and from farther East, and from Cambodia, Java and Thailand.

TRAVELLING TO ARS

Ars-sur-Formans lies in the southeastern part of France, fourteen miles north of Lyons (Lyon), the provincial capital. Lyons is well served by road and rail in every direction. Coming from Paris the journey time by high-speed train (TGV) can be as little as two hours,

covering a distance of 520 km. Naturally it costs more on the TGV than it does on a regular train, and all trains are frequent from Paris into Lyons. Once at Lyons there are local trains to either Villefrance-sur Saône or Trévoux. Both these stations are about five miles (8 km) from Ars, which is on the D904 road. There are bus services from the local stations to Ars, but a taxi is quicker although more expensive. By road from Paris/Dijon the N6 motorway passes through Lyons. To get to Ars leave the motorway at Villefranche and make for the D904 to the east. Approaching Lyons from Paris/Orleans on the N7, enter Lyons and exit north on the D933 to Trevoux, and then on to Ars. Lyons airport is Lyon-Satolas, 30 km southeast of the city. There are direct flights from London, Brussels, Zurich, Milan and Madrid by Air France.

ACCOMMODATION IN ARS

As in the days of the Curé, the village of Ars remains very small, with a main street and a few shops and hotels. The main hotel is *L'Hôtel de la Basilique*, Ars-sur-Formans 01480 Jassans-Riottier, tel: 74007376. Here the food is good, the atmosphere friendly and the prices reasonable. The Hôtel Basilique is adjacent to the church at Ars, so it is very convenient. There are a number of other hotels in Ars, all very small, notably the *Hôtel Regina*, tel: 74007367.

ACCOMODATION IN LYONS

Since the city is one of the major centres of history and culture in France there are plenty of hotels to choose from. For easy access to buses, trains and Metro, visitors are advised to choose a hotel in the centre. A three-star hotel near the station which serves bed and breakfast only is the *Grand*

Hôtel de Bordeaux. A two-star hotel on the same street is the *Normandie*; this hotel does not have a restaurant but there are plenty in the area for anyone wanting a good evening meal. A large three-star hotel called the *National* is situated on the Rue Cours de Verdun, the main thoroughfare that links the two rivers Saône and Rhône. Farther into the town there is a one-star hotel, the *Hôtel Alexandre*; this hotel is conveniently situated in the major shopping area. Because of the number of hotels in Lyons it should be unnecessary for the visitor to book in advance.

USEFUL ADDRESSES

Note: The telephone numbers as given here assume the caller is within France. When ringing from abroad, the appropriate International Code must be prefixed.

TOURIST OFFICE
Office du Tourisme
Place Bellecour 69002, Lyon
Tel: 78422575

HOTELS
Grand Hôtel de Bordeaux
1 Rue du Belier, Lyon
Tel: 78375873

Normandie
3 Rue du Belier, Lyon
Tel: 78373136

National
15 Cours de Verdun, Lyon
Tel: 78375548

Hôtel Alexandre
49 Rue du Victor Hugo, Lyon
Tel: 78377579

RAILWAY STATION
S.N.C.F.
Cours de Verdun, Lyon
Tel: 78921050

OTHER FACILITIES

The city of Lyons is situated in the centre of the wine country of Beaujolais. The area is famous not only for its wine but also for its cuisine, and the city has many restaurants where the visitor can eat a superb meal at a reasonable price.

There are plenty of garages where cars can be hired for a day or for longer periods. Pilgrims travelling to Ars may find it easier to hire a car in the area and travel by road.

Travelling about the city is comparatively straightforward. There is a good bus service and a recently opened Metro which runs across the centre of the town. It is best to buy a book or cachet of tickets at the start of your journey. These tickets can be used for each journey on all the varied forms of public transport. It is also very easy to walk about Lyon as many of the roads in the centre of the city have been made into pedestrian avenues on which all other traffic is prohibited.

JOURNEY TO LYONS

Since Lyons is the third largest city in France, access to it is easy. There is an airport some 30 km from the centre of Lyons with direct flights to and from London and other European capitals. Visitors flying into the airport can book hotels or hire cars there. For travellers by train there is a direct service five times a day from Paris, and now with the introduction of the new high-speed train that travels at approximately 162 miles per hour, the journey from Paris to Lyons takes two and a half hours instead of three hours 48 minutes. The Lyons–Paris line is the only one that carries the new train at the moment, and therefore is an extra incentive for any pilgrims who are also train enthusiasts.

LOURDES and NEVERS

On 16 April 1879 at the Convent of Nevers, about 180 miles due south of Paris, a 35-year-old nun called Sister Marie-Bernard died. I saw her body in a glass case in the chapel, lying clothed in her religious habit and with her hands clasped in prayer on her breast. It is said that the remains are incorrupt, and the face and hands are covered with a thin film of wax. Strangely enough, the sensation of seeing the body was for me in no way offensive; the lighting trained on the body is discreet, and the yellow reflection from the surrounding flickering candles danced about the gold framework of the casket, evoking an atmosphere of peace and tranquillity. For me it was like looking at a statue, similar to the one of St Thérèse that I had seen at Lisieux only a short time before. But this was not a statue, it was the remains of a real person – and a saint. It was the body of St Bernadette of Lourdes. Before this simple French peasant girl came to Nevers in 1866, she had set in motion at her home of Lourdes one of the most startling and lasting religious phenomena of our time. This reluctant celebrity was compelled to leave her place of birth and to hide away from an ever curious and intruding public who began to make life unbearable for her. But who could blame them? These people were eager to see, perhaps to touch and speak with the girl who had seen and spoken to the Virgin Mary.

Bernadette Soubirous was born in the Pyrenean village of Lourdes on 7 January 1844. She was the eldest child of François Soubirous and Louise Casterot, and she was baptised Marie-Bernadette. There were two further children born to the Soubirous family, a girl Marie-Toinette and a son Justin. The family was not too badly off from the mill they managed, called Boly. Because of bad business acumen and probably over-generosity, the family was broke by the time Bernadette was twelve. They were obliged to leave the mill and went to live in a hovel lent to them by a relation. It was a single room in the Rue des Petits-Fosses which had once been a prison cell. In spite of their misfortune and poverty, the Soubirous family was a happy one; the father sought employment where he could find it and the mother was a diligent person who kept her children as neat and as tidy as their poverty would allow. Bernadette often had the task of looking after her younger sister and brother whilst Mme Soubirous did what work she could find to try to make ends meet. In their reduced circumstances Bernadette soon came to know poverty, hunger, cold and hardship – and as a result she became asthmatic. She was a small child for her age, simple in her approach and always obedient to the wishes of her parents. Because she suffered from constant ailments Bernadette missed much of her regular schooling, and by the age of fourteen she could hardly read or write. She spoke only the local *patois* which was quite different from French.

On 11 February 1858 Bernadette, together with her sister Marie-Toinette and a friend called Jeanne Abadie, left the village to collect firewood down by the river. They eventually reached a place called Massabieille, which was an outcrop of rocks to the side of the river bank. To further their search the young girls had to take off their shoes and stockings because the ground was so wet. Bernadette was reluctant to do this because of her asthma, and she was left behind by her sister and their friend who were already barefoot. After a few moments of deliberation Bernadette decided that she, too, must bare her feet if the foray was to be worthwhile. Here is Bernadette's own account of what happened next:

I heard a distant murmur. I saw that the trees were quite still. I continued to take my shoes off. I heard the same sound, like a gust of wind. I looked up at the grotto. I saw a lady dressed in white. She was wearing a white dress and a blue sash and had a yellow rose on each foot, the same colour as the chain of her rosary. When I saw that I rubbed my eyes. I thought I was mistaken. I put my hand in my pocket and found my rosary. I wanted to make the sign of the cross, but I couldn't lift my hand to my forehead. My hand fell down limply. The vision made the sign of the cross. Then my hand began to tremble; I tried to cross myself and was able to. I began to say my rosary. The vision was running her beads through her fingers, but she didn't move her lips. When I had finished my rosary the vision suddenly disappeared.

Bernadette's two companions returned whilst she was still on her knees and they later said that there was something different about her as she knelt in prayer, with her gaze fixed on the rock face. However, the two girls scolded Bernadette for praying rather than collecting wood as they had done. They eventually dragged it out of Bernadette what she had seen. They gave faithful promises that they would not mention what she had told them. However, as soon as they arrived back home Bernadette's sister Marie-Toinette could not contain herself and blurted it all out to their mother. Bernadette was forbidden to go again to the grotto, because her parents decided what she had said was the product of her childish imagination. On the following Sunday, 14 February, after Mass, Bernadette obtained her parents' reluctant permission to visit the grotto once again. This time Bernadette was accompanied by more children. Again the vision appeared, visible only to Bernadette, who fell immediately into a state of ecstasy. All the children who were present at the time later testified to the beautiful transformation which overcame Bernadette's face as she looked at the vision in the rock face.

In all, Bernadette saw the apparition eighteen times, the last time on Friday 16 July, of the same year, 1858. During the third apparition the vision asked Bernadette to come to the grotto every day for two weeks, which she agreed to do. It was on this occasion that the vision spoke to Bernadette and told her, 'I do not promise to make you happy in this world, but in another.'

As word gradually circulated around the village, and beyond, of these strange happenings at the Massabieille Grotto, more and more people became interested. Towards the end of the visitations tens of thousands of people would gather all night at the spot in anticipation of the vision which the little peasant girl would see. It was on Thursday 25 February that Bernadette was instructed by the vision to scratch a hole in the ground, from which the famous

Lourdes. The Grotto

well sprang. That same well or spring, doubtless a tributary from the nearby river Gave, now yields tens of thousands of gallons of water every day. The overall message which Bernadette says she received from the 'beautiful lady', as she sometimes called her, was to pray for sinners and to do penance. During the thirteenth apparition, on Tuesday 2 March, Bernadette was instructed to tell the local clergy to build a chapel at the grotto and to hold a procession. Bernadette conveyed this matter to her parish priest, Fr Peyramale, who dealt out very short shrift, and Bernadette left his house in tears. By Thursday 4 March, and the eleventh apparition, the crowds had become so great that the civil authorities became concerned. Police and soldiers stood guard at the grotto, fearing

117

that the great excitement might generate some public disaster. Perhaps the most significant of all the visitations was the sixteenth, which occurred on Thursday 25 March. Until this time the identity of the vision was not known. Naturally there had been much speculation since the the first appearance, and most people had assumed that it must be the Virgin Mary. On this day Bernadette determined to ask the 'beautiful lady" who she really was. The regular visits to the grotto had now ceased, and Bernadette had not been there for three weeks. But now something urged her to go on that day. To Bernadette's delight the lady was already waiting for her, something which had never happened before. The third time Bernadette asked who she was, the lady answered, in the local *patois*, 'Que soy era Immaculada Councepciou,' which means, 'I am the Immaculate Conception.' This extraordinary statement was significant in two ways. Only four years before this date, Pope Pius IX had defined the dogma of the Virgin Mary's Immaculate Conception, which obliged all Roman Catholics to believe that the Virgin Mary was conceived in her mother's womb free from the taint of original sin. It was largely a matter for the theologians, and hardly likely to be the most discussed topic in and around the small village of Lourdes. Secondly, it is even more unlikely that the semi-illiterate Bernadette would have retained the rather complicated phrase in her mind – just supposing that she may have heard it during a sermon at the local church. What we do know is that as soon as she heard the rather strange phrase 'I am the Immaculate Conception' she had to keep repeating it over and over again to herself in case she forgot it. Before this Fr Peyramale had repeatedly asked Bernadette to ask the lady her name – and now she was able to tell him. Imagine the total astonishment of the man when the little peasant girl repeated that phrase which he barely understood himself! From that moment Fr Peyramale believed in Bernadette and what she had seen, and from then on he became her staunchest ally.

The final apparition took place on Friday 16 July, the feast of Our Lady of Mount Carmel. The grotto had been closed off to the public by the local authorities, so great had the crowds become. In fact Bernadette had to content herself with seeing the vision for the last time from the far bank of the river. Even though she had been some distance away from where the Virgin appeared, and not immediately in front of the spot, she said afterwards of the event, 'It seemed to me that I was in the grotto, no more distant than at other times. I saw the Holy Virgin.'

From the very beginning many had wondered if the whole business was not a figment of the child's imagination. Bernadette had, on many occasions, been rigorously interrogated by the police, the civil authorities and the clergy. Yet never once could she be persuaded to change her story, nor to deny any part of what she claimed she had seen. Medically speaking she was in perfect mental health, and apart from her asthma her health was sound. The clergy, particularly, are always suspicious of any supernatural claims, and they were unsympathetic to Bernadette's case. Yet Bernadette, no match intellectually for these men, was unbending in her determination to stick to the exact detail of her original story and to believe firmly in it. In later years, when Bernadette would read the latest account of the happenings at Lourdes in a newspaper or a magazine, she would often remark, 'The more simply one writes, the better it will be. . . . In trying to dress things up one only distorts them.' A short time after the apparitions the local bishop, Mgr Laurence, set up an inquiry on 18 January 1862, to examine the Lourdes phenomenon. The following text is taken from the official enquiry document:

We judge that Mary Immaculate, Mother of God, really appeared to Bernadette on 11 February 1858, and on following days to the number of eighteen days in all in the Grotto of Massabieille, near the town of Lourdes, that this apparition is endowed with all the characters of truth and that the faithful are justified in believing in it with certainty.

It seemed almost natural that Bernadette should become a nun when she came of an age to decide in which direction her life should now follow. When she did decide to become a nun, certain religious orders vied with one another for Bernadette's membership, presumably to enhance their own standing. She joined the Sisters of Charity of Nevers, partly as an escape. From the very beginning, news of the apparitions had spread like wildfire, and within a very short time Bernadette's life became intolerable; she was continuously pestered from every quarter by prying eyes, questions, finger-pointing and general harassment. Her life was not now her

119

own. There seems to have been a never-ending stream of people who wished to see Bernadette, to touch her, to ask the same questions and to ask her to recount the events at Massabieille. 'I am going to Nevers,' said Bernadette, 'because they did not lure me there.' Bad health kept Bernadette at Lourdes for a further year, and eventually, on 4 July 1866, she left Lourdes; she was twenty-two years old and she never returned to Lourdes.

Life as a nun for Bernadette was ordinary. Although never well-educated, Bernadette could now speak French, and she could also read and write tolerably well. The new member was warmly welcomed into the community at Nevers. She was directed to tell

Nevers. The convent

her Lourdes story once again to the whole congregation, with the condition that it was never to be mentioned again. Bernadette had come to Nevers 'to hide' and the sisters were going to make sure that this would be possible. But complete seclusion would never be possible, and for the most part of her convent life Bernadette still had to satisfy many inquiries relating to the Lourdes story. As far as life in the convent itself was concerned Bernadette showed no particular talent, so she was made the assistant infirmarian, and later convent sacristan. For most of the few years she spent at the convent as a nun Bernadette was content to minister to the sick in the infirmary. Through privation as a child her health was never very good, and slowly but surely those early days of poverty and damp accommodation began to take their toll. The asthma attacks became ever-increasing in number and severity. Bernadette began to spend time as a patient in her own infirmary. By 1878 she was bed-ridden, and her list of physical ills was a long one: chronic asthma, chest pains, a massive tumour of the knee and bone decay. Towards the end of her life Bernadette had little or no skin left on the lower part of her body and her back. Her body was one large sore, and to move even slightly was an excruciating agony. On Easter Monday of 1878 Bernadette remarked to a nun, 'I have been ground in the mill like a grain of wheat. I would never have thought that one must suffer so much to die.' Never once, through all her agonies, did Bernadette ever utter one word of complaint. About three o'clock on the afternoon of 16 April 1879 Bernadette, or Sister Marie-Bernard of the Sisters of Charity of Nevers, died quietly, clutching a crucifix. Her last words were, 'Holy Mary, Mother of God, pray for me a poor sinner, a poor sinner.' She was 35 years old. It was twenty-one years after the apparitions at Lourdes, and whilst the numbers of those who wished to visit the shrine were growing, Bernadette had long since been forgotten.

After Bernadette died her body was on view until Saturday 19 April and then placed in a double coffin of lead and oak. The final resting place was to be in the chapel of St Joseph in the grounds of the convent. Thirty years later Bernadette's remains were exhumed as part of the process for her beatification. On 22 September 1909 the remains were exhumed for the first time. The body was in a state of perfect preservation, and there was no trace of any unpleasant smell. The body was washed and placed in a new coffin lined with zinc and padded in silk. During those few hours that the body had been exposed to the air, there were signs that it had begun to turn black. The coffin was sealed and placed again in the chapel of St Joseph. Almost ten years later, on 3 April 1919, the body was again exhumed. This time an examining doctor reported that the body was still in a good condition: 'There was no smell of putrefaction, and none of those present experienced any discomfort.' In 1925 the body was exhumed for the third time, when relics were taken. It was found, even then, that the body was still ·remarkably well preserved. It was at this time that an imprint of the hands and face was taken, so that a wax face-mask could be made and a permanent covering for the hands could be accurately fitted.

What are we to make of Lourdes? Why do so many millions gather there, year after year, to visit the place where the Virgin Mary appeared? Quite simply, the principal drawing power of Lourdes is the healing of the sick. At the time of the apparitions in 1858 a woman claimed that her paralysed arm had been restored to health after she had immersed it in the spring which Bernadette started by scratching the soil, as instructed by the Virgin at Massabieille. Many cures were claimed in Bernadette's time, and many were authenticated at the time. Now the list of cures is a long one. It is likely that hundreds, if not thousands, of cures have happened through Lourdes. For a cure to be authenticated the whole case must be rigorously investigated by a team of doctors, not necessarily Catholic or Christian, who work through the Medical Bureau which is a permanent part of the Domain. To date over 60 cases have been authenticated at Lourdes which have been said to be beyond the explanation of medical science. Many more people simply use the word 'miracle'.

LOURDES/NEVERS

LOURDES

The town of Lourdes is the Christian Church's most famous modern place of pilgrimage. Situated in the southernmost part of France, in the French Pyrenees, it attracts pilgrims from all over the world. Lourdes is special because the sick and handicapped who come to this shrine on pilgrimage are treated as the most important people there. Lourdes caters for the handicapped in such a way that everything, except for the Château Fort and the Grottos of the Saracens, is accessible to those in wheelchairs via special lifts or ramps.

For most people the pilgrimage starts at the Grotto where Bernadette saw the apparitions of the Virgin. The Grotto is in an area called the Domain which is owned by the Church, and it includes most of the important buildings, churches and hospitals. Anyone entering the Domain is asked to remember that it *is* a place of pilgrimage and that people do go there in order to pray, or just to sit quietly, and that this should be respected.

The Domain, which is down by the river Gave, lies in the lower part of Lourdes and is well signposted. There you can walk along the beautiful avenue lined with horsechestnut trees until you reach the large paved area in front of the basilica. Then by turning right and going behind the basilica you arrive at the Grotto. Soon after Bernadette saw the apparition the river was diverted and a large concrete platform and path made so that pilgrims could gather round the Grotto. In the Grotto itself there is a small altar and above it to the right, standing in a niche in the rock, is the Fabisch statue of the Virgin Mary. It stands approximately in the place where Bernadette saw her apparition. Many pilgrims, both those on their feet and those in wheelchairs, form a queue and each takes a turn to touch, stroke, or even kiss the stone beneath the statue. There is also a place where pilgrims can leave written requests for help and prayers. These petitions are collected by the clergy at the end of the day and the prayers are said throughout the closed season from October to February. On the left behind the altar you can see the spring which Bernadette dug at the request of the apparition. The Grotto is a very extraordinary place, simply because of the atmosphere that surrounds it. There is always a large crowd near the Grotto, yet there is always silence. All that can be heard is the shuffle of feet, the quiet murmur of rosaries being said and the occasional squeak of a wheelchair. Beyond the Grotto are the Baths and on the opposite side of the river looking over to the Grotto is a large expanse of open land where many organised pilgrims hold open-air services of praise and thanksgiving.

THE BASILICA

The basilica at Lourdes is a large triple-spired church incorporating two basilicas, the larger Rosary Basilica, and above the Upper Basilica or Basilique Supérieure. The tall middle spire of the basilica can be seen from most vantage points in Lourdes. Built in a light-coloured stone it gleams white in the sunlight and shows no sign of wear or age.

Above the door of the Rosary Basilica, in a great arch, is a white marble relief showing the Virgin Mary as the Queen of Heaven. Lourdes is very much a 'Marian' shrine with statues and pictures of Mary dominating the exterior and interior of the basilica. The Rosary Basilica has a wide, almost round, interior with large frescoes on the walls. The pilgrim who has come from Lisieux and seen the basilica there may find the one in Lourdes disappointing. It is obviously older and the frescoes show signs of wear, the colours are paler and less discernible. The side aisles are wide so that wheelchairs can move up and down with ease. The Upper Basilica above is more traditionally Catholic in its ornaments and decorations. It is obvious that many skilled craftsmen were used to decorate the interior of the smaller basilica. In both basilicas there is an atmosphere of quiet contemplation rather like that in the Grotto.

123

Between the Rosary and the Upper Basilicas there is the crypt. After entering a door on the left the pilgrim walks along a marble corridor to a small chapel which is always kept in semi-darkness. There the pilgrim can sit quietly in silent meditation at any time of the day. The only light comes from a flickering candle on the altar. It is an extraordinarily peaceful place just to sit, and a great contrast to the noise and bustle of the pilgrims outside.

The most impressive building in the Domain is the Underground Basilica of St Pius X. When there is no service in progress it looks to the unsuspecting visitor like an enormous concrete underground car park. Wide ramps lead down into the centre, and plain benches face this centre. A raised platform supports the altar. Masses are held in the Underground Basilica on Wednesdays and Sundays, and those are a good time to see this vast building in its true light. The wide ramps enable the wheelchairs and stretchers for the sick to enter the basilica. The focal point is obviously the altar, which, because of the marvellous design of the building, can be seen from all parts of the basilica. So much so that the pilgrims, whether sitting, lying or standing, can feel part of the occasion and because the Mass is often said in Latin there is a unity and universality about the whole service. For many pilgrims this is the highlight of their stay at Lourdes.

For the pilgrim who only has one day to spend in Lourdes there is a special timetable organised each day, from July to September, for those who wish to be 'pilgrims for the day'. The starting point is to assemble at 0845 in front of the Crowned Virgin, which stands in the Domain opposite the basilica. Then at 0900 the pilgrims move to the Grotto where they can sit, or pray, or light a candle. At 0915 they move back up the hill behind the basilica, to hear the story of the basilica. At 0945 the Stations of the Cross are made, which are laid out on the hill to the south of the basilica in the open air. At 1130 there is a Mass at either the Upper Basilica or the Rosary Basilica after which there is a break for lunch. At 1630 there is the service of blessing the sick, which takes place in front of the basilica if the weather is dry or, if it is raining, in the Underground Basilica. At 2000 the pilgrims join in the torchlight procession that winds its way from the Grotto around the Domain and back to stand in front of the basilica for prayers. For those not taking part, the best vantage point from which to watch the procession is up in front of the Upper Basilica. From there the view is awesome; thousands of moving flickering lights winding their way round the Domain to the sound of the constant singing of the Lourdes hymn, 'Ave, ave, ave Maria, ave, ave, ave Maria'.

OUTSIDE THE DOMAIN

The two main thoroughfares outside the Domain are the Rue de la Grotte and the Boulevarde de la Grotte. Along these two roads you will find the biggest souvenir shops and bazaars, which sell every kind of religious trinket imaginable. On the Rue de la Grotte is the 'Musée de Cire' of Lourdes which is said to have the largest collection of religious waxworks in the world. It takes thirty minutes to see the whole exhibition, which covers five floors. Fortunately there are two lifts for those who find climbing stairs either difficult or impossible. The waxworks depict the life of Bernadette and the life of Christ. Bernadette's life begins with a display showing the hovel-like hut where she and her family lived. The rest of the display shows Bernadette's visions, her interrogation by Father Peyramale, her leaving Lourdes for Nevers and finally her death in the convent. The waxworks of the life of Christ are rather more spectacular. The two most impressive displays are the life-sized exact replica of Leonardo da Vinci's fresco of the *Last Supper*, and the crucifixion with its accompanying sound effects of thunder and lightening. At the top of the museum there is a souvenir shop and a magnificient view of the Domain. The entrance fee to the waxworks is expensive, but on the whole worth it. And there is plenty to see. It is open from 0900 to 1200 and then from 1300 to 1830.

PETIT LOURDES

After leaving the waxworks, carry on down the Rue de la Grotte towards the Domain, crossing the river at the bottom, then turn left along the Avenue Peyramale, and you will come to the 'Petit Lourdes'. Petit Lourdes is an exact facsimile in miniature of Lourdes as it was in 1858 at the time of the apparitions. There is the eleventh-century church of St Peter; the house of Father Peyramale; the Soubirous' hut and the Chateau Fort; and finally the Grotto exactly as it was the day that Bernadette and the other children went to gather wood.

THE CHÂTEAU FORT AND THE GROTTOS OF THE SARACENS

For the more casual visitor or independent pilgrim there are two outside attractions in Lourdes to visit. Neither has any direct connection with Bernadette, but are both interesting for the light they throw on the historical background of the area. The first is the Château Fort which stands on a rock high above Lourdes. In order to reach the fort you have to go up the hillside in a lift. There are two large lifts which

could take a wheelchair, but once up on the rock outside the Château it is difficult to negotiate the many steps and narrow paths.

From the very top of the fort the view is magnificent; to the west you can see across the whole Domain with a good view of the basilica; to the south and east you can see the whole town of Lourdes, and beyond that, the great mountain range of the Pyrenees.

Inside the fort there is a museum containing many examples of flora and fauna and other objects collected from the surrounding area. There are beautiful displays of butterflies native to the area, and stuffed animals which were once hunted for their fur or meat. Also in the museum are costume displays showing clothes that used to be worn by the people of the French Basque country, of which Lourdes is a part. There are displays of tools, beautiful hand looms and spinning wheels, old ploughs and yokes and donkey baskets. The donkey was the best pack animal for this area because they were considered to be far more reliable than horses on the narrow, tortuous paths through the Pyrenees.

Outside the Château Fort on the north side of the rock is a collection of miniature stone buildings standing about three feet high, which are exact replicas of buildings which could be found in the region. There is a replica of a Basque farmhouse and a small fort belonging to the Knightly Order of Hospitallers. Each building stands in its own grounds or garden, and altogether the whole display is very effective.

The other places of outside interest are the magnificent Grottos of the Saracens. They are situated quite a distance from the centre of Lourdes, and for the more adventurous they are worth visiting. However, anyone who

125

suffers even slightly from claustrophobia is advised to keep away, for the grottos of the Saracens are caves deep beneath the town, and in order to reach the bottom the visitor must climb down narrow, wet passages, often stooping to get under low ceilings.

The grottos were discovered in the 1920s, when men digging in a quarry came upon a vertical wall which led into the highest grotto beneath. They were said to be from 2,500 to 3,000 years old, and were caused by constant erosion of the rocks by water. In some caves there are stalagmites and stalactites, but the most impressive cave is the deepest, called The Great Hall, some 114 metres beneath Lourdes. Legend has it that during the sixth century Lourdes and the surrounding area was captured by the Moors, who ruled for the next 200 years. The Christian Emperor Charlemagne laid siege to Lourdes, and the Saracens in the Château Fort used the grottos beneath as a means of escape. They would go out to fetch food and other provisions, and thereby frustrated Charlemagne's plans. Hence the name the Grottos of the Saracens.

JOURNEY TO LOURDES

Most pilgrims coming to Lourdes travel either by train or by plane. There are scheduled flights from Rome, Dublin and Paris but none from Britain. Pilgrims from Britain either charter a plane and fly direct to Lourdes airport, or travel by rail via Paris or by special train from the coast. Throughout the season there are three trains each day and two at night from Paris to Lourdes, leaving from Paris Austerlitz Station. These arrangements are for people wishing to visit Lourdes in small groups. Anybody who is accompanying a handicapped person is advised to join a large organised pilgrimage which will arrange travel and accommodation for them. Throughout the spring and summer the British Roman Catholic newspapers *The Universe* and *The Catholic Herald* regularly advertise pilgrimages to Lourdes for various lengths of time. These package pilgrimages can often be far cheaper than independent travel.

ACCOMMODATION

For small parties of two or three, accommodation in Lourdes is comparatively easy. There are approximately 263 hotels in the town, ranging from a four-star hotel with restaurant to simple one-star hotels which only provide a room. Unlike larger groups, small parties need not book in advance unless they go during Holy Week, when every available bed is booked months in advance. Large parties from churches or clubs are advised to try to join one of the big city pilgrimages because of the organisational difficulties, or try the Roman Catholic press.

USEFUL ADDRESSES

Note: The telephone numbers as given here assume the caller is within France. When ringing from abroad, the appropriate International Code must be prefixed.

TOURIST OFFICE
L'Office Municipal du Tourisme
Place du Champ-Commun
Lourdes
Tel: 62941564

RAILWAY STATION
S.N.C.F.
Avenue de la Gare
Lourdes
Tel: 62375050

BUS STATION
Gare Routiers
Boulevard de Paradis
Lourdes
Tel: 62943115

OTHER FACILITIES

There are plenty of shops in Lourdes, hairdressers, clothes shops and grocers. There are also lots of restaurants for those staying in hotels with no dining room. Most shops and restaurants are open seven days a week and the restaurants are open quite late. In general, pilgrim hotel meals are served early: lunch at 1200 and the evening meal around 1800. These times are to fit in with the service and processions which take place down in the Domain almost every day.

NEVERS

There is no direct train journey from Lourdes to Nevers. The best route is to travel from Lourdes north to Toulouse, from Toulouse to Brive, from Brive to Clermont Ferrand and then on to Nevers. It is a long journey with possibly four changes and therefore could last all day, leaving the traveller little time in the evening to see much of Nevers. A two-day visit would be the minimum length necessary to see Nevers properly.

Nevers is the French equivalent of a county town with municipal offices and a cathedral. It has a population of 50,000 and lies 234 km from Paris. For pilgrims travelling by road from northern Europe it would be easier to visit Nevers first before travelling on to Lourdes.

Nevers is an interesting mixture of ancient and modern buildings, and apart from the convent where Bernadette lived and died the town has other attractions for both the casual visitor and the pilgrim.

CATHEDRAL OF ST CYR

The cathedral in Nevers is an interesting building both architecturally and historically. The exterior is a mixture of two styles, Romanesque and Gothic. In 1944 it was badly damaged in a bombing raid, but unlike Coventry Cathedral, which was also gutted in the Second World War and rebuilt in a contemporary style, it was decided that Nevers Cathedral should be restored exactly as it had been before. The restoration work has been so successful that it is difficult for the untrained eye to see where the old ends and the new begins. Inside the cathedral the stained-glass windows shattered by the bombs have been replaced by ordinary clear glass, enabling the sunlight to stream through and brighten the interior considerably. The stone of the interior is also new, which adds to the general lightness of the building. It is a very simple interior, large, empty of any ornate decoration, and some may feel it to be rather austere and bare. The furnishings are also very simple. The plain wooden altar has an equally plain crucifix on top. The organ loft is also made of wood, with gleaming new aluminium organ pipes. The most notable feature in the cathedral is the beautiful seventeenth-century clock with a face like the sun, which stands in the choir section of the cathedral.

THE CHURCH OF ST PIERRE

on the Place de M Ravel, is, in contrast to the cathedral, an ornate, highly decorative church. The Place outside is a noisy, busy thoroughfare, but the walls of the church are thick. Once the visitor has entered the church and shut the door, the noise is suddenly shut out, leaving the church strangely quiet. The interior is square and dark since there are only small windows high up in the side walls. Opposite the door is the

High Altar on which stands an elaborately decorated tabernacle. The ceiling of the church is painted with frescoes. Since the church is so central it is very busy with shoppers, some of whom have come to light a candle and others just to sit quietly for a few moments.

ST ETIENNE

is a church that stands in the older part of the town, in the road named after it, Rue de St Etienne. It is an eleventh-century church in the Romanesque style. The buttresses and windows are Norman, as is the square-shaped part of the building. Unfortunately this church is not always open to the public.

CHAPEL OF SAINTE MARIE

is in the centre of Nevers near the cathedral, and in contrast to St Etienne it has a highly decorated Italianate front. The front façade is made up of four columns with highly decorated fan-vaulting. On top of these is an ornately carved triangle of stone, on the apex of which is a cross.

ACCOMMODATION

There are a number of hotels in Nevers, so that it is usually unnecessary to book in advance, unless the stay coincides with one of the major festivals like Easter, or mid-April which is the anniversary of Bernadette's death. *The Auberge de la Porte du Croix* is a three-star hotel with restaurant situated near the railway station. Also near the station, on the Avenue Charles de Gaulle, is a two-star hotel with restaurant, *Hotel Terminus*. There are a number of small hotels without restaurants but which do serve breakfast. These are close to the convent where Bernadette spent her religious life. One of these is the *Hotel Verdun* on the Rue de Lourdes overlooking the park. In the very centre of town there is a one-star hotel without a restaurant, near the cathedral, the *Hotel Centrale*.

USEFUL ADDRESSES

Note: The telephone numbers as given here assume the caller is within France. When ringing from abroad, the appropriate International Code must be prefixed.

TOURIST OFFICE
L'Office Municipal du Tourisme
31 Rue du Rempart
Nevers
Tel: 86590703

HOTELS
Auberge de la Porte du Croix
Promenade des Remparts
Nevers
Tel: 86571271

Hotel Verdun
Rue de Lourdes
Nevers
Tel: 86613007

Hotel Terminus
57 Avenue General de Gaulle
Nevers
Tel: 86570922

Hotel Centrale
3 Place St Laurent
Nevers
Tel: 86570694

OTHER FACILITIES

Because Nevers is a thriving county town as well as a place of pilgrimage, it has a large shopping centre with all the usual shops. There are also plenty of restaurants for those who stay in hotels with only bed and breakfast. There are four cinemas and a large sports hall. In the centre of the town is a pleasant park.

ASSISI

St Francis of Assisi was born in 1181, the son of a French mother who christened him John. His father, Pietro Bernardone, was a cloth merchant and often travelled to France on business where he probably met his wife. Francis was born when his father was on one of his French business trips, and when he returned he insisted that his baby son should not be called John, a name suggested before his birth, but Francesco instead – the little Frenchman. Francis had the usual upbringing of an Assisian child. He became literate, although no great scholar, and he was probably bilingual, learning French from his mother. After his schooling it was natural that he should join his father in the cloth business. Francis worked hard alongside his father and the business prospered. Besides being diligent in his application to work, Francis also applied himself to play with equal concentration. He had plenty of money which he lavished upon himself and his friends. Imagine this young Assisian blade, strutting around the streets and visiting the taverns and having rather a good time of it! Touched by the French influence in his life, Francis was fascinated by the strolling minstrels and troubadours who wandered the countryside, and he imitated them by singing their songs of love and gallant deeds. Pietro Bernardone was proud of his son, this youth who outdid all his friends in expensive clothes and indulgent lifestyle, because Francis was a sign of the success of his father. To Francis money was no object, but he was also often noted to be a generous man, and even at that time in his life his instinct was to give, not only to his friends, but often to the poor.

However, amidst all this high living and easy spending there was one piece of the jigsaw which prevented the perfect picture from being complete. The Bernardone family lacked 'position' in society. It was all very well having lots of money, but they were not aristocrats, and therefore Francis could not become a knight, a thing which he wanted more than anything in the world. When Assisi went to war with nearby Perugia, this gave Francis the opportunity of proving himself in battle, which could eventually lead to becoming a knight. Dressed in the finest armour and sitting astride the finest horse – all supplied by his father – Francis, at the age of twenty-one, set out as a valet or apprentice knight to fight in Perugia. When battle commenced, things went badly for the Assisians, and Francis and others were captured and became prisoners of war. The defeated warriors languished in jail for many months (some of them for perhaps as long as two years) in Perugia before hostilities ceased and an amnesty was declared. Francis returned home to joyous parents, but he immediately fell very ill, probably due to his long imprisonment, and was confined to his bed for quite some time. He slowly became well again, and during this period of convalescence a great change was beginning to take place deep inside this disappointed knight. It was a change which was to turn the style of his former life completely on its head.

Meanwhile, another chance for military glory presented itself, and once again Francis joined a military expedition, this time to Apulia. Much to everyone's surprise he returned home two days later, totally disillusioned about the idea of going to war. The story goes that he gave away his fine military attire to a fellow combatant who was rather shabbily dressed (Francis was ashamed of the contrast between them). What is more important at this point in his life is that Francis had a vision on the first night away from Assisi in which he saw himself as a successful knight surrounded by an abundance of worldly goods. Gradually the opulence faded and he heard a voice saying, 'Who can do most for you, servant or master?' Francis answered, 'The master.' 'Why, then,' said the voice, 'do you follow the servant rather than the Master?' Francis put his own interpretation on this message, and returned to Assisi with some very different ideas.

Francis now spent his days in a kind of dream, and many of his friends accused him of being lovesick, and for convenience' sake he did not disabuse them of the idea. As he wandered alone in Assisi and the surrounding countryside, trying to work out what his life should really be about, he came upon the ruins of an old church just outside the town, called St Damian's. The church was in a bad state of repair, and the old priest who lived there was doing his best to keep the place viable. As Francis prayed at the chapel one day, a recently acquired habit, the figure of Christ on the cross spoke to him. 'Go, Francis, repair my church which, as you see, falls in ruin.'

At long last Francis felt that he had some guidance, some directive which would help him develop his life's work. Interpreting the message from the cross literally, Francis immediately went home, took a piece of cloth from his father's store, and went to nearby Foligno and sold it there in the market place, together with his horse and saddle. He then walked back to St Damian's and offered the money he had made to the astonished priest who, on hearing how it had been raised, refused to accept it. Francis was allowed to stay at the church and, for the moment, the money remained on a window sill where Francis had left it. Setting out from the little church each day, Francis decided to start begging for his bread on the streets of the town, which was all part of his plan to revolutionise his life. Imagine the surprise of the citizens at seeing the rich young playboy begging in the street, dressed as a beggar. Pietro, his father, was more disappointed than angry, and he flung his son into the cellar to let him cool off a little and come to his senses. After his mother had tried in vain to persuade him to come home and to stop this ridiculous stunt, Francis left his father's house for ever. On hearing this, Pietro was very angry that his son would not cease his shameful behaviour, so he took out a summons against him in the civil court, charging him with the theft of the cloth. Francis flatly refused to appear in court and appealed to the bishop, who knew him well. The bishop decided that the money, still at the church on the window sill, should be returned to Pietro. Francis immediately complied with this ruling, and he returned not only the money but also all the clothes he was wearing, as a sign that he was renouncing the world. 'Till now I have called Pietro Bernardone my father; but my purpose is to serve God, so I here hand over the money he is troubled about, and the clothes I had of him; and now I say: Our Father who art in heaven; not Father Pietro Bernardone.'

Although there was no malice in the heart of Francis, nevertheless it must have been a hard thing for his father to bear.

Francis had now embraced total poverty, and he set about his task of rebuilding St Damian's, which he managed to do with the proceeds of his begging. For the next two years this rich man's son turned beggar lived a solitary life – to many an eccentric way of life – begging in the streets and spending a lot of time alone like a desert father. Francis was certainly a very sensitive person, although his actions sometimes seemed to belie the fact. The decision to cut himself off from his family – and particularly his mother – was something which he felt very deeply.

It was 1208 and Francis was twenty-seven years old. For most of the last two years he had been busy helping out at various hospitals and churches in and around Assisi. One church which he often frequented was down on the plain below the town, called St Mary of the Angels (Santa Maria degli Angeli – the Portiuncula). During a spiritual experience there one day, it was revealed to

A street in Assisi

Francis what he was to do with the rest of his life. The Gospel of that day had been dealing with the twelve Apostles who went out and preached the word of Christ. Francis decided that this was exactly what he wanted to do. It was here that he finally made up his mind to dedicate himself to God and to convince as many people as he could that Christ was crucified and died for each and every one. The 'Morning Star of the Renaissance', as Francis is sometimes referred to, now began to burn brightly.

Francis was torn between two ideals; to preach the Gospel, and to pray and live a life of solitude. Somehow Francis seems to have done both praying and preaching very well, for besides becoming a very popular preacher, his spiritual life deepened as the years went by. In 1224, when he was praying in a cave at La Verna, he received the stigmata, the five wounds of Christ on his body, an indication of the depth of his spiritual union with God. Francis was not a learned man, yet he did have a knack of being able to keep people listening to what he had to say – which, we are told, was always delivered directly and to the point.

At this stage, it might help to have a detailed description of Francis from his biographer Thomas of Celano:

> He was of medium height, closer to shortness, his head was moderate in size and round, his face a bit long and prominent, his forehead smooth and low; his eyes were of moderate size, black and sound; his hair was black, his eyebrows straight, his nose symmetrical, thin and straight; his ears were upright, but small; his temples smooth. His speech was peaceable, fiery and sharp; his voice was strong, sweet, clear and sonorous. His teeth were set close together, even and white; his lips were small and thin; his beard black but not bushy. His neck was slender, his shoulders straight, his arms short, his hands slender, his fingers long, his nails extended; his legs were thin, his feet small. His skin was delicate, his flesh very spare.

Cimabue's painting on the ceiling of the lower church of the Basilica is said to be the nearest visual likeness to St Francis. As to his preaching, and the innate skills he employed to make people listen to him, we are again fortunate to have an account from Thomas of Spoleto, who saw Francis preach to good effect at Bologna in 1222:

In the same year, on the day of the Assumption of the Mother of God, when I was a student at Bologna, I saw St Francis preaching in the piazza before the Piazza Publico, where almost the whole town was assembled. The theme of his sermon was 'Angels, Men, Devils'; and he spoke so well and so wisely of these three rational spirits that to many learned men who were there the sermon of this ignorant man seemed worthy of not little admiration, in spite of the fact that he did not keep to the method of an expositor so much as of an extempore speaker. Indeed, the whole manner of his speech was calculated to stamp out enmities and to make peace. His tunic was dirty, his person unprepossessing, and his face far from handsome; yet God gave such powers to his words that many factions of the nobility, among whom the fiercer anger of ancient feuds had been raging with much bloodshed, were brought to reconciliation. Towards him, indeed, the reverence and devotion of men was so great that men and women rushed upon him headlong, anxious to touch the hem of his garment and to carry away bits of his clothing.

Francis attracted people to him for many reasons: he had a magnetic personality, he was an excellent and effective preacher, and there was also the poverty, something both eccentric and attractive. But much more important were the ideas which Francis stood for and which he preached. The time was right for people to listen and accept such new and revolutionary ideas. It was a war-torn age, the Church was scandalously rich and powerful, and people wanted to hear something different, sensing that there had to be a sweeping and fundamental change in society and in its attitude. Instead of war, therefore, Francis preached love; instead of the virtue of amassing great wealth and possession, Francis preached equality and that all things on God's earth were put there for everyone to share in equally. He also grasped the idea of harmony in the world and that everything had its part to play in it. This is why he used names like Brother Sun, Sister Moon, Brother Wolf and Sister Nightingale to illustrate the oneness he believed to be part of God's plan in creation. This was something to which Francis found people eager to respond – something new and exciting. It was the dawning of the Renaissance and the new ideas spread through every aspect of people's lives. St Francis was at the

Assisi. The basilica

very heart of it. In his *Civilisation* Sir Kenneth Clark said that St Francis 'changed the form of the Middle Ages.' I always remember a friar's comment on the same subject: 'Francis wasn't your average tapioca-pudding saint – people miss a lot when they confine him to the birds.'

In the short space of time after he had left his father's house and taken up his new way of life permanently, Francis soon attracted about a dozen men who were of a like mind. They wanted to be like Francis and they became his followers. Francis wrote out a simple rule by which they lived. This included absolute poverty, doing good works, preaching and trying to make people realise God's universal plan in which everything had a place. In 1209 Pope Innocent III approved the Rule which Francis had taken to Rome for his sanction, and from then on the little band of friars (brothers) were officially given permission to preach. Francis became a deacon and the others received their tonsure. At Assisi the Benedictine Monks let the new order of friars use the little church of St Mary of the Angels, the Portiuncula, down on the plain, where Francis had first understood what his life's work was to be. The Portiuncula was the Franciscans' first home.

There are many stories about Francis which tell us something of the character of the man – at times extremely inconsistent, yet engaging. At one point during my visit to Assisi I climbed the highest parapet of the friary at the Sacro Convento with a friar, and as we looked out on to the heat-hazy plain below, we could just see the huge dome of the Portiuncula in the distance. Over to our right we could also see the town of Perugia, almost invisible in the east. It is one of the most breath-taking views I have ever seen. As we both sat and took in this remarkable scene the friar told me of an incident in the life of Francis, early in his religious life, which was one of his great conversion moments. 'Down near to the Portiuncula Francis met a leper,' he began. 'He looked at him and was just on the point of turning away when he went towards him and kissed him. After that moment Francis always said that he never found anything difficult. Anything which he had found difficult before became sweetness for him now. His first work was with lepers, and because of this and the fact that he had genuinely thrown up all his wordly goods, people found it easy to follow him. They wanted very much to be like him – so they went with him.'

There is another famous story about Brother Rufino, a nobleman and cousin to St Clare, who was one of the first to join Francis. It seems that on one particular occasion Francis told Rufino to go up to the town centre and preach a sermon. Rufino, little practised in the ways of rhetoric, declined, saying that he could not do it. Francis flew into a rage and ordered the poor man not only to do it – but to do it in his drawers only! When Rufino left to do Francis' bidding, Francis was so overcome with remorse at the way he had treated the good Friar Rufino that he dashed off to the town and actually preached himself – stark naked. To complete his own humiliation, and to show that he was truly sorry, he had to go one better. There were no half measures with Francis! Blessed Rufino is buried in the crypt of the basilica in Assisi, alongside St Francis and in company with Leone, Masseo and Angelo, all faithful disciples of Francis. (Francis was originally buried in the church of San Giorgio. His companions were rediscovered in 1818 and reburied in the basilica, first in an ornate tomb, and in 1932 in a very simple one.)

One of the most famous people to have followed Francis in his lifetime was a woman, Clare di Offreduccio. On Palm Sunday, 18 March 1212, when she was in her late teens, Clare was received into the Brotherhood by Francis himself. She was from a well-to-do Assisian family, and had known Francis for a year or two prior to her entering the Order. Clare met Francis regularly during the two years before joining him, during which time he instructed her in the ways of the Franciscan life. Because her family did not know that she wanted to become a Franciscan, these meetings were held in secret. It is often said that Clare and Francis were in love, and perhaps they were, but it did not seem to interfere with their spiritual lives. The problem facing Clare was that there was no practical provision for a female to be accepted into the Order. So far membership had been exclusively for men, and it was clear that Clare could not be accommodated in Portiuncula. Instead she went to live with the Benedictine nuns for a while, but this arrangement proved unsatisfactory for Clare, who yearned to be a Franciscan. Eventually, along with her sister Agnes, Clare was installed at the little chapel of St Damian's, where she lived an enclosed life for 40 years. St Clare, canonised soon after her death in 1253, was always a great source of strength and sympathy for Francis when things were not going well for the Order. When he was ill Clare nursed him back to health, and she was with him shortly before he died. The basilica of Santa Chiara is over to the eastern side of the town, distinctive for its remarkable flying buttresses at ground level on the left-hand side. St Clare was buried in the basilica in 1260.

Francis always wanted to take the Gospel as far afield as possible. He certainly never intended that his activities should be confined to Italy. It was the time of the Crusades, and in 1212 he set off for the East to convert the Saracens. He was an optimist if nothing else. His plans were frustrated and he was driven on to the Dalmatian coast. Two years later he set out again, this time for Morocco through Spain, but illness forced him to return to Assisi. In 1219 he sailed for Acre where, to his horror, he discovered that the loose-living Crusaders were not the high-principled men he thought they should have been. Somehow Francis managed to get through the enemy lines and make contact with the Sultan, who was impressed by the rough-clad friar but unimpressed by Francis' attempts to convert him to Christianity. With some of his

companions Francis then spent a few months on pilgrimage in the
Holy Land, only to be recalled to Assisi to sort out problems which
had arisen because the Order was growing so quickly. The
Franciscans were now 5,000 strong, but with no real structure to
organise such numbers. Francis, always the realist, resigned as
head of the Order, realising that he was not an administrator, which
was what the Order needed if it was to survive. In 1221 Francis
revised the Rule and because this was not satisfactory he wrote
another which was approved by Pope Honorius II in 1223. Earlier
Francis had written a rule for lay people, married or single. This
rule became known as the Third Order, and those who joined it
became 'Tertiaries'. The Third Order still flourishes in many parts
of the world today.

By his early forties Francis' health was on the decline. When he
returned from Egypt in 1225, the year before he died, his eyes
needed to be cauterised if he was to keep his sight. This was a very
painful operation which he underwent at Greccio in the Rieti
Valley. It was St Clare who nursed him back to a better state of
health. Surprisingly enough, it was at this time, when he knew that
his life was coming to an end and when he was in great pain and
suffering, that Francis wrote his famous *Canticle of Brother Sun*:

Most high, all powerful, good Lord,
Yours are the praise, the glory and the honour and every blessing.
To you alone, Most High, they belong
and no man is worthy to pronounce your name.
Be praised, my Lord, with all your creatures,
especially Sir Brother Sun,
who is day and by him you shed light upon us.
He is beautiful and radiant with great splendour,
of you, Most High, he bears a likeness.
Be praised, my Lord, through Sister Moon and the Stars,
in the heavens you formed them clear and precious and beautiful.
Be praised, my Lord, through Brother Wind
and through Air and Cloud and fair and all weather,
by which you nourish all that you have made.
Be praised, my Lord, through Sister Water,
who is very useful and humble and precious and pure.
Be praised, my Lord, through Brother Fire,

by whom you light up the night;
he is beautiful and merry and vigorous and strong.
Be praised, my Lord, through our Sister Mother Earth,
who sustains and guides us,
and produces diverse fruits with coloured flowers and herbs.
Be praised, my Lord, by those who pardon for love of you,
and endure sickness and trials.
Blessed are they who shall endure them in peace,
for by you, Most High, they shall be crowned.

In the autumn of 1226 Francis fell seriously ill and was taken to the bishop's palace in Assisi. As the time of death drew near, the friars obtained permission to take their dying founder down the mountain slope to the Portiuncula, the place he had loved so much and which had played such a large part in his religious life. He certainly did not fear his end; he saw it as a natural part of God's creation, and so in honour of Death he wrote the final stanza to his *Canticle*:

Be praised, my Lord, through our Sister Bodily Death,
from whom no man living can escape.
Woe to those who die in mortal sin.
Blessed are those whom she will find in your most holy will,
for the second death will do them no harm.
Praise and bless my Lord
and give him thanks and serve him with great humility.

ASSISI

THE REGION OF UMBRIA
Assisi is situated in Umbria, which is known as the green heart of Italy. It is a somewhat isolated area of beautiful mountains and hills, rich vineyards and hilltop villages. Assisi is only one of a number of remarkable places in Umbria. Other places of interest include Perugia, Nocera, Orvieto, Loreto and Foligno.

HISTORY OF ASSISI
Assisi was one of the early settlements of the Italic people before it passed under the sway of Rome, when it became a municipality. Christianity was first preached in Assisi by St Rufino, who was later martyred. The city was destroyed and rebuilt over the years. It was devastated by the barbarians, razed to the ground by Totila and conquered by Charlemagne. Assisi's real fame began in the twelfth century, for it was at the end of this century that St Francis was born within the city walls. From that time onwards Assisi

has attracted Christian pilgrims from all over the world. However, even after the time of St Francis, Assisi did suffer some brutal sackings. It passed under the jurisdiction of one despot after another and was torn apart by rivalry between local factions, the Parte di Sopra (Upper Part) and the Parte di Sotto (Lower Part). It was not until the sixteenth century that Assisi found peace, when it came under the jurisdiction of the Papal States, where it remained, apart from a brief period during the Napoleonic invasion, until 1860.

MODERN ASSISI

Assisi is now an international tourist centre. There are many modern hotels with magnificent views over the Umbrian plain. There are plenty of attractive walks through the fields and woods, and Assisi's position at the centre of the Umbrian region makes it an ideal starting point for the many expeditions which can be made to the other Umbrian towns. Assisi abounds in religious festivals and folklore celebrations, and at almost any time of the year the visitor will have the chance to see one of these events. One of the most dramatic of these festivals is that of the Dead Christ on Good Friday evening. The chief celebration is, of coure, for the feast of St Francis, the patron saint of Italy, on 4 October. Every year a different region of Italy comes to pay special homage to the saint, and a representative of the Government sends a radio message to the whole country. During the summer the Tourist Agency organises concerts and folklore performances in the Public Gardens.

THINGS TO SEE IN ASSISI

The basilica in Assisi is dedicated to St Francis and consists of two superim-posed churches arranged to form a single building.

For pilgrims who do not speak Italian there are friars available to conduct tours of the basilica in many foreign languages. They can be found at the Portorium, just to the left of the main entrance to the lower church of the basilica.

The first stone of the basilica was laid on 17 July 1228, almost two years after the saint's death and the day after he was canonised. It was built on a hill which was commonly known as the 'Colle dell'Inferno' ('Hill of Hell') but was renamed the 'Hill of Paradise' because of the building there of St Francis' basilica. The building was completed in an amazingly short time, a mere twenty-two months after it had been started, and on 25 May 1230 the remains of St Francis were taken from the church of San Giorgio where they had been kept to the lower church of the basilica. They were laid in a small chapel at the centre of the transept and until 1442 they could be seen by pilgrims.

The lower church was intended as a place of meditation on the saint's earthly life with its poverty and sacrifice, while the upper church – dedicated to the cult of St Francis and his heavenly glory – was intended as a place of praise, and this is reflected in its magnificent triumphant atmosphere.

The pictorial decoration of the two churches of the basilica was begun immediately after their architectural completion and continued until 1369. Amongst the artists who painted there are such great names as Giunta, Jacopo Torriti, Pietro Cavallini and perhaps most famous of all, Giotto. The painters often asked for nothing for their services, such was the admiration that St Francis evoked in them. So great was their enthusiasm that they have given the basilica a rare collection of Italian art. Almost all the wall space is covered with frescoes.

The theme running right through these frescoes is the points of contact between the life of St Francis and the life of Christ. There is also a spectacular collection of stained-glass windows, most of which are contemporary with the frescoes.

Just to the left of the main door inside the basilica there is an altar screen by a glass partition. Above the altar is the tunic said to have been worn by St Francis. Also in the church, high up on one of the domes, is a faded frescoe of St Francis which is said to be the nearest likeness.

THE PORTIUNCULA (PORZIUNCOLA) CHAPEL

This chapel is situated within the basilica of Our Lady of the Angels, a monumental temple erected to preserve the Portiuncula and other chapels revered in the cult of St Francis. It is said to have been founded by four pilgrims to house a piece of the tomb of the Virgin which they claimed they had brought back from the Holy Land. The name Portiuncula is a vague name for a small portion of something, and was given to the chapel by St Francis because of its very small size. The chapel belonged to the Benedictines in the sixth century but was given to St Francis in 1211 when he chose it as his favourite centre. In return a bowl of fish from the Tescio river was given to the Benedictines each year and, curiously enough, this tradition still exists. St Francis himself restored the chapel, which was in a poor state of repair, and here he had the first little cells built for friars to live in. In 1212 St Clare sought shelter here after she had cut off her hair and fled from the rich

household of her father to begin a life of poverty and sacrifice.

After St Francis died in 1226 in the nearby Chapel of Death other chapels and small oratories were added to the cells. Like the basilica of St Francis, the Portiuncula chapel contains frescoes attributed to painters such as Martelli and Alunno, and a later fresco by J F Overbek of Lübeck (1829). The entrance door has fifteenth-century leaves and through it you pass into the bare interior, the walls blackened with smoke from the lamps and candles.

CAPELLA DEL TRANSITO (CHAPEL OF DEATH)

This chapel stands beside the Portiuncula on the place where St Francis died. Feeling he was near to death, St Francis insisted on lying on the ground as a demonstration that he had remained faithful to the principle of poverty until the end.

THE CHURCH OF ST DAMIAN'S (SAN DAMIANO)

It is said that one can hear the message of St Francis at St Damian's more than at any other church in Assisi. There seems to be a complete harmony between the simple little church and the soft, surrounding countryside. Its walls are interrupted rarely by plain windows, and with its humble little arcade the church seems to symbolise the virtue most dear to St Francis – poverty. St Damian's brings together the memory of both St Francis and St Clare. It was here in this humble oratory that St Francis heard the crucifix speaking to him, 'Go, Francis, repair my falling house.' Francis did not at first understand this command. He did not know which house the voice was referring to. It was not until later as he read the Gospel that St Francis understood the true message of the crucifix: he was to rebuild the invisible city of God.

Two years later Francis built the little convent for St Clare and her followers and for 41 years Clare lived there; her mother, Ortolana, also spent some years there with her.

The church has a single aisle with a single vault and a choir. On the right is a small window and three scenes of this episode in St Francis' life. After the voice of the crucifix had commanded him to repair the house, Francis collected money to give to the chaplain for the restoration of St Damian's. The chaplain refused the gift and Francis threw the bag of money out of this window. They are probably works by a follower of Giotto.

On the right is the chapel of the crucifixion. The wooden crucifix on the altar is supposed to change expression according to the angle from which you look. Above the High Altar is a copy painted on wood of the crucifix which spoke to St Francis.

At St Damian's the visitor can see St Clare's dormitory where she died on 11 August 1253; the cloisters; the refectory with old benches and a table marked with a cross where St Clare generally sat. On the floor above is the infirmary where St Agnes died three months after the death of her sister St Clare.

The energetic visitor could walk to St Damian's from the centre of Assisi in about half an hour. It is a distance of around two kilometres and is well signposted from the town centre. Buses go to St Damian's every day.

THE ROCCA MAGGIORE (GREAT FORT)

The Rocca Maggiore stands on the crest of a hill above Assisi, and is interesting not just in itself but in its contrast to the atmosphere of churches in the city below.

The first castle was erected in 1174 at the command of the archbishop of Mainz who was sent by Barbarossa to occupy Assisi. It was rebuilt after being destroyed in a popular uprising in 1198, and the enlargement and fortification went on until 1535. Today the fort consists of a surrounding wall with square defence towers at the corners, and a magnificent square towered castle in the middle from which you get a wonderful view of Assisi and the plain of Perugia.

RELIGIOUS EVENTS IN ASSISI THROUGHOUT THE YEAR

HOLY WEEK
Liturgical ceremonies are held in all the churches and basilicas of the town to commemorate the Passion of Christ.
HOLY THURSDAY
'The Deposition from the Cross' – a dramatic thirteenth-century mystery play re-enacted on Holy Thursday.
GOOD FRIDAY
'The Procession of the Dead Christ' – held by candlelight on Good Friday evening.
HOLY SATURDAY/EASTER SUNDAY
To conclude the Easter celebrations there is the Liturgy of the Easter Vigil and the Procession of the Sacred Veil.
22 JUNE
'Feast of the Vow'.
1–2 AUGUST
'Feast of the Pardon'. This pardon is one of the oldest and most renowned indulgences in Christian history, and is granted in the course of the feast which is celebrated every year.
11 AUGUST
Feast of St Rufino, patron of the town.
12 AUGUST
Feast of St Clare, patroness of the town.

3–4 OCTOBER
Feast of St Francis, patron of Italy.
25 DECEMBER–6 JANUARY
Many events to celebrate Christmas. St Francis popularised the crib figures, samples of which are on sale in the shops. The more expensive sets are hand-carved in wood and well worth the extra cost.

OTHER PLACES OF INTEREST IN THE UMBRIA REGION

PERUGIA

The mediaeval town of Perugia is set in the Umbrian hills and commands a wonderful view. Its National Archaeological Museum not only has one of the best Etruscan and Roman collections, but is also considered to be the most important museum of Umbria's pre-history.

The University of Perugia, founded between the end of the thirteenth and the beginning of the fourteenth centuries is one of the oldest in Europe. Today it has ten faculties, libraries and many student hostels. The university attracts students not only from all over Italy but also from abroad, mainly the Third World. Next to it is the university for foreign students. Thousands of students from all over the world come to learn Italian and to study the country's history and culture.

Perugia is also a musical centre. The Academia delle Belle Arti and the School of Music are situated there, and operas and concerts are performed in the Morlacchi Theatre.

Monuments of interest abound in Perugia. Amongst the most impressive are the Temple of St Angelo and the Palazzo dei Priori. The Renaissance fortress (the Rocca Paolina) is well worth a visit.

LORETO

The life of the small city of Loreto is devoted almost entirely to the Holy House which is one of the most venerated monuments of Christianity. Here the Virgin Mary is supposed to have been born. It is, according to legend, the place where Jesus lived his life until the beginning of his mission. The story is that the house was still intact in 1291 after the Moslem invasion of Palestine when, according to tradition, it was miraculously lifted and borne by angels to the hill of Tersatto in Dalmatia. In 1294 it is supposed to have crossed the Adriatic and come to rest in Loreto. From ancient times Loreto has been one of the great classical pilgrim places of Christianity.

The need arose for a sanctuary to accommodate the great stream of pilgrims who came from every country, and this sanctuary gradually grew into a great cathedral. Doubtless it was in connection with the miraculous story of the Holy House of Loreto that Pope Benedict XV proclaimed the Madonna of Loreto patroness of aviators throughout the world! The work on the basilica was begun in 1468.

The local tourist board in Loreto is in the Via G Solari 3; tel: (071) 97 276.

NOCERA UMBRA

Nocera is a typical mediaeval town surrounded by towered walls. The cathedral and the church of St Francis are important monuments as much for their artistic value as for their historical interest. The cathedral was destroyed by Frederick II in 1248 and was reconstructed in the late fifteenth century. The interior only dates back to the eighteenth century, and little remains of the original structure.

The church of St Francis has a Gothic portal built in 1386, but the interior only dates back to the fifteenth century. The interior is decorated with

143

frescoes, some of which are by Matteo Gualdo (1435–1503).

In addition Nocera has a city park, a playground for children, a tennis court and a bowling alley which makes it a very popular summer resort. Its main importance is, however, its mineral waters which are recognised for their therapeutic value.

ORVIETO

Of particular interest in Orvieto are the remains of the Etruscan civilisation. Remains of temples and temple decorations have been found in various parts of the town. Most of Orvieto's archaeological material is gathered in the Civic Museum of the Faina Foundation.

Other buildings of interest are the Palace of the Popes, now the seat of the Museum of the Opera del Duomo; the thirteenth-century churches of St Francesco, St Lorenzo de' Arari and St Domenico; and the impressive fortress built by Albornoz in the middle of the fourteenth century.

FOLIGNO

Foligno is famous for its jousting tournament which takes place on the second Sunday in September every year. The jousts were popular in the seventeenth century and were revived in 1946.

ADDITIONAL PLACES OF RELIGIOUS INTEREST IN THE UMBRIAN REGION

CASCIA. There is an important sanctuary dedicated to St Rita who is named the 'saint of impossible things'; she was born in nearby Roccaporena.
TERNI. Basilica of St Valentine, the patron saint of lovers.
NORCIA. Birth place of St Benedict, founder of Western monasticism. He was a key figure in the formation of Western civilisation.

HOW TO REACH ASSISI

Note: The telephone numbers as given here assume the caller is within the same country as the hotel, station, or other number. When ringing from abroad, the 0 at the start of each code must be omitted and the appropriate International Code must be prefixed.

BY RAIL: The station (five km from the town – good bus service) is on the line Foligno–Terontola (in connection with numerous international trains) with through trains from Rome and Florence, and in summer also from Ancona. The distance from Rome to Assisi is 182 km and the journey takes approximately two and a half hours.

ITALIAN STATE RAILWAYS

Italian State Tourist Office
1 Princes Street
London W1
Tel: 01-408 1254

Wasteels Travel
22 Gillingham Street
London SW1
Tel: 01-834 7066

L.R. Stanton Limited
23a Princess Street
Albert Square
Manchester
Tel: 061-236 7958

Stanton Travel Agency
Tel: (0606) 552772

Also by branches of Thomas Cook & Son.

BY CAR

The road from Rome reaches Assisi by the Autostrada del Sole to Magliano Sabina or Orte, and then by the Via Flaminia (179 km). The road from Florence comes through Chiusi or

Arezzo (by the Autostrada del Sole) and then through Magione and Perugia.

CAR HIRE

There are four car hire firms offering their services for travellers at the end of their train journeys: Autoservizi Maggiore, Avis, Eurotrans and Hertz. These firms have branches in all the main Italian cities and resorts. The railway stations will send a telegram on request to the nearest branch at a fixed rate.

TOURIST INFORMATION OFFICES IN THE UMBRIA REGION

Assisi: Piazza del Comune 27. Tel: (075) 812450
Perugia: Via Mazzini 21. Tel: (075) 61720. Corso Vannucci 30. Tel: (075) 65146
Terni: Via C. Battisti 7/A. Tel: (0744) 414 267

ACCOMMODATION IN ASSISI AND THE UMBRIA REGION

In the Umbria region hotel accommodation is very good and plentiful, with about 372 hotels and a capacity of 13,000 beds spread over areas of interest. There are also twenty camping sites on river and lake shores, and in hilly and mountainous areas. It is also possible to stay in hostels and holiday houses; this type of accommodation is usually chosen by students or people who wish to live with families.

ADDRESSES IN ENGLAND TO USE WHEN BOOKING

Italberghi, 104 North Road, Kew Gardens, Surrey. Tel: 01-878 2710.

The Italian State Tourist Office publishes the official list of all Italian hotels and pensions every year and can be consulted through your travel agent.

HOTELS IN ASSISI

Hotel San Francesco
Via San Francesco 48
Tel: (075) 812 281

Hotel Subasio
Via Frate Elia 2
Tel: (075) 812 206

HOTELS IN PERUGIA

Hotel La Rosetta
Piazza Italia 19
Tel: (075) 20 841

Hotel Brufani
Piazza Italia 12
Tel: (075) 20 741

BANKING HOURS

Banks are only open in the mornings from 0830 to 1300 hours, and are closed on Saturdays, Sundays and national holidays. Travellers' cheques and cheques can be changed at most hotels. Tourists can change money at main railway stations and airports.

SAN GIOVANNI

Padre Pio was born on 25 May 1887 in a small town called Pietrelcina near Benevento, about 50 miles northeast of Naples. His father was Grazio Forgione and his mother was Maria Giuseppa De Nunzio. On the day after his birth he was taken to the church and baptised Francesco. There were eight children in the family, all of whom received only a fair education which was paid for by their father, who went to America on two occasions to try to do better for his family. At a very early age Francesco showed signs of piety and an interest in religious things, and so it was no surprise to anyone that when he was fifteen, Francesco sought permission to enter the nearby Capuchin friary to become a friar. Much to his and his family's delight Francesco was accepted as ideal material for the priesthood. Francesco Forgione began his Capuchin novitiate at the friary of Morcone. Unfortunately he did not enjoy the best of health and was often ill. It seemed he was so devoted to his Christian faith and his love of God, and he fasted so rigorously, that at times his superiors became alarmed. The year after he entered the novitiate, Francesco made his religious profession and he took the name of Brother Pius or (in Italian) Pio, after Pope Pius V (1504–1572), the Dominican who struggled against the spread of the Reformation.

On completion of his novitiate Brother Pio began his studies proper towards the priesthood. During his philosophical and theological studies the young student came into contact with two friars, Padre Benedetto and Padre Agostino, two men who were to become very important to him in later life. But ill health constantly dogged Brother Pio's studies, so much so that on one occasion in 1909 his superiors sent him home to Pietralcina in the hope that the familiar air and surroundings would restore him to good health.

Eventually, on 10 August 1910, in the cathedral of Benevento, Brother Pio was ordained priest and became known as Padre Pio. It was at this time that the new priest began his correspondence with his two spiritual directors, Padre Benedetto and Padre Agostino. Fortunately Padre Pio's letters have been preserved and published in book form by the Friars at San Giovanni (*Padre Pio of Pietrelcina – Letters*).

Because clerics were not exempted from conscription into the Italian Army at the time, Padre Pio was called up in 1915. Army life with all its roughness and crudity so appalled the young and impressionable priest that he found his way back to his monastery. There was some administrative confusion with regard to Padre Pio's papers, and the military police were instructed to return the Friar to the ranks. In fact this order was never executed, and he never made any attempt to rejoin his company. In 1916 Padre Pio finally came to San Giovanni, and there he was to stay for the rest of his life. At that time it was an old, broken-down church set on the high mountains in harsh and arid country. All that was to change as the years went by.

So far, the life of Padre Pio had, to all intents and purposes, been uneventful. He was an average friar in many ways, apart, perhaps, from his exceptional piety. He did not enjoy good health, and for that reason there is no doubt that he was the cause of some concern to his superiors. After all, what do you do with a man who was constantly sick and in need of care and attention? However, on 20 September 1918, when the First World War was drawing to a close and a disillusioned world was counting the cost of all the horror and catastrophe, something happened at the friary of San Giovanni which was to make Padre Pio a marked man in both the literal and the figurative sense. The clue to what happened to Padre Pio is at the back of the friary church, in the choir loft. There, perched on a ledge, is a large crucifix, depicting the figure of Christ in all his agony; the nails in the hands are very large; blood pours from the feet, hands and side, and the face is spattered with blood which is coming from the crown of thorns. At this spot in 1918, Padre Pio received the stigmata, the five wounds of Christ upon his own body. Some time after this strange event, Padro Pio wrote to one of his spiritual directors, Padre Benedetto, telling him of what happened. Here is part of that letter:

On the morning of the 20th last month, in the choir, after celebrating Mass, I yielded to a peacefulness similar to a sweet sleep. All my internal and external senses, and even the very faculties of my soul, were indescribably serene. During this time absolute silence surrounded and invaded me: I was suddenly filled with a great peace and abandon which effaced everything else and became a lull in the turmoil. It all happened in a flash. I saw before me a mysterious person, similar to the one I had seen on 5 August, differing only because his hands, feet and sides were dripping blood. The sight of him frightened me; what I felt at that moment is indescribable. I thought I would die, and would have died if the Lord hadn't intervened and strengthened my heart which was about to burst out of my chest. The Person disappeared and I became aware that my hands and feet and side were dripping with blood.

Padre Pio was to carry those visible wounds for the next half century, wounds which caused him the same agony that Christ himself experienced at his crucifixion. Padre Pio was aged 33 when he received the visible stigmata. Later it became known that he had received the wounds 'invisibly', i.e. known only to himself, eight years previously, about a month after his ordination. It is extremely difficult to try to understand what the stigmata means, and why it happens. But what is certain is that Padre Pio did carry those wounds. The evidence for proof is overwhelming and consistent over 50 years. At one time a doctor from Rome came to examine Padre Pio and his wounds. He wrote:

All the wounds observed in Padre Pio are to be considered real and true anatomical wounds of the tissues whose persistent continuation, whose strong anatomical pathological pattern characteristics, with their capacity for continual bleeding, with the blood always fresh and perfumed and their locality corresponding exactly to the parts of the body that Our Lord suffered.

At the Friary I met and talked with two friars who had attended Padre Pio during the last years of his life. Both Father Joseph and Father Alessio gave me graphic accounts of the wounds which they both saw on many occasions, especially on his hands. Both priests emphasised the enormous physical suffering which

Padre Pio experienced through the wounds, and the humble way in which he accepted them and rarely referred to them. I also spoke to many other people who had seen the wounds on the hands whilst Padre Pio said Mass, the only time they were uncovered. Added to this there is also ample photographic evidence which testifies to the truth of this strange phenomenon. The wounds on Padre Pio's hands were through the palms, although according to Roman custom a crucified man would have the nails through his wrists. This would have helped bear the weight of the body on a cross, while nails through the palms would have ripped through and left a tear. However, the more traditional depiction is for the nails to go through the palms, possibly for artistic reasons, as on the cross from which Padre Pio received his stigmata. When Padre Pio died, the marks of the wounds, which had been very deep, were found to be completely healed. The remains were examined shortly after death by a doctor who had known Padre Pio well and was familiar with the wounds. The doctor declared that such perfect healing – with no sign of any scarred tissue – was beyond the explanation of his science.

Father Joseph explained what he thought Christ's wounds on Padre Pio meant. 'The stigmata is the most elevated of mystical gifts,' he said. 'Christ gives it to souls who are very closely united with him. Padre Pio found himself before the crucified Christ from whose body came rays of light which pierced open the hitherto unopened wounds on Padre Pio's body. I think it's important to note that those wounds remained open and bleeding for exactly half a century. Now that means that those wounds could not possibly have been natural, otherwise they would have become gangrenous. Doctors held several, protracted examinations of the wounds, always trying to heal them with ointment and bandages and fixing wax seals so that no one could tamper with them from one control to another. But the wounds continued to bleed. The doctors wrote that you could put your fingers through the holes in his hands. If Padre Pio held his hands up in front of you, you could see clearly through the hole the size of a penny.'

Father Joseph claimed that he had seen Padre Pio's wounds on many occasions. Father Alessio also helped Padre Pio dress his wounds. 'He usually looked after his wounds by himself and he used to change the bandages himself every other day. He would

San Giovanni. The church

usually say to me that he wanted to be alone for a little while in his cell, whilst he changed the bandages, and he would call me when he had finished. But on this particular occasion I waited for about fifteen minutes, and he didn't call me. So I became afraid and I ran to his cell door and I called in, "Father, are you all right? Did you finish?" but he didn't answer me for a moment. Then he said, "Come in, my son, help me." I went in and found Padre Pio half on the bed and half on the floor. He had no gloves on his hands and the blood was pouring from the wounds. I was scared so I lifted him up on to the bed and tried to dry the blood with some of the bandages. Then I put on his gloves, but every time I touched his hands he would draw them away from me because of the pain.'

Father Alessio guessed what had probably happened to Padre Pio as he began to tend his own wounds. 'The blood would come out of the wounds and form a crust. This crust would break into pieces and those pieces would raise up and give Padre Pio a lot of pain as he tried to remove them. The agony of doing this must have been so intense that he fainted. And that's the only time I saw the wounds.'

Which of the wounds gave Padre Pio the most pain? 'His feet, except when people squeezed his hands, trying to kiss them. In these cases he always pulled his hands away.' The wounds disappeared shortly before Padre Pio died; how did that happen? 'It's something that I can't explain, but to see his hands when he died – there was not even a scar. They were rosy and smooth like a baby's. You know how a baby's hands are rosy and beautiful and smooth; well, Padre Pio's hands were just like that when he died. Now I saw those wounds right through his hands – yet somehow they had disappeared.'

What was the purpose of Padre Pio's stigmata? 'The purpose,' according to Father Alessio, 'was that after the First World War the world was in a mess, and I think that God had to give a light so that everyone would believe more in the mercy of God and also to bring people back to their Faith.' But why did Padre Pio have to suffer all that agony? 'Well, didn't God send his own Son to be crucified?' replied Father Alessio. 'It's for the same reason. He could have chosen another way for Redemption. God sees the perfect soul as a victim – we've got to accept that. God never spares people who offer themselves for suffering. It's a mystery why God wants suffering to save souls, or to increase people's faith in him. I can't explain it.'

As though the stigmata were not enough, there are many other startling aspects to Padre Pio's life which equally defy explanation. For example, there are hundreds of stories about his power of bilocation. This means that in some supernatural way Padre Pio was able to be in two places at the same time. It has often been claimed that while he was at the Friary at San Giovanni (in fact he hardly ever left the precincts except to vote, to visit the sick and say Mass down in the town), he appeared to people in far-off places to offer them spiritual assistance. Many have sworn that in their hour of need, Padre Pio had been visually with them and helped them through some particularly trying situation. Padre Alessio assured me that on many occasions he was certain tht Padre Pio 'journeyed' through the night to distant places in a quest to save souls. During his lifetime there are many accounts of blind people who were able to see again through the intercession of Padre Pio; of diseased people almost on the brink of despair, but who gained new hope and health through the Capuchin friar, including some who had never met the man, yet were convinced that he had intervened on their behalf. I met Geraldine from Ireland who originally had come most reluctantly to San Giovanni, where she found peace and tranquillity and the way out of a nervous breakdown and acute agoraphobia. On the main street one day I fell into conversation with a woman, a Dutch lady, whose first son had died of a congenital heart condition. Her second son was also threatened with the same fate, at which point the lady came to San Giovanni to pray to Padre Pio. That second son is now studying to be a Capuchin friar. As she told me her story there was sheer joy and happiness on her face. That woman now lives permanently in San Giovanni. I also met a woman from New York who used to come to the village when Padre Pio was still alive. She told me what it was like to see Padre Pio saying his Mass. 'He was elevated, as though in ecstasy – like he was not present and as though he was very close to someone else. His eyes were so fixed to the host in a saintly sort of way.' I met a girl called Maria who helps to run the family hotel, very close to the friary. She remembers with great fondness the old monk because she was baptised by him over twenty years ago. Maria's father had told her, as she grew up, about the many instances of the healing powers of Padre Pio. She also mentioned that often those who believed themselves to be possessed by evil spirits came to San Giovanni to be exorcised. Maria also told me of a doctor who once came to stay at the hotel and who was suffering from terminal cancer. As a last resort he had come to see what would happen if he came to San Giovanni. That doctor returned to the hotel many months later, a cured man.

According to Father Joseph, Padre Pio also possessed another gift. 'Padre Pio had what is known as the gift of perfumes. I would say that he had at least a half a dozen kinds. It's not technically the "odour of sanctity" but these smells were supernatural perfumes, which Padre Pio still uses after his death. It's a sort of calling card. For example, he'll send a pleasant flower perfume to announce the arrival of a grace; or to remind someone to pray for someone else he'll send the smell of incense. Whilst you were with Padre Pio you never experienced these odours because the perfume did not come from him; it's a supernatural quality which, if I understand it correctly, is the enlightenment of the mind carried by an angel. In point of fact you could hold your fingers to your nose and pinch the nostrils, and still experience the perfume. That perfume could be a flower, incense or an acid smell which means mortification.'

As well as the stigmata, Padre Pio also had another source of suffering, which was both mental and physical: the devil called upon him many times during his lifetime and tormented him with spiritual doubts and physical violence. Father Alessio often found the old friar in a state of deep distress with a bloodied face, black eyes and lying helpless on the floor of his cell. This was at a time when the old and tired man could hardly move or do anything for himself, not even rise from his own bed unaided. 'During his lifetime there were many occasions when the evil spirits actually took physical forms in front of him. They actually beat him so badly that in July 1974 a doctor had to come in at ten o'clock at night to put two stitches in his brow. His eyes were black and he was beaten badly on the upper part of his body. Padre Pio could not even celebrate Mass the next day. He said to me that it was the devil who had done this to him.'

In his many letters to his spiritual directors throughout the years, this theme of the devil and his torments is not an uncommon one. Here is part of a letter written in July 1912:

I had a very bad time the night before last; from about ten o'clock, when I went to bed, until five o'clock in the morning, that *wretch* did nothing but beat me continually. He presented to my mind many diabolical suggestions, thoughts of despair, distrust in God. But praise be to Jesus, for I defended myself by saying to him repeatedly: your wounds are my merit. I really thought that that was the last night of my life, or that if I did not die I should lose my reason. But may Jesus be blessed, for nothing of the sort occurred.

The letter goes on to describe that when the devil had left him, Padre Pio became cold and trembled from head to toe. This coldness lasted for two hours. Padre Pio also spat blood at the end of this ordeal.

One way of getting as close as possible to Padre Pio after his death is to examine the things which he held dear all his life. In his cell, in the friary, his simple effects have been frozen in time within the tiny space where he spent the greater part of his life. The bed, the chair and the wash-stand have all been covered in a thick see-through plastic which both helps preserve the artefacts and also prevents 'holy stealing', as Father Joseph described the pilfering in the early days after Padre Pio's death. This tiny cell is a shrine within a shrine, and the entrance has been sealed off with a glass door and partition, through which the pilgrim can look and see into Padre Pio's cell. In the middle of the floor there is a glass case which holds the sandals Padre Pio wore. They are enlarged slightly to accommodate his swollen feet. Up against the window there is now an illuminated wooden cross, so that people down below in the courtyard can still see the spot from where Padre Pio would look out and bless the many pilgrims who came to catch a glimpse of him. There are bandages which were used to bind the wounds, all faintly stained with the remains of washed-out blood. It is a simple cell with a few rather pathetic personal belongings: a pocket watch once received as a gift, a comb and a hairbrush.

Father Joseph described the character of Padre Pio. 'I came into the picture during the last four years of his life and by that time he was quite withdrawn, having prophesied his own death several times – once nine years before – to the exact day. He was preparing for death and his wit was drying up. On top of all that he was suffering terribly with his wounds. There was also a great deal of moral and spiritual suffering, and his age began to tell on him. So the man I knew wasn't the funny man that the other friars had known most of his life here in the friary. However, that's not to say that there were no moments of joy and laughter. Padre Pio had a wonderful sense of humour, a delicious wit in his younger days and he even liked a good practical joke at times. He was always kidding and joking with the Friars. For example, when the crowds would press all around him he would turn to his companions and say, "Why are they all here?" and then a friar would say something like, "Oh! didn't you know that they have all come to see me!" and Padre Pio would smile with a twinkle in his eye. Certainly what St Teresa of Avila said about "long-faced saints" was in no way true about Padre Pio. He was a beautiful, simple and very humble human being.'

There is also another story connected with Padre Pio which concerned Pope John Paul II. It was said that Padre Pio had foretold to the then Father Wojtyla that one day he would be the Pope. I asked Father Joseph about this and he was able to tell me exactly when and how this extraordinary meeting took place. According to Father Joseph, back in 1947 Father Wojtyla was sent to Rome as a young priest to study for a degree in philosophy. At one time he made the journey to San Giovanni with a professor from Rome University. During a private chat Padre Pio drew the young priest aside and they had a lengthy conversation. Afterwards Father Wojtyla reported to the professor and other companions that Padre Pio had told him that one day he would be Pope. Father Wojtyla commented that this could not possibly happen because he was Polish and not Italian.

From 1916 until his death in 1968 Padre Pio remained at San Giovanni, living the life of a Capuchin friar. During half a century

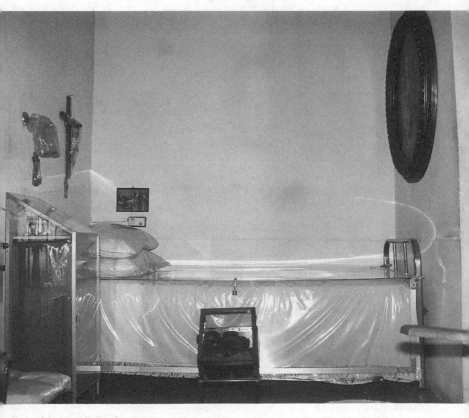

San Giovanni. Padre Pio's room

he never took a holiday and, notwithstanding his terrible suffering through his stigmata, his daily routine was very rigorous; he would spend most of his day in prayer. He rose at 2.30 am and he prayed until his Mass at 5.00. He would celebrate another Mass during the day and then pray in front of the Blessed Sacrament for seven hours each evening until midnight. As to his eating habits, the doctor who attended Padre Pio told Father Joseph that a one-year-old child could not exist on what he ate. He slept only two hours each night and he bled from his wounds every day for over fifty years. However, this routine was more and more interrupted as Padre Pio's fame spread. This fame, which mystified and exasperated him, had its penalties. The faithful demanded more and more of his time and much of Padre Pio's day had to be given over to hearing endless confessions. Pilgrims came in their tens of thousands to be heard by this man who had a gift of insight, and who could read people's souls like open books. His advice was always sound and to the point. In the early days he would spend up to twelve hours in the confessional, as pilgrims unburdened their sins upon him. Perhaps it was this long experience in the confessional which gave Padre Pio his loathing of sin and, indeed, his great fear of it. His life's work, as he saw it, was to win souls back to God and to save them from eternal damnation. To illustrate just how important he considered this work in the confessional, here is part of a letter he wrote to Padre Benedetto in 1919:

> I haven't a free moment. All my time is spent in setting my brothers free from the snares of Satan. May God be blessed. Please don't afflict me further, like the others, by appealing to charity, because the greatest charity is that of snatching souls from Satan so as to win them for Christ. This is precisely what I am doing constantly by night and by day. Innumerable people of all classes and of both sexes come here for the sole purpose of making their confessions and I am only sought for this purpose. There are some wonderful conversions.

There is no doubt that such was Padre Pio's gift for returning souls to God that he rejoiced in doing this work, even though the strain was considerable. Those with particular difficulties went to great lengths to get to San Giovanni, and they never went away disappointed. However, this arrangement was a double-edged sword; so quickly was the fame of Padre Pio spreading that, in 1921, the Church authorities tried to move him away from San Giovanni but, two years later when the decision was confirmed that Padre Pio should go to another friary in the March Province, there was an outcry by the faithful and the plan had to be abandoned. Ten years later Padre Pio was actually confined to his cell for a period of two years by the Vatican. He was not allowed to say Mass in public, nor to hear confessions, nor even to appear in public. Naturally this affected the friar deeply, and once, in floods of tears, he stated to his Superior that it was not for himself that he grieved but 'for all those souls I cannot help'. Years later, in 1960, Padre Pio was investigated by Rome and again attempts were made to remove him from San Giovanni. This idea was once more defeated and Padre Pio remained to cope with the ever-increasing numbers of pilgrims who constantly sought him out.

One reason for which he came under Vatican scrutiny involved the hospital at San Giovanni. If you stand on the piazza with your back to the door of the friary church, a hundred yards over to the left is an immense building which dwarfs everything around it, including the church and the friary. It is the hospital of the Casa Sollievo della Sofferenza (House for the Relief of Suffering). In 1944 Padre Pio expressed a wish for a hospital to be built near to the friary. Such was his fame throughout the world by this time that the money flowed in from many countries. The United Nations granted a big sum through a post-war rebuilding scheme and, in 1956, the great hospital was inaugurated. Starting with a few beds, the Casa Sollievo della Sofferenza now has 1,000 beds, and is recognised to have the best medical equipment in the whole of southern Italy. All treatment is free of charge and of the highest standard. The running of the hospital has now been taken over by the Vatican, which owns the building and is responsible for its day to day management. Because such huge amounts of money were involved at the time of building the hospital, critics were not hard to find who found fault with the 'rich monk' who was supposed to have taken a vow of poverty. There were mutterings about large contracts going to unqualified people, and that the wrong builders were hired. However, Padre Pio came out of the investigation unscathed. Enough money was also collected to build a new and larger church (1959) for the increasing crowds (where changes are still being made to accommodate more and more pilgrims), and also to build a massive Way of the Cross which starts between the hospital and the church and climbs farther up the mountainside.

In the closing years of his life Padre Pio grew old and slow. According to Father Joseph his wit was drying up and he was preparing for death. The day before he died his lavish marble tomb was completed in the crypt under the church. After a normal day of early rising and saying Mass, Francesco Forgione, known during most of his life to millions simply as Padre Pio, died peacefully at 2.30 am on 23 September 1968. On the night of the 26th his venerated body was interred in the marble tomb and 10,000 pilgrims mourned his passing. He actually died of an old man's bronchial complaint, having also suffered from asthma towards the end of his life. There was no need to tend the wounds on his hands, feet and sides; they had all disappeared.

SAN GIOVANNI

THE REGION OF APULIA

Apulia (Puglia) is often called the 'heel' of Italy and is one of Italy's largest regions, and the first to be colonised and civilised by the Greeks. Dominated by a rocky landscape, it is almost completely flat with coastlines on the Adriatic and the Ionian Seas. This contributes to its mild climate and long summers. Its warm weather, from February to October, makes it an attractive area for tourists.

The Gargano, the spur on the 'heel', is a magnificent peninsula on the edge of the Umbra forest. There are 11,000 hectares of woodland which cover the heights of the Gargano, as well as a coastline of beaches and rocky coves. Also of great interest and unique to Apulia is the *trulli* area with its bright, white cone-shaped houses and dark roofs. Apulia has an outstanding number of historical, artistic and religious relics, and whilst some of these can be seen in the numerous art galleries and museums, there are plenty of others in Romanesque cathedrals, castles and rock settlements.

Some of the finest Italian cooking can be sampled in this region. It is famous for its cheese, pasta, rice and veal, and it claims to provide over fifty varieties of fish. The main dishes are *coniglio al capperi* (rabbit cooked with capers), *zuppa di Cozze* (mussel soup with white wine and tomatoes) and *ostriche* (fresh oysters baked with breadcrumbs). The region's excellent wines include San Severo, Castel del Monte and Locorotondo.

SAN GIOVANNI

The little village of San Giovanni Rotondo has a population of 21,000 and lies in a fertile valley at the centre of the Gargano. It has become famous in recent years because of Padre Pio, and every year people from all over the world flock to San Giovanni to enjoy the peace and spiritual refreshment there. The focal point of the religious activity is the church of Santa Maria delle Grazie, which adjoins the Capuchin convent where Padre Pio worked as a priest. The Casa Sollievo della Sofferenza, the House for the Relief of Suffering, is a large and well-equipped hospital very close to the church and friary. It was built at the instigation of Padre Pio whose reputation ensured that funds from all over the world were available.

Under the church at San Giovanni is the crypt which contains the remains of Padre Pio. They lie in a marble tomb surrounded by a wrought-iron enclosure decorated with fresh flowers, and the area is always busy with visitors and pilgrims praying at the tomb. In addition to the crypt, the visitor can visit Padre Pio's cell which is now preserved like a museum and remains exactly as it was when he died. His personal effects are in the same positions as he left them, including his hairbrush which still lies beside the washbasin, near the window where pilgrims often waved to him. In one of the side chapels there is the confessional where Padre Pio spent many hours listening to the pilgrims who wanted him to help them.

Tourist accommodation in San Giovanni is very reasonably priced and in most cases caters specifically for pilgrims. The surrounding scenery is harsh and rocky, but is not without its attractions when one drives on the good roads around San Giovanni and Foggia.

OTHER PLACES OF INTEREST IN THE APULIA REGION

LECCE

Lecce is not only the chief town of Salento but also its spiritual, cultural and economic centre. It is 11 km from the Adriatic coast and twenty-three from the Ionian coast.

The origins of Lecce are very mysterious. Legend has it that it was founded by Malennius, the son of Dasumnus and the first king of the Salentines, in the year 1211 BC. It is said to have been occupied by Lictius Idomeneus after the destruction of Troy, and the word Lecce is said to be derived from Lictius, who also introduced Greek culture.

Lecce fell into a decline with the end of the Roman Empire and beginning of the Middle Ages, but in the late Middle Ages the town began to flourish again under the Counts of Enghien.

The city then housed important institutions such as the Consistorium Principis which ruled over the whole region of Apulia and part of Lucania. The bi-weekly market which still flourishes today traces its origins to those times.

The city gives the impression of being very old, even though it has undergone many changes since ancient times. Its style is predominantly Baroque and it has many works of architecture which are unique to Lecce. It is due to this wealth of architecture that Lecce has gained for itself the title 'The Florence of the Baroque'.

It consists mainly of buildings constructed between the end of the sixteenth century, when the Renaissance style was about to give way to the Baroque, and the early eighteenth century. During this time, thanks to the patronage of the Church, Lecce was given its most magnificent ecclesiastical buildings. Of particular interest in Lecce are the complexes of the Piazza del Duomo with the seminary, the bishop's palace, the cathedral and the bell tower. The most important monument of the period is the Basilica of the Holy Cross. The central Piazza Sant' Oronzo is dominated by a Roman column bearing a statue of St Orontius, tutelary saint of the city. It is now largely occupied by the excavated Roman amphitheatre which was discovered beneath it. On the Piazza's western side is the former town hall and the chapel of San Marco with its lion over the doorway. Opposite is the Baroque church of Santa Maria delle Grazie, behind which lies the sixteenth-century Castello.

Lecce is well worth a visit. Its architecture has been described as 'a kind of embroidery which decorates the whole city with the lightness of lace'.

BRINDISI

Brindisi is a modern provincial capital which has the safest harbour on the Adriatic and is consequently important as a trading port with the East. It is built between the two arms of a land-locked bay. Brundisium was the chief port of the Romans and the place where their armies embarked. It was the final point in the tour of the poet Horace and his patron Maecenas, described in one of Horace's poems. Here Cicero landed in 57 BC on his return from exile; Octavius first assumed the name of Caesar; Virgil died in 19 BC on his return from Greece; and Agrippa landed bearing the ashes of Germanicus. At this time it had an outer and an inner harbour, the outer one sheltered by the islands of Barra. Brindisi was the chief place of embarkation in the Crusades but fell into disuse when they came to an end. Lately, great efforts have been put into restoring the port.

Brindisi has many connections with the Crusades. Its church of San Giovanni al Sepolcro was built by the Knights Templars in the eleventh century on their return from the Holy Land. They were also responsible for the building

of Santa Lucia with its charming Basilican crypt and the cloisters of the church of San Benedetto. The cathedral in Brindisi is also worth a visit. Consecrated by Urban II in 1089 and rebuilt in the reign of King Roger, it has been ruined several times by earthquakes and little remains except the mosaic pavements.

The ancient church of San Giovanni Battista is circular, built of large stones without mortar, and has a beautiful portal and pillars resting on stone lions. At the same time the tourist can see the fourteenth-century portico of the Knights Templars which is close by.

The castle is a magnificent building and was begun by Alfonso of Aragon and completed by Charles V.

Twentieth-century history is also represented in Brindisi. The Sailors' Monument was built in 1933 as a memorial to those who died in the First World War. Shaped like a rudder, it towers over the city at a height of 52 metres.

Ferries are available every day for trips to Corfu, Ithaki, Igoumenitsa, Paxi and Patras. The international airport, the railway and the high-speed expressway which takes road traffic to the motorway all link Brindisi to the leading cities of Northern Europe.

VIESTE

Vieste is one of the oldest and prettiest fishing ports in the Gargano, with a good beach for tourists. The town itself is on top of a high cliff which gives some wonderful views of the coastline. From here you can visit the great forest in the hills as well as famous pilgrimage shrines such as Monte Sant' Angelo, and of course San Giovanni Rotondo.

Vieste has an important mediaeval cathedral, said to have been built by Frederick II. The cathedral boasts interesting external architecture and contains a wealth of art treasures, including the Holy Trinity with Angels by Giuseppe Tomaiuolo who was born in Vieste, a wooden triptych by the Genoese Michael Manchelli, and a low-relief marble of the dead Christ.

There are a series of sepulchres in natural cavities which are worth seeing. The most interesting tombs are those of Salata and Caprarezza in the neighbourhood of Merinum, those at St Nicola at Panatanello, and at the Spanish Grotto to the south of Vieste.

About twenty caves, some of which are extremely beautiful, can be explored between Vieste and Mattinata. Excursions to these caves are conducted regularly by local experts.

FOGGIA

Foggia is a modern-looking city of 122,800 inhabitants and important for its paper mills. Now the marketing centre of a vast agricultural region, it is also the communication centre for northern Apulia because of its important railway junction. It was founded by the people of the abandoned Italic town of Arpi. The name of Foggia probably comes from the 'foveae' or trenches made to store corn. Lautrec took the town and massacred the inhabitants and it was almost totally destroyed by an earthquake in 1731. Foggia's cathedral was also destroyed by an earthquake, which are common in Italy, and it was largely rebuilt in the last century but retained its ancient crypt and its original western front.

If you leave the cathedral by the west door and turn right, you will find a Norman arch in a wall near the town gate. The arch is supported by eagles and bears. An inscription reads that it was the gate of the palace of Frederick II who often stayed here. It also says that his third wife, Isabella, daughter of Henry III of England, died in child-birth in 1341. Charles of Anjou died at Foggia in 1285.

HOW TO REACH SAN GIOVANNI

Note: The telephone numbers as given here assume the caller is within the same country as the hotel, station, or other number. When ringing from abroad, the 0 at the start of each code must be omitted and the appropriate International Code must be prefixed.

BY RAIL

There is a frequent train service from Rome to Foggia and the journey takes about five and a half hours. At Foggia there is an hourly bus service to San Giovanni which leaves from the station forecourt. The bus journey is one hour.

BY CAR

It is always possible to rent a car through the Italian State Railways, at the same time as buying your rail ticket. San Giovanni is very easy to reach by car because it lies at the centre of the Gargano and the road leads through the Gargano Peninsula and is a good starting point for the Tremiti Islands, the Umbra Forest and Gargano coast. Most people who visit San Giovanni travel from Rome. The most direct route is the A24 motorway (autostrada) to Pescara and the A14 to Foggia. The distance between Rome and Foggia is 375 km and the journey should take about four hours.

ITALIAN STATE RAILWAY OFFICES

Italian State Tourist Office
1 Princes Street
London W1
Tel: 01-408 1254

Wasteels Travel
22 Gillingham Street
London SW1
Tel: 01-834 7066

L.R. Stanton Ltd
23a Princess Street
Albert Square
Manchester
Tel: 061-236 7958

Stanton Travel Agency
Tel: (0606) 552772

Also branches of Thomas Cook and Son.
Italian State Railways have offices in most capital cities of the world, including the U.S.A.

CAR HIRE

Self-drive car hire is always available in most cities and resorts. Many international and Italian firms operate this service with different rates and conditions. Generally, small local firms offer cheaper rates, but cars can only be booked locally. Some firms restrict hire to drivers over 21. Generally speaking you should have a valid driving licence for at least one year before applying for car hire. Hire of motorscooters can be arranged locally in most cities and resorts at approximately £5 per day. Railway stations will send telegrams to the nearest car-hire branch at a fixed rate.

TOURIST INFORMATION OFFICES IN THE APULIA REGION

San Giovanni Rotondo: Piazza Europa 104, Tel: (0882) 856 240
Lecce: Via Oberdan 63, Tel: (0832) 56194
Brindisi: Via Duomo 4, Tel: (0831) 26862
Vieste: Piazza S.M. delle Grazie 9, Tel: (0884) 78755

ACCOMODATION IN SAN GIOVANNI AND THE APULIA REGION

Hotel accommodation is very good and plentiful in the Apulia region. There are also a great many attractive camping sites. The address to use when booking is Italberghi, 104 North Road, Kew Gardens, Surrey, tel: 01-878 2710. The Italian State Tourist Office publishes the official list of all Italian hotels and pensions every year, and can be consulted through your travel agent.

HOTELS

SAN GIOVANNI
Hotel Pace (one-star) (0882) 856234
Hotel Sollievo (one-star) (0882) 856134
Hotel San Gaetano (one-star) (0882) 856244
Hotel Gaggiano (three-star) (0882) 856650
Hotel V7 (three-star) (0882) 856883

LECCE
Patria Touring
Via Umberto 1
Lecce
Tel: (0832) 29431

Delle Palme
Via Di Leuca
Lecce
Tel: (0832) 647171

BRINDISI
Bologna
Via Cavour 41
Brindisi

La Rosetta
Via San Dioniso 2
Brindisi
Tel: (0831) 23423

VIESTE
Hotel Degli Aranci
Vieste
Tel: (0884) 78558

Hotel Gargano
Vieste
Tel: (0884) 78685

BANKING HOURS

Banks are only open in the mornings from 0830 to 1300 hours, and are closed on Saturdays, Sundays and national holidays. Travellers' cheques can be changed at most hotels. Tourists can change foreign money at main railway stations and airports.

FATIMA

The story of Fatima starts in 1916, the year in which most of Europe was engaged in the First World War. In the spring of that year an angel appeared to three children; Lucia dos Santos, aged nine, and her two cousins, Francisco, aged eight, and his sister Jacinta, aged six. Only after Francisco and Jacinta had died was it revealed that this apparition had taken place. The three companions had been looking after the family sheep at a place called Loca do Cabeco, just outside the village, when they saw a luminous cloud gliding towards them from across the valley below. As the cloud approached it formed into the shape of a boy aged about thirteen. Lucia described him as 'very beautiful' and 'more dazzling than a glass of crystalline water penetrated by the rays of the most burning sun'. The angel spoke to the children and said, 'Don't be afraid, I am the Angel of Peace. Come and pray with me.' The astonished children knelt down with the angel as he said the following prayer: 'My God, I believe, I adore, I hope, I love you. I ask pardon for those who do not believe, nor adore, nor hope, nor love you.' Then he told the children that this was the way in which they should pray. He then left them. A few months later he appeared again near a well in Lucia's garden, where all three were playing. This time the angel impressed upon the children the urgency of prayer in reparation for the sins of the world. This idea of reparation for sins is a constant theme which runs through the subsequent messages which the Virgin was to impart to the children. When Lucia commented on this second apparition, later in her life, she explained how she and the other two were made to understand the real value of sacrifice and how sinners could be converted through prayer.

The angel appeared for the third and last time at the Loca,

where they had first seen him. On this occasion he was holding a chalice and a host in his hands. He told the children to follow him in prayer: 'Most Holy Trinity, Father Son and the Holy Spirit, I adore you profoundly, and I offer you the most precious Body, Blood, Soul and Divinity of Jesus Christ, present in all tabernacles of the world, in preparation for the outrages, sacrileges and indifference with which he himself is offended. And, through the infinite merits of his most Sacred Heart, and the Immaculate Heart of Mary, I beg of you the conversion of sinners.' The angel then gave the host to Lucia, and the chalice to Jacinta and Francisco. He then repeated the prayer prostrated on the ground. It seems remarkable that the children did not tell anyone of the angel's appearances as soon as they happened. One can only surmise that the experience made such a profound impression upon them that they felt naturally inclined to keep silent.

The main story of Fatima happened in 1917. From May until October that year, the Virgin appeared to the three children on the 13th of each month (except one) at noon, in the Cova da Iria, which is two kilometres from Loca do Cabeco where the angel first appeared to them. The three children who were involved in this extraordinary drama were of simple and straightforward peasant stock who had little education, and spent much of their time on the land helping their parents. Lucia was the eldest of the three and she was born in March 1907. Her parents were Antonio dos Santos and Maria-Rosa. Lucia's cousins, Francisco and Jacinta, were the children of Lucia's father's sister, Olimpia. Francisco was born in June 1908 and Jacinta in March 1910. Neither family was very poor; each had a little land and a few livestock, and they were able to make a hard but adequate living. On 13 May 1917 the three children went to the Cova da Iria, a little way outside the village, to look after the grazing animals. As usual at noon they started to say their rosary. Hardly had they begun when a 'flash of lightning' lit the sky around them, and, looking up into a small tree nearby, they saw a young lady hovering above it. According to the children's description the lady was surrounded by a dazzling white light and she looked to be about fifteen years of age. She wore a long white gown tied at the neck by a long golden cord. Her feet were uncovered and they appeared to be not quite touching the branches of the tree. A long, white veil covered her head and fell down to her waist and she held a rosary in her hands. The two girls were enraptured as she spoke to them. She told them not to be afraid. Francisco, meanwhile, could see nothing, and he was quite upset that he couldn't see what the others were looking at in the tree. The little boy immediately started to say his rosary (which he may not have been doing at the beginning), and then he, too, saw the apparition. The lady then told them that she had come from heaven, and she made them promise that they would come to the Cova on the 13th of the month, at the same time of day, for the following five months. Since the lady said that she came from God and from heaven, Lucia took a chance and asked if she, too, would some day go to heaven; the vision assured her that she would. The lady promised that Jacinta, too, would go to heaven, and that if Francisco would say his rosary more often, then he, too, would go. The lady then warned that each of them would suffer a lot because they had seen her, but that if they offered it up to God they would save many souls from eternal damnation. When the lady disappeared, Lucia cautioned her cousins not to tell anyone of what they had seen for fear of disbelief. However, when they arrived home, the resolve of little Jacinta gave way, and she told her mother of what had happened. Her mother, Olimpia, was slightly disturbed at the news and hurried to see Lucia's mother, where she discovered that Lucia had been telling the same story. Both parents came to the conclusion that the children were fantasising and telling lies. They were admonished not to speak of the incident again.

By the time the next rendezvous with the lady came, the children were excited and very eager to go to the Cova. For a whole month the village had been buzzing with this news, and many of the villagers had taunted and teased the children about the 'lady' and that she couldn't possibly exist. It was the feast of St Anthony, the patron saint of Portugal, and the children set out for the Cova, together with sixty or so curious villagers. When they arrived, the children knelt down at the same spot in the Cova in front of the tree and began to say their rosary. For a while nothing happened and then Lucia cried out, 'See over there, a flash of lightning, she's coming!' Then both Jacinta and Francisco looked up into the tree and saw the lady. This time the apparition spoke of the importance of saying the rosary, and she made the children promise to be at the spot at the same time the next month. Those people who had accompanied the children failed to see the lady, but they did see beautiful colours flickering and waving across the sky and landscape. They also noticed that the air began to grow cool and the sun began to lose its light, so that they could see the stars shining.

Word now spread quickly; some thought that this was an act of divine intervention, while others claimed that it could only be the work of the devil. Olimpia forbade her children to go to the Cova again, and Lucia's mother also had grave misgivings about the whole affair. However, by the time 13 July came around, opinions had changed and the children were allowed to go to the Cova again. On this occasion 6,000 people went with the children to see the lady. Again she appeared but did not reveal her true identity, promising to do so eventually. She also guaranteed a great miracle so that others would believe she was there. It was at this apparition that the three children were taught to say the now famous Fatima prayer, which is said by millions today around the world.

> Jesus, forgive us.
> Save us from the fires of hell.
> Lead all souls to heaven,
> Especially those most in need.

Although the multitude of 6,000 had not seen anything specific, most of them seem to have left feeling that something extraordinary had taken place. News of the Fatima apparitions now began to spread through the whole of Portugal. It was a story which angered the very anti-clerical Government of the day. Ever since 1910 the Government had said that it intended to wipe out Christianity in Portugal, and it viewed the events at Fatima as a countermeasure to these intentions.

The Church, treading a cautious line, chose to ignore Fatima and the clergy were forbidden to have any dealings with it. National newspapers even carried stories which attempted to discredit the children.

On 11 August, just two days before the third apparition was due to take place, a local and powerful sub-prefect of the area heard about the children's claims and he ordered them to come to his office at Ourem, some eight miles away. Artur Oliveira Santos was an unpopular man because of his anti-Christian attitudes, and his

Fatima. Aerial view of the basilica and the crowd of pilgrims celebrating the fiftieth anniversary of the apparitions

aim now was to extract a confession from the children to say that they had been telling lies. He was also anxious to extract the 'secret' which everyone was talking about, and which the lady had told to the children at the second meeting. He picked on Lucia as the one most likely to break under questioning, and during an interview with her he shouted and screamed that he would have the confession. He threatened to kill Lucia and the other two, and he also threatened their parents who went to Ourem with them. He tried to make them all promise that they would not go to the Cova again. The children refused, saying that they had promised to be there, and that they would be there. The children returned home, but Santos hatched a plot to kidnap them so that they would be unable to go to the Cova on the thirteenth. When the day dawned, Santos turned up at Lucia's house and said that he wanted to go to the Cova the next day to see for himself what happened. He arranged to meet the children at the priest's house to make it look as though he was acting in good faith. He offered to take the children to the Cova in his carriage, but instead of going there he turned around and took all three back to Ourem. After another terrifying interview, all three were thrown into jail with criminals. The children simply hung a medal of the Virgin on the cell wall and said their rosary. It is amazing to think that at this point the children had not, in any way, given in, having been through such an ordeal and separated from their parents. Cruellest of all was that Santos had threatened to have them all boiled in oil – which they believed. At such perseverance even Santos was amazed, and he had the youngsters examined by a doctor to see if they were mentally sound. The doctor declared that they were perfectly well, apart from the state of shock which his treatment of them had induced. Eventually Santos had to admit defeat, although he had ensured that the children had not been able to be at the Cova on the thirteeth. Even though the children had not been there, 18,000 other people had. Some said that they saw a cloud which settled over the tree and, staying a few moments, disappeared again. Six days later the Virgin did appear to the three 'seers' as they now became known. This time the spot was Valhinos, near the Loca do Cabeco. It was at this apparition that the children were told that the already-promised miracle would not be as great as first planned, but that something would happen on 13 October. By the time the next apparition was due, on 13 September, a staggering 30,000 people were present at the Cova. Led by Lucia, they all began to recite the rosary as on all previous occasions. At noon a globe of light appeared from the east and seemed to settle above the oak tree. It was raining heavily on 13 October 1917 and the crowd had now swelled to between 70 and 100 thousand; people from all over Portugal and Europe were anxious to see what the 'miracle' was going to be. What actually happened has been documented many times over, in both religious and secular records. The crowd saw the sun behaving in a very peculiar way.

When I was in Fatima on 13 May, I met an elderly lady who had been part of that great throng in 1917. This lady was a retired nurse, and when I spoke to her she was tending those who had fallen ill or fainted on that hot day. Most of her work, as with all the medical staff on duty at Fatima, was binding the swollen and bloody feet of the pilgrims who had walked long distances to be at the shrine. I sat down with the old nurse, and with the help of an interpreter she told me what she had seen.

'It poured down with rain for hours and hours, like I'd never seen it rain before, and none of the people had any protection and they were completely soaked. Suddenly all the umbrellas were being folded, and then the rain had stopped and the sun began to shine. The clouds opened in a circle around the sun; it was a big blue circle, and there was no way that those clouds were going to hide that sun. The funny thing was that although the sun was very bright we could look right into it without being blinded. But at the same time we could see it spinning. I can't think of anything to compare it with; it wasn't like silver; it wasn't like the moon; it wasn't like anything else and it was coming away from the sky – spinning and coming down. People began to cry and scream and they started praying because we were all afraid that it was going to fall on us. But I wasn't afraid like that – I was cheerful and happy because it was a miracle. Instinctively, I climbed on to my seat in the carriage and I stood on it with both feet. I was happy. I turned to my cousin and said, "Didn't I tell you it was going to happen? This is a miracle." I also saw all the colours and it looked like a rainbow, and the colours kept repeating over and over again.'

It is also interesting to note that not everyone saw what happened on that day; some saw everything, others saw a part of the phenomenon, whereas others saw nothing at all.

Ever since the events of 1917 at Fatima, crowds have been coming to this shrine. About twenty years ago hotels and hostels began to spring up in the village to cater for the increasing numbers of visitors and pilgrims. For many years now, the Portuguese pilgrims turn up and camp out for the night around the great square. As evening approaches on the twelfth, out come the plastic sheets and the blankets, and rows and rows of people – thousands and thousands of them – sleep in their makeshift tents and gather around little fires to pass the night away and to keep vigil until the celebrations on the following day. All evening the square is illuminated with endless torchlight processions, wending their way around the concourse, singing and saying the rosary. This continues most of the night and the whole atmosphere becomes lively and exciting.

Before dawn broke on the day that I was there the square was filled to capacity with over 350,000 people. As the morning progressed, High Mass was celebrated on an open-air altar on the steps of the basilica, overlooking the people. One of the traditional penances at Fatima is to walk down the centre of the square on your knees. Many people were doing this, in great pain, especially those who spurned the wearing of knee-pads. There was a lot of blood on that hard concrete. I saw one woman in excruciating pain, largely because she was carrying a child of about eight in her arms. That woman had travelled on her bare knees at least 500 yards. The child seemed to be mentally handicapped, and obviously the woman was hoping for a cure.

As the ceremonies come to an end, the vast crowd wave white handkerchiefs as the statue of Our Lady of Fatima is carried around the square. When the 'Adeus' has been sung, the Virgin disappears into the little Chapel of the Apparitions, and slowly the square empties. It is all over in the space of twenty-four hours. At one moment you are looking at the largest crowd of people possible, and the next moment it seems as though nothing had ever happened.

In the basilica are the graves of Francisco and Jacinta who died shortly after the Virgin appeared to them; both had been assured that they would join the Virgin in heaven very soon. In 1918 Francisco caught Spanish influenza, an epidemic at the time; after five months of great pain and suffering he died on 4 April, aged eleven. His sister Jacinta also caught the same infection and she died in a Lisbon hospital on 20 February 1920; she was not quite ten years old. At the time of writing Lucia is still alive and lives in an enclosed convent in Coimbra, a town further north up the coast from Fatima. Lucia is now in her eighties. It was not long after Lucia had seen the visions that she expressed her wish to become a nun. At the age of fifteen she joined the Dorothian Order and took the name Sister Mary Lucia of the Sorrows. In 1946, wanting to follow a more contemplative way of life, she joined the Carmelites at Coimbra. At the ceremony of the Golden Jubilee of the apparitions Pope Paul VI was at Fatima, together with Lucia. Pope Paul came to Fatima as a pilgrim to a shrine. 'I have come,' he said, 'like any other humble pilgrim, for peace in the world, and for communist countries and unfree populations.'

The secret which was disclosed to the children by the Virgin has always been a subject of great controversy. According to Lucia it was revealed to the children in three parts, one of which was confided to them on 13 June, and the other two parts during the third apparition the following month. The first part concerned devotion and reparation to the Immaculate Heart of Mary, which Lucia was permitted, by the Virgin, to reveal in 1927. The second concerned a vision of hell in which the children saw souls burning and crying out in great agony. The third part of the secret has never been revealed. It was written down by Lucia and is now kept in the Vatican Archives. It was read in 1960 by Pope John XXIII and some of his aides, but they declined to make public what they had read.

In direct response to the Virgin's wishes that the world should pray specifically for the conversion of Russia, a movement began in Fatima in 1946, called the Blue Army. It is now a world-wide organisation and its aims are to pray and to make sacrifices for the conversion of Russia. What the Virgin said to the children was of a very personal nature, for it concerned, for the most part, their own spirituality. It is often said that whereas Lourdes is a place of physical healing, Fatima is a place for those who seek spiritual wholeness. That is not to say that spectacular healing miracles have not taken place at Fatima. They have on many occasions, and there are records in Fatima which are available for inspection, as they are at Lourdes. Father Luciano Guerra, Rector of the Sanctuary, was born and bred at Fatima. 'Fatima does not belong to the deposit of faith,' he told me, 'it is not absolutely necessary to believe in it. But if you have the authority of the Church for it – especially if you know what happened – and you have no reason to disbelieve it, then in that way you are almost naturally obliged to believe in it. And that's the case with me. I know not only from the authority of the Church, but also from the people. My kind mother herself was in Fatima on 13 October, in 1917, and she saw the sun spinning – and also my father used to tell me about the stories. I knew the parents of Francisco and Jacinta, so you see the story is very strong in me, and I believe it.'

FATIMA

The Sanctuary at Fatima has become one of the most celebrated places of pilgrimage in Europe since the apparitions of Fatima occurred during the First World War. The first appearance of the Virgin was on Sunday 13 May 1917, and since then, on the thirteenth of each month from May to October an enormous crowd, sometimes numbering over 300,000, has gathered to commemorate the apparitions and their consequences. Camps are set up by pilgrims around the Sanctuary and they prepare to pray in the morning in front of the altar which is in the open on the huge esplanade in front of the church.

Each evening there is a torchlight procession and Masses are celebrated throughout the whole of the thirteenth; at the end of the ceremony, the host is elevated before the sick and the disabled.

The fiftieth anniversary of the apparitions of the Virgin was celebrated here in 1967 in the presence of Pope Paul VI.

At the end of the esplanade is a chapel which marks the spot where the apparitions took place, and candles are always kept alight there. In the basilica itself are the tombs of two of the three shepherd children who saw the apparitions, Francisco and Jacinta. The tower of the basilica is 200 feet high and has a carillon of 43 bells.

The Chapel of Perpetual Adoration is worth visiting and is situated behind the Chapel of the Apparitions. The visitor can also see Aljustrel, the home of Francisco and Jacinta. The third shepherd child's house (Lucia's) is also there, with its well where the angel appeared for the second time. Lucia is now a Carmelite nun living in Coimbra.

Because of Fatima's importance, both as a tourist centre and as a place of pilgrimage, large numbers of hotels, inns and shops have sprung up to cater for the visitors.

HOW TO REACH FATIMA FROM LISBON

There are two possible routes from Lisbon to Fatima, the shorter is 147 km and the longer is 158 km.
The longer route. This route runs from *Lisbon* through *Alenquer* with its beautiful castle and numerous churches, and from there to *Obidos* with its famous Usseira aqueduct; the castle, the city walls and the whole of the architecture of the village are well worth stopping to see. From *Obidos* the route travels through *Caldas da Rainha* to *Alcobaca*. It is worth stopping to visit the Alcobaca monastery which dates back to the twelfth century. From *Alcobaca* the traveller passes through *Batalha* with its museum dedicated to the unknown soldier, to *Fatima*.
The shorter route. This route also goes through *Alenquer* but branches off at *Salvador* and passes through *Rio Maior* and *Venda das Raparigas* (instead of Obidos), and rejoins the longer route at *Alcobaca*. As with the longer route, the traveller reaches *Fatima* directly from Alcobaca.

THE RELIGIOUS LIFE OF FATIMA

From 1 May to 31 October there are at least eight Masses a day between 0730 and 1830 hours. Every day except Sundays there is a Rosary and Candle Procession at 2130 hours. On Tuesdays, in the colonnades, the Stations of the Cross are walked, and on Fridays this takes place at Valinhos, west of Aljustrel where the Virgin appeared on 19 August 1917. Confessions are heard daily in the basilica from 0700 to 1930 hours.

PILGRIMAGES OF THE 12th AND 13th – TIMETABLE

12th: 2100 hours – Eucharistic Vigil.
13th: 1030 hours – Rosary and Procession from the Chapel of the Apparitions.

1100 hours – Mass. Blessing of the sick and farewell ceremony.

LISBON

The Roman town of Lisbon – known as Felicitas Julia – was built on one of the hills above the right bank of the Tagus where the Castelo de S Jorge is now situated. It was an unimportant town and in 711 fell into Moslem hands and was called Lashbuna, still only a small regional capital remote from the main traffic routes of the Moslem empire.

Lisbon's period of prosperity began when King Alfonso Henriques captured the town with the help of British and Flemish crusaders in 1147. It then expanded beyond its walls to the west and north and acquired a number of great buildings. The first of these was the cathedral, erected on one of the city's other hills. In 1148 Lisbon beat off a large Moslem expedition and thereafter attracted a further influx of settlers.

In 1256 Lisbon became the capital of the kingdom. Whilst the town has suffered several earthquakes throughout history it has, nevertheless, continued to be extended.

It was not until the early sixteenth century that the city reached its largest extent, not surpassed until very recent developments. Lisbon became one of the greatest markets of the world, a crowded cosmopolitan city of luxury and splendour. The union with Spain (1580–1640) brought few changes and in the absence of a court the great mansions of the nobility became the centres of literary and artistic activity.

During three very bad earthquakes in the sixteenth century Lisbon was almost completely destroyed. It is thought that 20,000 people died in this disaster, and it left the town in a mere heap of ruins. An almost entirely new city had to be built, and this was achieved by the Marquis de Pombal.

During the nineteenth century the city grew little. It suffered during the invasion of Napoleon's armies, and it also suffered from the loss of Brazil and the civil wars occasioned by dynastic disputes.

Today Lisbon has begun to grow again. Whole new districts have grown up in the last thirty years and older residential areas have gradually been swallowed up in the Greater Lisbon of the present day. Lisbon now extends a long way along the banks of the Tagus (Tejo) estuary and the Sea of Straw (Mar de Palha), a small island in the sea. It has a population of over 1.5 million. The town, rebuilt by the Marquis de Pombal and called the Baixa, follows a rigid grid plan. It lies behind the Praca do Comercio on the sea front and follows the line of a narrow valley with well-defined sides, and is dominated by the Castelo de S Jorge.

Pombal's town is now a large, modern, vital city, especially around the Praca D Pedro IV or Rossio, the real centre of the town from which two avenues, the Avenida da Liberdade and the Avenida Almirante Reis, lead to the residential districts in the northern parts of the town. The older parts of the town are centred around this point, with their ancient palaces, winding lanes and small gardens.

The Judiarian (the old Jewish quarter) is an interesting part of the old town. It is situated on the southern slopes of the castle hill. There is also the old Moslem quarter which is worth visiting, the Mouraria. The new districts, particularly spacious around the magnificent Parque Eduardo VII, are situated around the centre of Lisbon on the basalt plateau.

One of Lisbon's greatest problems has been that of communication. This is because Lisbon is spread over such a large area on a very chaotic plan. This, coupled with the complex geographical and topographical structure of the area, has proved a headache to numerous planners.

LISBON CATHEDRAL
(12th century)

Founded by King Alfonso Henriques in 1147 on the site of an earlier mosque, this is the oldest church in Lisbon. It was partially destroyed in the 1755 earthquake, when its Romanesque lantern tower and Gothic choir collapsed. The façade, however, with its massive crenellated towers, survived.

The central aisle, the triforium and the lateral aisles belong to the original Romanesque structure. The Gothic rose window has been restored. Within the church is the chapel of Bartolomeu Jones, with a recumbent figure of the founder and a nativity group by Machado de Castro.

In the seventeenth-century sacristy is a small museum of sacred art. The cloister is Romanesque and one chapel has a very beautiful Romanesque wrought-iron grille. The treasury is also interesting but can be visited only with special permission.

BELÉM

Belém is the contracted form of Bethlehem and was formerly a separate suburb of the capital. One of the most interesting features of Belém is its Hieronymite monastery (Mosteiro dos Jeronimos) founded by King Manuel I (1495–1521). It comprises the church of Santa Maria, the cloisters and various associated buildings. It seems to have been built over three different periods and so the monastery is a compound of different styles and cannot properly be given the unqualified label of 'Manueline'. Only the work of the first architect, Boitac, is strictly entitled to be so described. The rest shows Renaissance influence and perhaps some Plateresque features.

The interior is astonishingly light. Soaring columns over 200 metres high separate three aisles and support a vaulted roof with ribs in the form of arabesques. The cloister, one of the most famous in the world, is a quadrilateral with sides 55 metres long and consisting of two superimposed galleries. The Belém cloister has been described as more of a palace than a place of prayer. It has lawns and flower beds which add to its charm.

COIMBRA

The Roman city was called Conimbriga, from which Coimbra is derived. It was occupied by the Moors at the beginning of the eighth century but was recaptured in 1064, and became the capital of Portugal under the kings of the first dynasty. The university was founded in 1290 and until 1911 was the only university in Portugal.

Today Coimbra stands above the Rio Monego, with its centre on the north bank. Its population is only 80,000, but its buildings are so fascinating that it is worth stopping to explore. Coimbra is so impressive because during the Romanesque and Renaissance periods it was the centre of a flourishing school of architecture and sculpture. Coimbra is also Portugal's university town. Recently there has been some industrial development, particularly in textiles and foodstuffs.

THE UNIVERSITY

The university was founded in 1290 and was transferred several times to Lisbon and back to Coimbra, but was eventually transferred permanently to Coimbra by King John III who donated his palace so the university could be installed there. The most important monumental centre of the town is the buildings of the old part of the university, where the central offices and Faculty of Law are installed. Of special importance for the tourist are Saint Michael's Chapel, the Old Library, the Tower and the Via Latina.

THE OLD CATHEDRAL (Sé Velha)

This is the most important Portuguese Romanesque building. The first stone was laid in 1162 and it was designed by the famous French 'Maître' Robert. Not only is it most impressive from outside but it also contains exceptional works of art on the inside, such as Gothic tombs from the thirteenth and fourteenth centuries.

The west doorway is magnificently decorated with a window and a balcony above the porch. The doorway or Porta Especiosa was built around 1530 by Norman builders and is also splendidly decorated.

The cathedral has an austere façade with crenellations, buttresses and slit windows which give it the aspect of a fortress. A particularly interesting feature is that the cathedral has three aisles, each of the five bays having different kinds of roofs. In the centre aisle there is barrel vaulting and in the side aisles groined vaulting.

Other places of interest in Coimbra are the *Monastery of the Holy Cross*, which contains tombs of Alfonso Henriques and Sancho I, and whose choir loft is one of the most beautiful to be seen in Portuguese churches; and *St Sebastian's Aqueduct*, built at the end of the sixteenth century. Its architect took advantage of the outline of the previous aqueduct, which most probably dated back to Roman times.

RUINS OF CONIMBRIGA

The largest Roman archaeological site found in Portugal, its first known inhabitants were the Conii, a pre-Celtic tribe that lived here until the Roman conquest. It was occupied until 1465 when it was conquered and destroyed by the Swabians.

NAZARÉ

Nazaré is one of the most typical fishing villages in Portugal, and is always overwhelmed in summer by tourists. It can be divided into three parts: *Pederneira*, which is gradually being abandoned by fishermen. It has a sixteenth-century church and an ancient pillory. *The Praia*, an area with no buildings of special importance, but it is interesting to walk along the shore and watch the fishermen in their costumes. It is worth waiting to see the return of the fishing boats in the evening. There is no harbour and the boats have to be drawn up on to the beach. *The Sitio* is on the top of the 110-metre-high cliff and can be reached by car. The seventeenth-century church of Nossa Senhora da Nazaré is situated here, and nearby is an interesting old palace which is now a hospital. At the far end of the cliff is a small chapel at the point where a miracle is supposed to have saved the life of D Fuas Roupinho; the story goes that he was out hunting a stag in misty weather when he was about to ride over the edge of the cliff. Something made his horse stop sharply at the brink and it was heralded as a miracle.

ERICEIRA, MAFRA AND SINTRA

These three places can be visited in one day.
Ericeira, 50 k from Lisbon on the Atlantic coast, 12 km from Mafra and 22 km from Sintra, is a picturesque fishing village famous for its shellfish and also a popular thermal resort. It is an impressive place with sheer cliffs and a little harbour. The coast is indented with excellent sandy beaches, such as Praia do Sul. Its history dates back to

the first quarter of the thirteenth century, which is noticeable in the Moorish lines of the architecture of the houses. The parish church of S Pedro is very interesting with its painted ceilings, as are the chapels of S Antonio (1634) and S Sebastiano (seventeenth-century).

Mafra. From Ericeira, Mafra is 12 km on the N116, passing through the village of Sobreiro which is famous for its pottery. It is a small town of only 4,000 inhabitants and well known for the magnificent and enormous monastery. The town consists of two parts, the old town (*vila velha*) and the newer part (*vila nova*). The monastery was built by King John V to fulfil a vow that he had made that he would do so if his wife bore him a child. He employed a German architect, Friedrich Ludwig, for the work which went on for about thirteen years. It occupies 40,000 square metres and the front is 220 metres long. At its high point there were 300 monks in Mafra. In the centre of the main front is a chapel with a double row of columns and a dome above the transept. The interior is magnificent with its different coloured marbles, black and white in the vestibule and all colours in the rest. It is advisable to leave at least an hour for the visit since there are a large number of rooms to see, such as the pharmacy, the infirmary and the library, with their beautiful paintings and furniture. The library is particularly impressive, containing 38,000 volumes.

In the Vila Velha of Mafra is the parish church of St André from the thirteenth to fifteenth centuries. It is worth having a look; a priest from this church, Pedro Juliano, became Pope John XXI in 1276.

Sintra, 29 km from Lisbon, is situated in a depression in the northern slopes of the Serra de Sintra. The town is divided into a number of distinct districts.

Perhaps the most interesting features of Sintra are its castles. The castle of La Pena, built in the middle of the eighteenth century to satisfy a whim of Prince Ferdinand of Saxe Coburg-Gotha, is extraordinary to look at, with its domes and minarets. G Pillement's description perhaps sums up La Pena best: 'It is a hybrid and eccentric structure, the work of a misguided Romantic, an abortion of make-believe with its Gothic keep, its Arab minarets, its Renaissance domes, its Manueline windows, its Baroque doorway; a building altogether without rhyme or reason'. Perhaps the most interesting portion of the building is the remains of the Hieronymite convent which are built into the structure.

Sintra also has its Moors castle (Castelo dos Mouros), built on a rocky spur in the seventh to eighth centuries, and frequently altered and rebuilt. It was captured from the Moors in 1147 by Alfonso Henriques, the first King of Portugal. In the early fifteenth century John I commissioned various works for the castle which he chose as his summer residence. There are also several fine churches. Worth visiting are Santa Maria (19th century), Sao Pedro (16th century), Sao Martinho (built originally in the twelfth century and completely rebuilt in the eighteenth century).

USEFUL ADDRESSES

Note: The telephone numbers as given here assume the caller is within the same country as the hotel, station, or other number. When ringing from abroad, the 0 at the start of each code must be omitted and the appropriate International Code must be prefixed.

HOTELS IN FATIMA
Hotel Santa Maria (three-star)
Reu de Santo Antonio
Tel: Fatima (049) 97215

Hotel de Fatima (two-star)
Reu Jacinta Marto
Tel: Fatima (049) 97251

Hotel Pax
Tel: Fatima (049) 97412

There are also many pilgrim hostels in Fatima, and a list of these can be obtained from the Information Centre, Sanctuario de Fatima, Fatima, Portugal.

PORTUGUESE TOURIST BOARD
1 New Bond Street
London
Tel: 01-493 3873.

CZESTOCHOWA

Czestochowa is an industrial town in southern Poland which produces steel, textiles and plastics. For most of the year it is an ordinary, rather drab sort of place; but on certain feast days through the summer months, Czestochowa is transformed by a flood of pilgrims which multiplies the resident population many times over. The focal point for these vast crowds is the Pauline Monastery of Jasna Gora, built high on a hill above the town. Together with hundreds of local people I stood on the Avenue of Our Lady (Al. Najswietszej Marii Panny) and watched an endless river of pilgrims arriving at Jasna Gora after a nine-day trek. They had walked from the Polish capital, Warsaw, 300 kilometres away, and now they had reached their destination. As we all clapped and cheered them as they passed, they were singing to the accompaniment of their own instruments, including guitars and flutes, tambourines and maracas. It was a wonderful, happy sound, in spite of the arduous hike of 300 kilometres; there was a carnival atmosphere and everybody was joining in. The pilgrims were pouring along the street in an endless line and, as they swept up a gentle incline beyond the shops and buildings, they arrived on a flat field at the foot of the monastery walls. A white-robed Pauline monk was there to bless them as they passed in front of him. Flying above him were two flags, one the flag of Poland, and the other, white with bold red letters splashed across it which read 'SOLIDARNOSC'. Most of the walkers were young people, including young priests and nuns who were leading the groups. Although pilgrims have been visiting this shrine for six centuries, it was not until 1710 that people began to walk the great distance from the capital; in that year an influenza epidemic ravaged Warsaw and claimed many lives. The people prayed to the Virgin and promised to walk to Czestochowa if the epidemic ceased.

For over 270 years people have walked from Warsaw to the shrine, and the year I was there over 80,000 made the nine-day hike. In recent years the Communists had made things difficult for pilgrims and had tried to frustrate all their efforts to have a pilgrimage. But in the year of Solidarity it was different, because the free trade union, the first in any Eastern-bloc country, came itself as a group and there was no interference or intimidation. The Assumption of Our Lady is certainly a great day at Czestochowa, but the feast on 26 August, eleven days later, is even greater. That is the feast of Our Lady, Mother of God of Jasna Gora, and half a million people regularly gather at the monastery. For the Assumption the figure is around 300,000, and most arrive on the Friday evening and stay until the Sunday morning when they begin to drift away.

I saw very few facilities at or near the monastery for the pilgrims. Apart from a few people who had tents over in one corner of the grounds, the rest had neither tents nor blankets and many not even an overcoat. They all slept out under the stars for two consecutive nights. Those who had walked from Warsaw had also slept out most nights. What little food people had they brought with them, for there was nothing to buy apart from vinegar-soaked gherkins in huge steaming wooden barrels and the odd bread roll from a vendor. The one blessing in all this was that the weather was fine, but I did hear that bad weather in the past had no effect on the numbers. If the field was a mud-bath in the wet, then so be it, they made the best of it. To the left side of the monastery there were a few rather impoverished stalls selling the usual pious trinkets. Most prominent, reigning supreme amongst the cheap and plastic toys and the thin rosary beads, were copies of the famous picture of the Virgin or the Black Madonna of Czestochowa. Every Polish household has one, and there must be as many versions of that picture as there are households. Some of them are decorated and some are plain, others are garish and others tasteful. All bear an unmistakable resemblance to the Virgin and Child in the famous picture at the centre of the shrine. A similar picture hangs in many other churches throughout the world, and it is often known outside Poland as Our Lady of Perpetual Succour. In that picture there is a story which, in a sense, is the story of Poland and of the unswerving loyalty of its people to their Christian faith.

According to legend, the Byzantine picture of Our Lady of

Czestochowa was painted by St Luke the Evangelist. It was hidden away during the persecution of the early Christians, and then brought by St Helena (255–330), the mother of the Emperor Constantine, to Constantinople. In the eighth century, during a massive destruction of all religious art by iconoclasts, the picture was secretly removed from Constantinople to what is now Romania. It managed to survive a Tartar invasion and eventually found its way to Czestochowa in 1382. In the early part of the fifteenth century a cathedral was built to house the picture, but in 1430 the Hussites (followers of the heretic John Hus, 1369–1445) looted the cathedral and stole the picture. The robbers, finding that they were too overburdened, threw the image into a ditch, first slashing it with their swords. The picture was recovered and restored. The two slash marks now to be seen on the canvas were added later by Italian restorers, which accounts for its pre-Renaissance appearance.

One of the greatest moments of glory came to Czestochowa in 1655, when the invading Swedish Army of King Carl X Gustav entered Poland and met with little resistance. Soon the whole of Poland had been occupied, except for the immediate area around Czestochowa. From nearby Kraków the Swedish king decided that he would storm the monastery of Jasna Gora to make his victory more complete. At the time there were a mere 168 soldiers in the monastery, together with some refugees and their families, and 68 monks. The Swedes were 10,000 strong and they had the reputation of being one of the most efficient and fierce armies of the day. The man who led the monks was their Prior, Father Kordecki, who later became a national hero. When the news of the impending Swedish attack first reached the monastery, the Prior set about preparing Jasna Gora in a military-like fashion; he sent for guns and powder and ammunition, in the hope that Poland's most important shrine should not pass into the hands of soldiers who would loot and desecrate it. On a cold night, late in November, the Swedes arrived and demanded that the little garrison surrender to overwhelming odds. The monks replied that they would rather die than give up the sanctuary into the hands of Lutheran Swedes. With that, the Swedes rolled their cannons into place and made ready to commence battle.

Meanwhile, the Prior had gathered everyone in the chapel of the monastery, where they prayed together for victory. Presently,

181

they all went outside and processed around the inside of the monastery walls, with Prior Kordecki holding aloft the sacred host, and the congregation sang a Polish hymn with the ancient words: 'Holy God, strong God, holy and immortal God. Have mercy on us.' Later, the cannon were blessed and the monks and their soldiers prepared to die if necessary. By this time, the Swedes had completely surrounded the monastery and had dug an encircling trench close to the walls. The battle began and the Swedes rained shot and fire on the monastery unceasingly for several days. Many Swedish shots went wide of their mark, and the monastery sustained little damage. This infuriated General Muller, the Swedish commander, who had the trenches dug even nearer to the walls. The general had the cannon redouble their efforts to bring down the monastery. As the battle raged Prior Kordecki was to be seen rushing around the ramparts and encouraging the soldiers and fighting monks to do their utmost. The older monks were instructed to pray in the chapel for a victory. As the days went by, the Swedes decided to employ the latest and biggest cannon that had yet been seen on a battlefield. In the first week of December, six of these monsters were brought up and they roared their destruction out towards the monastery. This time the new guns had the desired effect, and the masonry began to crash down, and fires started in many parts of the monastery and its outbuildings. General Muller again gave the monks a chance to surrender, and when they again refused, the cannon roared once more. One of the worst moments came when the great double doors of the chapel were brought off their hinges and destroyed a whole section of the building. Seeing this, some of the monks pleaded with Fr Kordecki to surrender but he flatly refused. As Christmas day approached, General Muller, at the suggestion of Prior Kordecki, agreed to hold a cease-fire on Christmas morning. Soon after noon, however, on Christmas day 1655, the battle started again. As the day wore on and darkness was beginning to fall, there was a terrific roar, louder than had been heard at any time before, and certainly loud enough to be heard over the noise of the battle. The largest of the Swedish cannon had exploded – the one doing the most damage to the monastery.

Czestochowa

That evening General Muller sent word to the Prior, offering terms. In reply Father Kordecki, who was not without a sense of humour, sent the general a Christmas gift which was a history of the Jasna Gora, reminding the general that the exchange of gifts at Christmas time was a good and Christian thing to do. There is a diary still preserved at Jasna Gora, and the entry of the Prior's gift is made there in his hand. On St Stephen's day, the day after Christmas, the Swedes abandoned the siege of Czestochowa as a hopeless task. The gallant resistance which the monks and their soldiers had shown filled the rest of Poland with courage and renewed purpose. The Swedes were harried on all sides by the people they had previously conquered so easily. Eventually, the once proud Swedish Army was expelled from Poland, broken and defeated. The Polish people looked upon this victory as a miracle, brought about by the Virgin. The Polish king, John Casimir, who returned from exile when the Swedes had left, solemnly committed his country to the protection of the Virgin Mary, naming her Queen of Poland. Nothing further is recorded of the real hero of this event, Prior Kordecki; presumably, he went back to the quiet and contemplative life of a monk in his cloisters.

For the next 300 years the Polish people firmly believed that their state security and welfare was identified with the picture of the Black Madonna at Czestochowa. King John Sobieski (1624-1696) paid homage at the shrine on his way to war to drive back the Turks from the gates of Vienna in 1683. The whole of Europe was fearful that if the Turks were not defeated, Islam would supersede Christianity in western Europe. In a military alliance with the Duke of Lorraine, the Polish cavalry crossed the Danube and made its way to the Turkish camp outside Vienna. The attack came on 12 September 1683 and the Christian army, under the command of John Sobieski, routed the Turks who outnumbered the Christians two to one. Sobieski sent a message to the Pope, 'Veni, vidi, Deus vicit,' accompanied by one of the flags captured from the Turks, to Rome, where it still hangs in the church of the Lateran.

Adolf Hitler visited Jasna Gora in the 1930s, no doubt with designs on its great treasures and realising its importance as a national rallying point. Later, when Germany knew she had lost the Second World War and her occupying troops were leaving Poland before the Russians came, orders were given to destroy Jasna Gora.

High explosives were placed under arches, in the church and library, intending to raze it to the ground. However, good sense seems to have prevailed even then, and instead of detonating the explosives, the soldiers lit great fires in the monastery courtyards and in the nearby fields, so that from a distance it would look to their commanding officers that they had done the job. During the Nazi occupation pilgrimages to Jasna Gora were forbidden, but in 1945 half a million people came to the shrine to thank the Virgin for their liberation, and they continued to come to pray that they would not to be overtaken by Communism. However, as we now know, history tells another story.

On the other hand, it could be argued that their prayers *were* answered; throughout the many centuries of wars, occupations and unspeakable hardship (including the wholesale murder of millions of both Jewish and Christian Poles by the Nazis) the faith of the Polish people has always remained very strong. Jasna Gora, particularly, has evolved into the unique focal point which stirs religious and national identity. To be a 'good' Pole, i.e. an anti-Communist, is to be a Roman Catholic. To be a good Roman Catholic is to hold the Virgin of Jasna Gora in the highest regard. The intense religious fervour at Czestochowa must be seen to be believed, and much of it has to do with Polish patriotism, faith and a deep sense of values – and the right of the Polish people to take charge of their own destiny.

I found the Polish people to be most charming and hospitable as well as having a truly religious nature. To illustrate this, allow me to tell what happened soon after I arrived at Czestochowa. The main, state-owned, hotel in the town is called the Patria. Most of the employees who work there are paid more or less the same wages, whether they be chambermaids or managers. Although I had booked a reservation by telex from Warsaw, when I arrived the hotel was completely full. I realised it was no use arguing when I was greeted by hopeless and mystified looks from the people behind the reception desk. There was positively no room at the inn. As I tried frantically to think of some alternative – of which there was none – the male receptionist said he had an idea, and if I could hold on for a while he would see what he could do. Five minutes later he came back and asked if I would care to lodge with a hotel employee? Yes, I would. I soon found myself with a very hospitable and kind family and immediately I was accepted almost as one of them. It was only later that I realised that the man of the house and his wife actually let me have their bed, and they went to sleep elsewhere in a friend's flat. They lived in a grey block of flats in an even greyer street, but the flat itself was cheerful and spotlessly clean. Living space in Poland is at a premium; the sitting room becomes one bedroom at night, and the dining room becomes another. Couches are let down, blankets are brought from wardrobes in the dining room, and all is made ready for sleep. The whole household was very devout, and whatever was going on up at the monastery was the topic of conversation. In the flat, suitably accommodated, were friends from Warsaw. Together, we all went up to Jasna Gora two or three times a day to attend services.

On the morning of the Assumption I set out early. I arrived at the flat field in time to see people still asleep and slumped in heaps, a few were just beginning to stir. Apart from crumpled clothing no one seemed any the worse for wear. Some began to have a meagre breakfast of what they had brought with them, for there was little to buy.

As the day wore on, Masses were celebrated on a balcony on the monastery ramparts overlooking the great throng that had now gathered in the flat field and beyond, stretching down the Avenue and way off into the town. I made my way around the left-hand side of the great building, and into the monastery precincts. It is a maze of outbuildings, chapels, museums and an enormous Way of the Cross which leads off behind the buildings. The white-robed Pauline Fathers, who advise, direct and generally help the pilgrims find their way, try hard to keep the vast crowds moving all the time through the various parts of great halls and chapels, as they all gaze at the wonderful Baroque architecture. Candles are in profusion all around at side altars where people keep up a constant round of prayer. At every corner and under every archway are impromptu confessionals, and streaming from each, on both sides, the inevitable queues. The monk sits in the centre of the open box, and shifts from one side to the other as one penitent finishes and another begins. In a side chapel to the left of the huge main church is the picture of the Black Madonna. Immediately before the sanctuary steps there is a wrought-iron grille which seals off the altar completely from the congregation. The altar is black marble, with massive pillars on each side supporting a canopy overhead. The shining marble is delicately fringed with fine silver work running along every border, edge and moulding. Rosary beads hang like icicles from all possible points, together with Solidarity emblems and badges. Set back in the altar, above the tabernacle, is the picture itself in a solid silver frame. Age, as well as constant varnishings to preserve it, have made the faces a deep brown, almost black. The two figures have clothes attached to the canvas, so that the faces are recessed from the surface some one and a half to two inches. The whole clothed part of the picture is a mass of gold and jewels and precious stones. The atmosphere is oppressive and highly charged as people pray out loud and offer rosary beads in outstretched arms to the Virgin. The chapel is too small to accommodate such a crush of people, and the hundreds of burning candles use up the oxygen. An elderly lady began to scream hysterically and was led away from the centre of the crowd. At four o'clock a screen is gently lowered in front of the image, and trumpets begin to play as the picture slowly disappears from view. For a moment the canopy glistens in the candle light as the last notes of the trumpets die away and evaporate high above in the vaulted roof. The congregation relaxes and people begin to leave.

CZESTOCHOWA

Czestochowa is situated 290 km south of Warsaw and 80 km north of Kato-wice on the Warsaw Road (Highway No 16) in the Kraców–Czestochowa Upland, often called the Jura. It is the chief town of the district and has 164,000 inhabitants. The landscape consists of deep ravines and towering craggy rocks often topped by ruins of castles of the twelfth to fourteenth centuries.

The town itself is dominated by the limestone hill of Jasna Gora. There have always been settlements here; indeed, archaeologists have found agri-cultural settlements in the area dating back to the Neolithic period and a burial ground of the Lusatian culture which dates back to 700–400 BC. Within the borders of the town are sections of a settlement dating back to the period of Roman influence (third and fourth centuries).

Czestochowa is said to have taken its name from Czestoch, who is supposed to have been the first owner of this land. It seems that the settlement developed on two sites, one on the bank of the Warta river at the junction of important trade routes, and one on the hill where an imposing Pauline monastery grew up and has existed ever since.

The two settlements were mutually dependent but each lived its own life.

Czestochowa really flourished in the fifteenth and sixteenth centuries. The town was surrounded by fortified walls and the houses were built of stone and brick. However, in the seventeenth century Old Czestochowa (the area around the Warta river) fell into decline as a result of the plague which wiped out a vast amount of the population. In addition to the natural disaster of the plague, Czestochowa was at the mercy of brigands who put much of the town to the torch. This was followed by the Swedish invasion which led to the siege of 1655 which brought the town to ruin.

Only in the nineteenth century did the modern development of the town begin. Old Czestochowa and Czestochowa were merged into a single complex connected by a communication road called the Avenue of Our Lady (Al. Najswietszej Marii Panny), along which a new town centre has developed. Czestochowa gradually became an industrial centre with the extension of the Vienna Railway line in the nineteenth century. After the Second World War, Czestochowa was included in the general plan of nationwide regional development. So today Czestochowa is the capital of the Czestochowa Industrial Region, a centre of the metallurgical, textile and building material industries, the chief town of Poland's communication network.

Czestochowa contains a number of fine buildings. The most impressive are the monastery and church of Jasna Gora (Mountain of Light) set on the previously fortified hill. The fortress is built of brick; the monastery was never captured during the Swedish invasions in 1655 and it played an important part in the country's liberation from the invaders.

In the town itself the Town Hall, some seventeenth-century houses and the church in the Old Square are worth seeing.

JASNA GORA

Jasna Gora is the magnificent Pauline Monastery in Czestochowa, where the Pauline Fathers took possession in June 1832. A wooden church dedicated to Our Lady, Virgin and Mother, was in existence already. There were sixteen monks at first who had all come from the church of St Lawrence near Buda in Hungary. The turning point in the history of Jasna Gora came with the appearance of the picture of Our Lady in 1382. Hallowed by legend, it has made Jasna Gora the centre of pilgrimages for nearly six centuries.

According to legend it was painted by St Luke the Evangelist on a wooden plank which had served as a table top in the house of the Holy Family at Nazareth. The fame of the monastery spread enormously after the attack by Polish and Czech Hussite Brothers on Jasna Gora in 1430, during which they slashed the picture with their swords. From this time the monastery at Jasna Gora came under the special protection of the Jagiellonian dynasty, beginning with Ladislaus Jagiello who conferred grants of land and privileges on the monastery. During the Reformation in the sixteenth century Jasna Gora declined in popularity, but towards the end of the century, when Catholicism gained a victory in Poland and the Counter-Reformation reigned supreme (placing special emphasis on the cult of Mary), it gained ground once more. Again Jasna Gora was surrounded by special royal protection.

The seventeenth century brought Poland again into a difficult period of wars in the East, North and South. The

Swedish 'deluge' submerged the whole country. It was then that an event occurred which was to have incalculable consequences. In November 1655 a Swedish army, under General Muller, began a siege of Jasna Gora which lasted for several weeks. The monastery garrison was tiny, but put up such a defence that the Swedes were forced to lift the siege and depart. The attack on Jasna Gora was held to be an insult to the country's religious feeling and its successful defence was attributed not to the strength of defences but to the supernatural powers and protection of the Holy Virgin, to whom the shrine was dedicated. A legend grew up around the defence of Jasna Gora and on his return from exile, John Casimir made a vow in Lvov Cathedral, placing the country under the protection of Our Lady and declaring her Queen of the Crown of Poland. The Madonna's picture at Jasna Gora became the main symbol of her sovereignty over the country. When peace with Sweden was concluded, the monastery became the goal for mass pilgrimages and the treasury of Jasna Gora was swamped with precious gifts. It is to these gifts that we owe the outstanding collection of works of art which can be seen today in the monastery. Both the church and the monastery are a treasury of national heirlooms and with the passing of time, legends have grown up around some of the most precious offerings.

The treasury at Jasna Gora contains the art of gold and silversmiths, together with tapestries, armour and weapons. The monastery, church and chapel of Our Lady are filled with mural paintings and pictures. There is also an exceptionally fine library in the monastery containing many ancient books and manuscripts, rare and unique editions both Polish and foreign; in fact, the monastery had its own printing works where books on many subjects were published. There is also a magnificent collection of rare illuminated manuscripts with hand-painted illustrations.

Apart from its value as a national monument, the Jasna Gora complex, because of its situation, offers a commanding prospect of the Warta Valley, especially from the high, slender monastery tower which rises above the surrounding town to a height of 348 feet. Other historical buildings worth seeing in Czestochowa include the Gothic church of St Sigismund and two early Baroque churches built by the Pauline monks in the mid-seventeenth century.

WARSAW

Warsaw lies on the banks of the Vistula at an altitude of 328 feet. It is almost in the very centre of Poland in the centre of Europe. The date of the foundation of Warsaw is not known although recent archaeological research has led to the discovery of traces of a ninth–tenth-century township, but everything else seems to suggest that the town was not founded before the end of the thirteenth century.

History has not been kind to Warsaw. During the six years of Nazi occupation 700,000 inhabitants lost their lives and in 1944–45 the city was totally ruined. So when we visit palaces and monuments, churches and mansions in the old town, we must remember that all have been painstakingly rebuilt and the smallest fragment that could be saved has been preserved and put back in its place in the reconstructed monument.

The first big step in the rebuilding in 1949 was a thoroughfare which joined the Praga district on the lower right bank of the Vistula river to the western districts of Warsaw passing in part

189

beneath the old town. From then on Warsaw became a massive reconstruction yard, new buildings springing up, such as the whole of the residential quarter of Marszalkowska in the town centre, the reconstructed old city, and dozens of large industrial concerns and new residential districts.

The Poles say that Warsaw has literally risen from the dead. They pay great heed to the local legend which tells of a mermaid rising from the waters of the River Vistula and telling a fisherman by the name of Warsz that here on the banks of the Vistula a prosperous, beautiful and happy town would rise. Today the visitor can see the Vistula mermaid, a statue half fish and half woman in silver, and she is also the symbol immortalised on the town's coat of arms.

As already mentioned, the river Vistula divides the city into two parts, left-bank and right-bank Warsaw. The part on the right bank of the Vistula, which suffered comparatively little during the war, is called Praga and is identified today by big industry and new housing estates. Left-bank Warsaw consists of the Old Town, the Royal Way, the castle, offices, schools of higher learning, the embassies and some industrial enterprises.

THE OLD TOWN

Whilst the history of the Old Town dates back to the Middle Ages, it is in fact quite new and rebuilt between 1949 and 1960 exactly according to old architectural plans, and reconstructed brick by brick from war ruins. The restoration of the Old Town to its former splendour freed it from its nineteenth- and twentieth-century slum quarter.

The Old Town market square surrounded with burghers' houses is a bustling, colourful area with cafes and shops. It has a horse-drawn cab stand and open-air art gallery where artists display their paintings on the pavement.

WARSAW HISTORY MUSEUM

The Warsaw History Museum nearby is definitely worth a visit, as is the Museum of Literature. In 1947 the History Museum was founded in the 'Little Negro' house, one of the best known houses in the old quarter of Warsaw. The 'Little Negro' house was the only one in the old Market Square that had been spared in the war. Seven neighbouring houses were reconstructed and when they had been joined together inside (a process which took eight years) and arranged as a museum, it was opened to the public. This was in 1955, ten years after the liberation of the capital.

It contains many items illustrating the history of Warsaw from oldest times to views of modern building projects and future planning. There are a number of models of various places in the town made by the staff of the museum on the authority of old iconographic documents.

The museum is also a scientific centre for research into the history of Warsaw.

CASTLE SQUARE, ROYAL CASTLE AND SIGISMUND'S COLUMN

Close to the Old Town is the Castle Square with the Royal Castle and Sigismund's Column. In the centre of Castle Square is a column bearing the bronze statue of King Sigismund III (1566–1632). It was erected in 1644 and regarded as a symbol of the city. The monument was destroyed at the end of the last war but rebuilt in 1947. As well as being the oldest monument in Warsaw it is also the most typical.

The Royal Castle dates from the first half of the seventeenth century. Bombed and partly burned in 1939, it was destroyed completely in 1944. Luckily it was possible to rescue many fragments of the interior decoration from the ruins and preserve them in the new. In 1971 it was restored and reconstructed in the same manner as the Old Town, exactly as it was before.

THE ROYAL WAY

The Royal Way is the favourite walk in Warsaw. It starts at Castle Square and leads along Krakowskie Przedmiescie and Nowy Stwiat streets along Aleje Ujazdowskie to the Lazienki Park. Along the Royal Way is the University of Warsaw, the Laboratory of Physical Sciences and the church of the Holy Cross. Inside the church are two urns sealed in pillars; one contains the heart of Frederick Chopin and the other the heart of Ladislaus Reymont, the novelist who was awarded the Nobel Prize in 1924. The interior of the church was completely destroyed during the rising of 1944, when bitter fighting took place in the church and its ruins.

Further on is the Ujazdowski Park and the Botanical Gardens founded in 1819 by Michael Szubert, a professor of biology at the University of Warsaw. Next to it is the Lazienki Park and Palace, the private residence of the last Polish king, Stanislaw August Poniatowski.

The Neo-Classical Palace on the Water is surrounded by a park in which there are many picturesque pavilions and buildings. In the park is the Chopin monument under which concerts of Chopin's music are organised in the summer.

The other interesting summer palace is Wilanow, which is also surrounded by a magnificent park and belonged to King John III Sobieski, who conquered the Turks at Vienna.

Once you are in Poland you may realise that many of the streets and squares are named 'Kopernika'. This is, of course, in memory of the famous Polish scientist, Nicholas Copernicus, the astronomer who discovered that the sun did not revolve around the earth and consequently that the earth was not the astronomical centre of the universe, as had previously been thought.

MUSIC

Warsaw has five musical theatres, of which the Wielki Opera and Ballet Theatre is the biggest and most magnificent in the country. Warsaw's twenty-three stages present classic and contemporary plays, Polish and foreign repertoire.

KRAKÓW (CRACOW)

Kraków is the former capital of Poland and the residence of the kings of Poland between the eleventh and sixteenth centuries. It has a wealth of historical remains and is largely famous for these.

Kraków is situated at the heart of the Upper Vistula basin in southern Poland at the foot of the Carpathians. Unlike Warsaw, it did not suffer badly in the last war and now has a population of almost 500,000.

To many the name Kraków means learning, culture and tradition. A city of historical monuments, it is also the capital of Polish steel and a centre of industry. One of the oldest cities in Poland, it dates back to the early Middle Ages. Until the tenth century it was the residence of the chiefs of a tribe called 'Wislanie' which dominated the lands of 'Little Poland'.

The city's history pre-dates that of the Polish kingdom by several centuries, and it did not become the capital of

Poland until the second half of the eleventh century. The beginning of the fourteenth century marked a particularly fortunate period for the growth of Kraków. The town became the centre of the political and economic life of the state, and was at this time an important transit place for the trade between Ruthenia in the east, Hungary in the south and the Rhenish countries and England to the west. It grew rapidly and when Casimir the Great founded a university in 1364, he ensured the future of Kraków as an important city. It became a centre of arts and sciences and one of the most famous, most powerful and richest towns in Europe.

It was not until the end of the sixteenth century that Kraków's Golden Age began to decline. The great Jagiellonian dynasty died out and was followed by the unhappy time of the Swedish Vasa dynasty. The end of the Jagiellonian dynasty marks the beginning of great wars and civil disturbances, of epidemics and fires.

During the seventeenth century the citizens of Kraków began to lose their former privileges. At this time, however, the old Kraków bourgeoisie were struggling hard in an effort to keep their position in the cultural and economic life of the city, but domestic struggles, followed by murderous wars with Sweden and then a disastrous plague, reduced Kraków to ruins during the seventeenth century.

At the end of the eighteenth century the abandoned houses, ramparts and fortifications were demolished and only a few buildings, such as the tower of the Town Hall, the Barbican and St Florian's Gate, have survived.

During the nineteenth century Austria granted a measure of autonomy to the part of Poland it occupied. Kraków began to grow and, in a short time, again became one of the largest and most prosperous towns in Poland. Since then Kraków has remained a scientific and artistic centre.

THE OLD TOWN

In the centre of the Old Town stands the main market place (or square), often known as Kraków's drawing room. Many experts claim that it is one of the biggest and most impressive market places in Europe, covering four hectares. The 100-metre-long Cloth Hall with charming arcades stands in the middle of the market place. It was built as a place of commerce and the ground floor is still used for trade today. The first floor, however, contains the gallery of Polish paintings of the eighteenth century and includes works by Piotr Michalowski, Henryk Rodakowski and Jozef Chelmonski. In June each year a 'Night of Poets' is held in the market place at the monument to Adam Mickiewicz, the great nineteenth-century Polish poet.

ST MARY'S CHURCH (12th–14th centuries)

St Mary's Church (Mariacki) contains the magnificent altar piece carved by Wit Stwosz, the brilliant German–Polish woodcarver. The church stands on the site of an earlier Romanesque church, and of another Gothic church from the beginning of the fourteenth century. The oldest part of the present church is the choir built towards 1365 which is distinguished by its slender walls and high narrow windows. The main body of the church dates from 1497, but the two towers were built in the first half of the fifteenth century and are 266 feet high.

THE TOWN HALL

The Town Hall, with its dominating slender tower, is also situated in the market place. High up on top a gilt eagle keeps watch over the seat of the town's council. The interior of the tower has been made into a museum and the display there tells the story of the municipal authorities. The cellars of the tower are also interesting. They used to serve as dungeons and torture chambers but now offer a cup of coffee by candlelight for the weary tourist!

THE JAGIELLONIAN UNIVERSITY

It was established in 1364 by King Casimir the Great and is now one of the oldest centres of learning in Europe. In the fifteenth century 45 per cent of the students were foreigners and, today, students come from all over the world to study there.

The University's most illustrious student was Nicholas Copernicus and in 1912–1914, Vladimir Lenin used to come to read in the library.

The oldest building of the Jagiellonian University is known as the Collegium Maius and today houses the museum of the history of the University. With its arcaded courtyard it is a magnificent example of Gothic architecture.

Today the university has eleven schools of higher learning and provides an education for 60,000 students.

WAWEL

Wawel is a limestone hill situated near the market place dominating the whole town and topped by Wawel Castle, a cathedral and towered fortifications.

Wawel took its name from the canons of Wawel Cathedral who used to live here. It is, in the opinions of specialists, one of the finest museums in the world and certainly one of the most popular in Poland. Its 71 magnificent rooms contain just under 5,000 works of art and objects of historical interest, and some of the exhibits are of great value.

The large court of the castle is today the centre of open-air performances; the Gothic walls and the Renaissance arcades form a perfect background for modern music and old Polish poetry.

The most precious of the Wawel Castle collection's exhibits are the priceless Arras tapestries. It was the idea of King Sigismund Augustus to have the tapestries made, and he commissioned the best Flemish weavers and supervised the work, which lasted for twenty years. At his death the collection comprised 356 tapestries but, unfortunately, only 136 pieces of the collection survive, and today they adorn the interior of Wawel Castle.

MODERN KRAKÓW

Kraków is today the capital of Polish steel and an important centre for industry. The Lenin Steel Works situated in Kraków is the biggest Polish industrial enterprise. Annually it can make seven million tons of steel and employs about 35,000 people. It is fully self-sufficient with its own power station and a cement plant processing the furnace slag.

A modern town was built around the Lenin Steel Works in the 1950s called Nowa Huta. It provides accommodation for the employees of the complex and is the biggest and most modern district of Kraków, with 200,000 inhabitants.

Metallurgy, however, is not the only industry in Kraków. There are also industries producing electrical engineering goods, cables, pharmaceutical products, food, timber and electronic components.

CURRENCY EXCHANGE

Currency Exchange desks are open in branches of the National Bank of Poland and major hotels. Currency exchange outside the foreign currency offices is illegal and punishable according to the regulations valid in Poland.

POLISH CURRENCY

The unit of currency in Poland is one zloty which is divided into 100 groszes. Bank notes are issued in denominations of 20 zlotys, 50 zlotys, 100 zl, 500 zl and 1,000 zl; coins in circulation are: 1, 2, 5, 10, 20 and 200 zlotys; small change coins are: 5, 10, 20 and 50 gr. Import, transit and export of Polish zlotys is forbidden. Tourists who have not spent all their Polish money during their stay in Poland can change the Polish zlotys back into foreign currency, provided they present a receipt of legal exchange. If they are unable to produce such a receipt they can deposit the money at a border customs house and, within one year, draw the sum during subsequent visits to Poland at any border customs office on presentation of the deposit receipt. Visitors are usually obliged to spend a minimum amount of money whilst in Poland (usually pitched quite low so that you would have to spend more anyway), but if this minimum amount is not spent, then you may have to forfeit the balance when you leave the country. In spite of constant approaches offering huge rates of exchange, far exceeding the official rate, do not be tempted; such exchange is illegal.

USEFUL ADDRESSES

Note: The telephone numbers as given here assume the caller is within the same country as the hotel, station, or other number. When ringing from abroad, the 0 at the start of each code must be omitted and the appropriate International Code must be prefixed.
Travel Lines
154 Cromwell Road
London SW7 4EF
Tel: 01-370 6131

TOURIST INFORMATION OFFICES

Tourist Information Offices in Czestochowa, as in the rest of Poland, are marked with the sign 'it'. In Czestochowa 'it' centres are to be found at tourist offices and hotels.

Polish Travel Office (Orbis)
11 Aleja 40/42
Tel: (034) 420 56 and 417 69

Cooperative T.O. (Turysta)
ul. Zawadzkiego 12
Tel: (034) 447 16

National Tourist Cooperative (Gromada)
ul. Armii Ludowej 14/16
Tel: (034) 455 01

Polish Tourist Society (PTTK)
11 Aleja 39
Tel: (034) 467 55

Youth Foreign Tourist Office (Juventur)
ul. Raclawicka 2
Tel: (034) 417 02

RAILWAY STATION (Inquiries)
ul. Swierczewskiego
Tel: (034) 413 37

COACH STATION (Inquiries)
ul. Wolnosci
Tel: (034) 466 16

HOTELS
Orbis – Patria
ul. Starucha 2
Tel: (034) 470 01
Telex 037269

Centralny (Category two)
ul. Swierczewskiego 9
Tel: (034) 440 67

Motel (Category two)
ul. PPR 181
Tel: (034) 326 28

Note: The Czestochowa area code (034)
should have replaced the old code
(0331) some time during 1988.